W9-ATD-590

SELECTED PAPERS FROM THE FIFTH WORLD CONGRESS OF
CENTRAL AND EAST EUROPEAN STUDIES, WARSAW, 1995

Edited for the International Council for Central and East European
Studies by Ronald J. Hill, Professor of Comparative Government, Trinity
College, University of Dublin, Ireland

Titles in the series include:

Sue Bridger (*editor*)
WOMEN AND POLITICAL CHANGE
Perspectives from East-Central Europe

John Dunn (*editor*)
LANGUAGE AND SOCIETY IN POST-COMMUNIST EUROPE

William E. Ferry and Roger E. Kanet (*editors*)
POST-COMMUNIST STATES IN THE WORLD COMMUNITY

Graeme Gill (*editor*)
ELITES AND LEADERSHIP IN RUSSIAN POLITICS

Paul G. Hare (*editor*)
SYSTEMIC CHANGE IN POST-COMMUNIST ECONOMIES

Mark S. Johnson (*editor*)
EDUCATION IN TRANSITION

Anthony Kemp-Welch (*editor*)
STALINISM IN POLAND, 1944–56

Stanislav J. Kirschbaum (*editor*)
HISTORICAL REFLECTIONS ON CENTRAL EUROPE

Carol S. Leonard (*editor*)
THE MICROECONOMICS OF POST-COMMUNIST CHANGE

Kevin McDermott and John Morison (*editors*)
POLITICS AND SOCIETY UNDER THE BOLSHEVIKS

John Morison (*editor*)
ETHNIC AND NATIONAL ISSUES IN RUSSIAN AND EAST
EUROPEAN HISTORY

Judith Pallot (*editor*)
TRANSFORMING PEASANTS
Society, State and the Peasantry, 1861–1930

Richard Sakwa (*editor*)
THE EXPERIENCE OF DEMOCRATIZATION IN EASTERN
EUROPE

Barry P. Scherr and Karen L. Ryan-Hayes (*editors*)
TWENTIETH-CENTURY RUSSIAN LITERATURE

Ray Taras (*editor*)
NATIONAL IDENTITIES AND ETHNIC MINORITIES IN EASTERN
EUROPE

Ian D. Thatcher (*editor*)
REGIME AND SOCIETY IN TWENTIETH-CENTURY RUSSIA

International Congress of Central and East European Studies
Series Standing Order ISBN 0–333–71195–5
(*outside North America only*)

You can receive future titles in this series as they are published by placing a standing order.
Please contact your bookseller or, in case of difficulty, write to us at the address below with
your name and address, the title of the series and the ISBN quoted above.

Customer Services Department, Macmillan Distribution Ltd
Houndmills, Basingstoke, Hampshire RG21 6XS, England

Elites and Leadership in Russian Politics

Selected Papers from the Fifth World Congress of Central and East European Studies, Warsaw, 1995

Edited by

Graeme Gill
Professor of Government and Public Administration
University of Sydney
Australia

First published in Great Britain 1998 by
MACMILLAN PRESS LTD
Houndmills, Basingstoke, Hampshire RG21 6XS and London
Companies and representatives throughout the world

A catalogue record for this book is available from the British Library.

ISBN 0–333–69544–5

First published in the United States of America 1998 by
ST. MARTIN'S PRESS, INC.,
Scholarly and Reference Division,
175 Fifth Avenue, New York, N.Y. 10010

ISBN 0–312–21347–6

Library of Congress Cataloging-in-Publication Data
World Congress of Central and East European Studies (5th : 1995 :
Warsaw, Poland)
Elites and leadership in Russian politics : selected papers from
the fifth World Congress of Central and East European Studies /
edited by Graeme Gill.
    p.   cm.
Includes bibliographical references (p.) and indexes.
ISBN 0–312–21347–6 (cloth)
1. Elite (Social sciences)—Russia—Congresses.   2. Political
leadership—Russia (Federation)—Congresses.   3. Russia
(Federation)—Politics and government—1991– —Congresses.   4. Post
-communism—Russia (Federation)—Congresses.   I. Gill, Graeme J.
II. Title.
HN530.2.Z9E49 1995
305.5'52'0947—dc21   97–49885
                                                            CIP

Selection and editorial matter © International Council for Central and East European
Studies and Graeme Gill 1998
Chapters 1 and 7 © Graeme Gill 1998
General Editor's Introduction © Ronald J. Hill 1998
Chapters 2–6, 8 © Macmillan Press Ltd 1998

This book is printed on paper suitable for recycling and made from fully managed and
sustained forest sources.

10   9   8   7   6   5   4   3   2   1
07 06 05 04 03 02 01 00 99 98

Printed and bound in Great Britain by Antony Rowe Ltd, Chippenham, Wiltshire

Contents

General Editor's Introduction

It is a great pleasure for me to introduce these volumes of papers that originated in the Fifth World Congress of Central and East European Studies, held in Warsaw in the week 6–11 August 1995, under the auspices of the International Council for Central and East European Studies and of the Institute of Philosophy and Sociology and the Institute of Political Studies of the Polish Academy of Sciences.

In the period since the previous world Congress, held in Harrogate, England, in July 1990, that part of the world that is the focus of Slavists' special attention had undergone the completion of changes that were already in train but the outcome of which was still uncertain. Moreover, given the inevitable time-lag between the conception of a major scholarly event and its occurrence, the major concerns at the beginning of the decade were not yet those of charting and analysing the transition from communist rule to some other form of political, economic and social entity and the impact of this on the societies and cultures of Russia, the Soviet Union and the countries loosely referred to as 'Eastern Europe': far less ambitious expectations were still the order of the day. Even though Poland had led the way in abandoning communist rule, shortly followed by all the other countries in 'Eastern Europe', it took some considerable imagination and conviction for the Executive Committee of the International Council to take the bold decision to hold the 1995 Congress in Eastern Europe, a decision that evoked a very positive response from our colleagues in Warsaw.

The different international climate immediately made itself felt, as scholars from the region were able to attend in large numbers a conference organised by a body that had been almost exclusively 'Western' in its previous experience. No longer were they specially invited guests (who on previous occasions had sometimes been denied exit visas to attend such Congresses), and it was a moving experience for me, as General Editor of the Congress proceedings, to receive letters and other communications by fax and e-mail from countries that in 1990 had no separate existence, or from provincial cities in the heart of post-Soviet Russia. Moreover, the opening of archives and the opportunities for new kinds of research, by scholars based in the countries concerned and by those entering from outside, meant that by 1995 there was much new information available, and scholars from the two 'sides' inevitably had much to say to one another.

The traditions in which the different groups had been trained meant that the styles of scholarship were not totally compatible, and there is a learning process in train that is likely to continue for some years. However, both the Congress itself and, more especially, the collaborative ventures such as this series of volumes containing selected papers, give opportunities for professional colleagues from around the world to make their own contributions to the new (and sometimes old) scholarly debates in ways that were hitherto impossible.

While not every paper that was presented or offered for publication was considered suitable for inclusion in the various thematic volumes, and individual editors sometimes had to make difficult choices and disappoint some authors, the endeavour as a whole must itself be seen as part of the global process of learning about the Slavic, Eurasian and Central and East European world: its peoples, its languages, its literature and cultural life, its history, politics, societies, economies, and its links with the rest of the world. Interest in the region is likely to grow, with new opportunities for contacts at various levels, and these volumes will, I am certain, serve both to educate and to inspire scholars and students anxious to understand.

It is very pleasant indeed to acknowledge once again the association of the Congress and the International Council with Macmillan, who will be publishing these volumes in the United Kingdom, and particularly the highly professional support and the keen personal interest of Tim Farmiloe for the whole project. If I may add a personal note, I should like to express my gratitude to John Morison and the Executive Committee of the International Council for charging me with the function of General Editor; to the editors of individual volumes, to whom fell the difficult tasks of assessment and selection followed by the tedium of editorial preparation; to my wife, Ethna, for her assistance in keeping track of several hundred typescripts, letters, faxes and e-mail messages; and to the many scholars who have patiently (and sometimes not so patiently – such are the pressures of modern academic life!) contributed to this complex international publishing venture. The collapse of communist rule has contributed sharply to globalisation, and the creation of this series of volumes has placed me at the hub of a world-wide enterprise, with editors on several continents and authors located in many countries of the world. It has provided me with a new kind of learning process for which I am humbly grateful.

Trinity College, Dublin RONALD J. HILL

List of Contributors

William A. Clark, Louisiana State University, Baton Rouge, USA.

Graeme Gill, University of Sydney, Australia.

John Higley, University of Texas, Austin, USA.

Leslie Holmes, University of Melbourne, Australia.

Olga Kryshtanovskaya, Institute of Sociology, Russian Academy of Sciences, Moscow.

Judith Kullberg, Ohio State University, Columbus, USA.

Martha Merritt, Notre Dame University, Indiana, USA.

Jan Pakulski, University of Tasmania, Australia.

Stephen White, University of Glasgow, Scotland.

John P. Willerton, University of Arizona, Tucson, USA.

1 Introduction

Graeme Gill

It is now a commonplace for people to suggest that the world as we know it was transformed at the end of the 1980s–early 1990s. The cold war, which had been the principal factor structuring world politics in the post-war period, ended, and with it a discernibly new era dawned. One writer saw the fall of communism, first in Eastern Europe and then in its heartland the USSR, as defining the end of what he called the 'Short Twentieth Century'. Hobsbawm's terminology is useful. It highlights the way in which the collapse of communism effectively brought to an end the pattern of international politics (at least in Europe) generated by the outcome of the First World War. The great contest between the capitalist West and the communist East, a contest focused on Europe but the effects of which were to be found in all corners of the globe, had ended, with some Western triumphalists interpreting this as the complete victory of their way of life. As events soon showed, particularly in the Persian Gulf and the former Yugoslavia, such views not only were optimistic, but may also have significantly under-estimated the cost of the Western 'victory'. But even if these sorts of judgements are problematic, what is not in question is that the dynamics of international politics have been altered.

In domestic political terms too there has been fundamental change. The fall of international communism was simply the international manifestation of the collapse of communist regimes throughout the Soviet and East European region. While the patterns of collapse were different in different countries and the sort of regime which emerged in the various states differed, the fact of change cannot be disputed. How different the new regime was from that which it replaced varied considerably: compare Uzbekistan where the ruling communist party was renamed, little scope was given to opposition activity, and the communist-era leader confirmed in power, with the Czech Republic where the democratic process has become entrenched. In Russia too the changes have been substantial. Russia has become an independent country instead of part of the larger Soviet federation. The political monopoly of the communist party has been replaced by a political system in which broadly free and

fair elections determine the political leadership. The economic monopoly, never of course complete, has been replaced by a system in
which market mechanisms play a much larger role, even if they are not
functioning in all spheres in the classic fashion. In its values and beliefs,
the contours of its social structure, and even its physical appearance,
Russian society is significantly different from its Soviet predecessor. Of
course there are also important continuities and similarities, and it is the
balance between continuity and difference which is crucial in defining
the sort of system that is emerging. But within this complex picture of
continuities and differences, one thing has remained of enormous importance: leadership.

The Soviet political system was one in which the top leadership
played a central and crucial part not only in the continuing functioning
of that system, but also in its establishment and subsequent transformation. Of course all political systems will be affected and even shaped
by their leadership, but in few has the impact of that leadership on
the system been as great as it has in the USSR. From the outset, the role
of the individual leader and the group around him has been decisive.
The decision to seize power in October 1917, the form taken by the
new government and the mix of policies evident during his lifetime
are all owed in significant measure to Lenin personally and to his immediate entourage. But the form which the Soviet Union took owed most
to Stalin. His role in the initiation of collectivisation and forced-
pace industrialisation, in the purges and terror, in the conduct of the war,
and in setting the tone during the post-war period, was enormous. The
way the system reacted to and coped with Stalin's death, and thereby
with the removal of the principal pillar of the system, was clearly
affected by the personality of the leader who had to guide this process,
Nikita Khrushchev. The ambiguities and uncertainties implicit in this
situation were personified by Khrushchev, the increasing arbitrariness of
his behaviour being a pertinent factor in defining the way the system at
large functioned. The systemic response to this arbitrariness, reflected in
a drive for regularity and routinisation, found its perfect spearhead
in Leonid Brezhnev. The leadership style fostered by Brezhnev was
perfectly attuned to this sort of reaction to the Khrushchev period, and
enabled the system to settle into a much more routinised and regular
pattern of functioning than it had enjoyed at any time in the past. And
finally, the problems that had accumulated during the Brezhnev period
demanded a vigorous response, and this sort of response was forthcoming from the new Soviet leader, Mikhail Gorbachev. It was Gorbachev who led and provided much of the initial impetus for the reform

movement which, ultimately, escaped his control and destroyed the Soviet Union.

The representation of Soviet history summarised above would be accepted for what it is by most scholars. It does not tell us everything of importance that played a part in shaping the Soviet experience. The massive levels of social mobility, the growth of an urban society and an industrial economy, the development of high levels of hostility and competition with the West, the emergence of the microchip revolution, and many other broader socio-economic and historical processes, all fundamentally shaped the course of Soviet development. But the way in which the Soviet system responded to and handled these was fundamentally shaped by the orientation of the political leadership. It may not be too much to say that, more than in other systems, the phases of the Soviet experience were a reflection of the changing orientations of different Soviet leaders. Any understanding of that experience therefore requires an appreciation of the role of leadership.

A similar point can be made for the post-Soviet period. Historically, in periods of institutional uncertainty or ambiguity, forceful leaders are able to place their imprint firmly upon the course of development. Lenin was able to do this in the early years of the Soviet regime, and Yeltsin has been similarly placed in the post-Soviet period. Yeltsin was personally important in shaping the outcome of all of the major questions: the defeat of the August 1991 coup, the dismantling of the Soviet Union, the introduction of a form of economic shock therapy, the closure of the legislature and drafting of a new constitution, the search for a military end to the Chechen situation, and the continuing composition of the government and nature of policy were all intimately associated with Yeltsin personally and those immediately around him. Again while the focus on the leader and his group does not explain everything, nothing else can be explained satisfactorily in the absence of at least some attention being paid to the leadership group.

Recognition of the role of leadership is a long-established principle of political analysis and has been applied to the study of all kinds of political systems. It has been an especially strong and fruitful theme in much of Soviet studies, and given the extent of the continuities which remain between the Soviet past and Russian present, there is no reason to believe that such a focus will not continue to be useful. The utility of such a focus on leadership is also suggested by that body of theoretical writing which many have sought to use in an endeavour both to understand and to bring a comparative dimension to the recent Soviet–Russian experience, namely, the 'transition to democracy' literature. One of the principal themes of this literature (some of which is referred to in the chapters which follow) is the way in which elites play a crucial role in structuring the transition from authoritarian to democratic rule. Indeed, for many writers from this school, democracy is best ensured by the exclusion of the masses from the transition process and the crafting of democratic institutions by political elites. It is the elites who organise the dismantling of the authoritarian structure and consequent shift of the system in a democratic direction. By ordering their own relationships in ways which will facilitate the growth of democratic norms and values, the elites thereby foster the emergence of a democratic culture which can sustain a set of democratic political arrangements. While this sort of elite-focused analysis may be criticised on a number of grounds, including its lack of attention to broader socio-structural and historical factors and the problems for theorising posed by the importance many writers attach to contingency, it is undeniable that at one level it does have considerable explanatory power. It does provide an explanation for transition which, although incomplete, enables the sort of comparison across cases which ultimately can only enrich our understanding. Despite its limitations, this literature is useful in helping us understand the course of developments in Russia.

Thus both a more traditional Soviet studies approach and the use of broader theoretical methodologies to study the Russian transition attest to the importance of a focus on leadership and elites. The papers collected in this volume, most of which originally were presented at the V World Congress of Central and East European Studies in Warsaw in August 1995, approach this issue of elites and leadership from a variety of directions. Some adopt a methodology very familiar to those whose pedigree lies in the Soviet studies field; others use the transition to democracy literature. Regardless of approach, all recognise the importance of a focus upon those at the upper echelons of society for an understanding of the more general course of development that society is experiencing.

The first three all acknowledge the importance of structural factors in moulding the contours of political life. Martha Merritt analyses the course of development of a system of parliamentary checks and balances on the issue of presidential appointments. She compares the way this developed under Gorbachev and Yeltsin, showing how the latter has been able to avoid parliamentary checks, but at mounting cost. William Clark looks at Yeltsin's appointment policy in the regions, more specifically the Heads of Administration and Presidential Representatives. He shows how this has been affected by the interplay between central authority and local government, reflected in a mix of bringing in new people and confirming local people in situ. He concludes by arguing that many of Yeltsin's appointments now sit in the Council of the Federation, thereby perhaps strengthening Yeltsin's hand, and by suggesting that a strong centre (president?) may be necessary to bring about economic transformation.

John P. Willerton analyses post-Soviet mobility norms through a study of the recruitment patterns of the Yeltsin federal executive. The focus of his investigation is patronage, and the obvious comparator the Soviet period. He argues that, over time, Yeltsin has become increasingly reliant on clients and allies rather than protégés, with the implication that the top levels of political power may better be seen in terms of shifting alliances than of the dominance of a patronage-based political machine. Part of this alliance strategy is seen to be Yeltsin's building of personnel-based links with important sectoral interests, or lobbies, in the economy. Olga Kryshtanovskaya and Stephen White are also interested in this political–economic linkage. They trace the way the Soviet *nomenklatura* was able to use its privileged position to acquire property and wealth and, through the construction of new economic structures, to become inter-linked with the state. The authors argue that the new Russian elite is triple-layered, comprising politicians, entrepreneurs and people involved in security, but it is the link between the new Russian business elite and the state which is crucial for shaping the Russian future.

Judith Kullberg, John Higley and Jan Pakulski seek to combine elite and institutionalist accounts of transition to explain the different trajectories of the former communist regimes. They too point to high levels of continuity in both personnel and behavioural norms, and argue that this does not facilitate democratic consolidation. Rather it can lead to presidentialism, which is antithetical to the development of the pluralistic and accommodative patterns of elite relations historically associated with the emergence of representative democracy. Graeme Gill draws upon the transition to democracy literature to analyse whether the course of elite relations in independent Russia is consistent with the sort of conditions which facilitate democratic consolidation. The major focus here is the resolution of elite conflict, and the conclusion is that while elite relations may have fallen into a relatively stable pattern, it is by no means clear that this is a pattern based solidly upon elite commitment to democratic principles.

In conclusion, Leslie Holmes provides a descriptive model of post-communism and thereby a dynamic context within which the earlier analyses can be placed. He shows how post-communism is a situation very different from that in which other transitional societies find themselves, and that even though in certain respects Russia is *sui generis*, in many ways it is less different from other post-communist societies than is often claimed. What is important for Russia, as for none of the others, is the identity crisis stemming from the loss of empire.

These studies raise many issues, but answer few of them definitively. This is in part because it is not clear that Russian conditions have stabilised; a decade hence, trends which appear significant today may appear to have been of relatively little importance. But it is also because a society undergoing the sorts of changes Russia has experienced throws up very large research questions, in terms of both the substantive issues to be addressed and the methodology through which they can be addressed. Such large questions cannot be answered overnight. In this context, the chapters in this volume represent not only examples of where research is currently being conducted, but an ambitious research agenda for the future. They offer signposts to questions which the scholarly community must address. We hope that they will be seen as useful therefore not only for the substantive material and arguments they present, but also as stimulants to further work in this area.

2 If Checks Won't Balance: Parliamentary Review of Ministerial Appointments

Martha Merritt

In *Dom knigi*, Moscow's major bookstore, the shelf marked 'Constitution of the Russian Federation' has a tiny gummed attachment reading '12 December 1993'. This constitutional impermanence writ small has profound significance writ large across Russia's political landscape, at least for those accustomed to more secure constitutional arrangements. The embryonic political institutions and conventions associated with the 'Yeltsin' Constitution reflect many shortcomings of a document adopted by a slim margin through popular referendum, and without the benefit of what might be called robust institutional give-and-take.

President Boris Yeltsin's rout of parliament in 1993 and the subsequent streamlining of the constitutional process reintroduced a frequent source of unease in Russian politics: will the current Russian chief executive, as with his tsarist and communist predecessors, continue to dodge potential checks on his power before undertaking major initiatives? When parliament is 'unable or unwilling to fulfil its constitutional role of extracting accountability from the government',[1] the expected result is unrestrained exercise of executive power. Although at least one analyst provides an upbeat assessment of the relative stability of Russian politics after the adoption of the Constitution,[2] others focus on the 'unchecked power this Constitution accords a Russian President'[3] and lament the example set by executive fiat with the unpopular conflict in Chechnya.[4]

An examination of the review of ministerial appointments by parliament – one form of executive accountability that became more meaningful in the late Soviet era and that continues to raise high expectations in the new Russia – provides valuable insight into both the limitations of the present constitutional arrangement and the informal norms developing between President and parliament. And the continuing struggle between President and parliament on ministerial appointments seems a good test of the principle of checks and balances: time and again the niggling issues of appointment, approval and removal of government ministers occupy the attention of the State Duma and the presidential inner circle. Restrictions on the legislature's ability to challenge presidential appointments could be seen as undermining the ability of the Duma to hold the executive, chiefly the President, to account. Certainly the Russian press continues to point out the discrepancy between presidential appointment activity and parliamentary participation.[5]

In fact, members of the Duma have missed few opportunities to challenge Yeltsin's appointments, often in extra-constitutional fashion. This chapter considers the persistence of legislative pressure on appointments despite considerable efforts by the executive branch to discourage such interference. It is worth noting at the outset that, however petty the conflicts detailed below, contention between executive and legislature over personnel appointments lay at the heart of the development of responsible government elsewhere. When responsible government is understood to include practices that serve to make ministers accountable to legislative rather than to executive authority,[6] the role of parliamentary review of ministerial appointments is a key to balance in governing.

The focus here is on tension in the relationship between Presidents and their respective legislatures, Soviet and Russian, over ministerial appointments; a more complete survey would include review of judicial appointments and tsarist-era precedents, including Nicholas II's ministerial controversies, but this awaits a more comprehensive work on the struggle for responsible government in Russia. I shall instead begin with the late-Soviet legacy for review of ministerial appointments, continue with Yeltsin-era checks and balances relevant to this tension between executive and legislature in contemporary Russia, and finally undertake an examination of the complex incentives for the Russian executive to compromise on appointments.

Right of Review in the Gorbachev Era

In 1989 the power of review of ministerial appointees abruptly gained meaning after decades of ritualised approval (under Article 129 of the

1977 Constitution). Although there was widespread agreement in the Soviet period that parliament should have the right to review at least some appointments, most political actors were surprised at how vociferously the newly constituted Supreme Soviet seized its first meaningful weapons against government ministers.[7]

A curious amalgam of presidential and parliamentary-style procedure in the conduct of the Supreme Soviet was strongly in evidence during the process of ministerial review. That the appointments were subject to legislative review at all, and sometimes to harsh rejection, suggested the kind of checks and balances associated with separate branches of government. Chairman of the Council of Ministers Nikolai Ryzhkov submitted the initial nominations for members of his government. But successful ministerial candidates could not also be members of parliament,[8] offering a further contradiction to parliamentary practice. And the main reason for the peculiar flavour of the proceedings was that the mightiest chief executive, President Mikhail Gorbachev, hovered over the proceedings without taking direct responsibility for them.

Ryzhkov's own appointment was subject to Supreme Soviet approval, and in the course of answering deputies' questions he revealed that:

> In contrast to the previous practice, now there will be a very careful examination of each nomination in committees, commissions, and the houses of the Supreme Soviet. ... If the Supreme Soviet does not confirm a minister, then the Chairman of the Council of Ministers should agree with this. If he is convinced that the minister can fulfil his function, then he is required to prove this to the deputies.[9]

Asked if he personally supported the procedure of ministerial review, Ryzhkov rather bookishly responded that the practice accorded with the constitution because the Council of Ministers was said to be appointed by the Supreme Soviet.[10]

This upheaval in the conventional understanding of cross-institutional approval for decisions made by executive authority belied somewhat the charge by the radical deputy Yurii Afanas'ev that the Congress had elected a 'Stalin-style, Brezhnev-style' Supreme Soviet, one with an 'aggressively obedient' majority. Nevertheless, the initiative for change, albeit in a democratic direction, appeared to have come from above. There was much hedging when it suited the chair and intricate manoeuvring on the part of the leadership. The newly belligerent Supreme Soviet persisted on many occasions, however, and ultimately rejected nine candidates.[11]

The Supreme Soviet proved to have a mean bark when reviewing its own officers and committee members, with candidates grilled on their departmental and occasionally personal records. Charges of nepotism caused particular controversy. Even so, the bite came down unexpectedly sharply when Ryzhkov submitted his list of government nominees for approval. Since over 60 per cent of the candidates were incumbents, many were vulnerable to the charge of being 'yesterday's minister' (the epitaph of the 15-year incumbent Minister of the Timber Industry, M. Busygin). The total number defeated was unusually high for any country with ministerial review, and the significance of this check by the legislature was lost on no one. The Communist Party leadership's domination of decisions on key appointments, first shaken by the 1989 general elections, had been further eroded.

Most important among those rejected was V. Kamentsev, the incumbent Chairman of the State Committee for Foreign Economic Relations. His appointment only two and a half years earlier meant that he had been hand-picked by the current leadership. Ryzhkov and Gorbachev kept the nomination alive after one negative round of voting with the pretence that a significant number of deputies were not in the chamber at the time of the vote, but the second round sealed the defeat more definitively: 200 (for), 172 (against), 47 (abstentions).[12] Kamentsev's rejection despite leadership pressure to support his candidacy was a notable assertion of legislative independence. Ryzhkov made no secret of his unhappiness with the result: 'I am convinced ... that I was not mistaken when I submitted the proposal on Kamentsev's candidacy.'[13] Asked if he considered it a loss for the government, he took the question on a level more literal than symbolic and responded affirmatively ('Now a new man must be found').

On the other hand, the case of N. Konarev, the incumbent Minister for Railways, was a peculiar victory for the government. Konarev, who was appointed by Andropov to oversee a major shake-up in railway personnel, was credited (in the West, anyway) with having achieved a considerable improvement in railway transport.[14] The legislative rumbling during his questioning session was therefore less about Konarev's performance than it was due to the widespread fear of a rail strike looming in the wake of the coal-miners' strike. One deputy temporised:

> What will people think of us if we vindicate him, if we even praise him? ... I realise that he is not to blame and that he probably should be elected ... [but] we must make it understood that we are able to protect the people's interests from this department.[15]

Konarev was a scapegoat in the making for a legislature terrified of unrest. More officially, his candidacy was defeated because 'he did not understand the crucial nature of social problems and paid for this with his ministerial portfolio.'[16]

One month later, after the threatened strike had failed to materialise, a group of deputies led by Boris Yeltsin recommended that Konarev's candidacy be reconsidered. The move generated a storm of protest, led by the cry that reviewing a rejected candidate would undermine the credibility of the Supreme Soviet. The session became so unruly that Gorbachev was called to the chair to restore order. The administration's argument for reconsidering Konarev ran as follows: no one could be found who wielded as much authority or had as much experience as Konarev, and thus a month had passed with no one in charge of railways. The voice of the people was also said to have spoken, but via traditional party means: letters and telegraphs from voters protesting at the rejection of his candidacy.

These reasons failed to sway those who objected on procedural grounds, so after a recess Gorbachev produced a letter from the Council of Ministers deeming it possible to return to a consideration of Konarev's candidacy 'in the light of the opinion of a significant number of USSR People's Deputies and of representatives of labour collectives and managers of the country's railroads'.[17] The candidacy was voted upon once again, and a majority of deputies (245) voted in favour of Konarev. On what authority the Council of Ministers was able to instruct the Supreme Soviet in this manner was a more salient question than whether or not Konarev was abandoned for the wrong reasons the first time around.

The candidacies of two incumbents named Gusev provide examples both of the issues that were raised by the deputies and the importance of a good defence. S. Gusev (incumbent First Vice-Chairman of the USSR Supreme Court) met with hostile questioning about the shortcomings of the legal system, as did every candidate for the bench. Some of the nominees responded with a ringing condemnation of current practice; Gusev instead launched the shaky defence that 'telephone justice', the widespread practice of party officials interfering with court cases by telephoning and instructing the judge, had been done away with and that he himself had never submitted to it.[18] The ridicule with which the deputies received this unlikely information, joined with queries about Gusev's age and abilities, led to a rejection.

V. Gusev (incumbent Vice-Chairman of the Council of Ministers and head of the Bureau of the Chemical and Timber Complex) faced an equally strong challenge based on his record. Ecological issues were raised repeatedly at the sessions as a critical concern for the population, as indeed they had been throughout most of the deputies' campaigns.

One of the first candidates rejected by the Supreme Soviet had been P. Polad-zade, for the post of Minister for Water Resources Construction.[19] This Gusev, while not as notorious as Polad-zade, none the less headed a bureau associated with heavy polluting. After a sharp discussion, managed adequately by the nominee, Ryzhkov intervened to state that no matter who was made head of the complex, problems would remain. The appointment was approved.

Some of the wiser candidates tackled controversial issues in their preliminary statements to the Supreme Soviet. M. Shchadov, incumbent Minister of the Coal Industry, headed off strong potential criticism about miners' living conditions by delivering a speech on social problems. A.Volkov, incumbent Minister of Civil Aviation, promised – with excessively high hopes, as it transpired – to introduce competition for Aeroflot.

The Defence Minister, Dmitrii Yazov, admitted to corruption and waste in the military, but came across as singularly unwilling to propose changes which would address these problems. A voice from the floor interrupted at one point to ask what his salary was, and from there the proceedings turned into a rout. Repeated queries were made regarding who should monitor sales of weapons abroad (with the expressed intent of seeking a more prominent role for the Supreme Soviet); speakers pressed issues summed up by one account as concerning 'favouritism, nepotism, bureaucratism, bribe-taking, window-dressing and hoodwinking'[20] in the army.

Yazov, a Gorbachev appointee, was clearly out of his depth. The session lasted for over four hours – far longer than the allocated time period – and many deputies evidently relished the opportunity to interrogate an incumbent Minister of Defence, a position which would have made Yazov untouchable under the old regime. The range of complaints (many of which deputies had heard as candidates for office) received an airing that was talked about in the country for days afterwards. Perhaps the public felt more gratified than did Gorbachev, who looked impassive but called upon Marshal Sergei Akhromeev towards the end of the session. Akhromeev, a respected figure who could be counted on to defend Yazov (as well as the honour of the military and the USSR before his despairing suicide in 1991), was unable to mute the hostility of subsequent speakers. From the chair, Gorbachev felt it necessary to close the discussion with an impassioned defence of his candidate.

The primary import of Gorbachev's remarks was to refuse the deputies the symbolic role which they wished to attribute to Yazov and his candidacy and to define the Defence Minister's responsibilities relatively narrowly. With the scope of Yazov's accountability thus limited, Gorbachev could then discuss the Defence Minister's background and performance as a 'courageous and principled Communist', words which – for this transitional group of deputies – still held a sufficiently positive meaning in 1989. With the preference of the Chair having been made forcefully and at length, 256 deputies voted for Yazov's appointment and a total of 143 withheld their support. Although the Supreme Soviet relented on this occasion, it had become clear that any candidate could become a target; Gorbachev closed the session with a hopeless call for more polite treatment of candidates.

The wisest candidates of all may have been those who refused to take up a new position, head of the State Committee for the Protection of the Environment. Ryzhkov told the press that his first five choices turned him down. The post was finally accepted by N. Vorontsov, who at least left his mark on history as the first non-party member to take up a position in the Council of Ministers (and later as the only Cabinet minister openly to oppose the August 1991 coup).

Although the focus here is review of ministerial appointments, it is worth mentioning that among the most controversial candidates was A. Vasil'ev, nominee for the post of First Deputy Prosecutor and former head of the Leningrad prosecutor's office. Vasil'ev faced hostile questioning on the still-simmering controversy over Gdlyan and Ivanov, the freewheeling prosecutors (and later members of the Congress of People's Deputies) who led investigations into corruption in Uzbekistan and in 1989 levelled charges of corruption at senior central officials, including Politburo member Yegor Ligachev. Vasil'ev was able to overcome the negative recommendation he received in committee and was eventually approved, but the session became so embittered that a majority of deputies voted not to have it televised in full.

That the legislature was inventing its powers *vis-à-vis* the Council of Ministers as it went along is clear from another close call, suffered by V. Bykov, Minister for the Medical and Microbiological Industry. Bykov received one negative recommendation from the three committees which questioned him before the session, with the final consensus among them that he receive conditional approval for the post, subject to a one-year review. It is unheard of for a parliament to put a minister on probation in this way – much less for an executive to agree – but it suited Soviet political norms sufficiently to avoid objection.

Two figures who did not pass review, perhaps not coincidentally, headed important sectors for the public, the Ministry of Culture and the Ministry of Physical Culture and Sport. V. Zakharov and M. Gramov were considered by the deputies to be out of step with the times. Zakharov had clashed repeatedly with the reformist group Memorial on their efforts to erect a monument to the victims of Stalin. Gramov went down quickly with his sloganeering and refusal to discuss sports problems such as drug use among athletes. Perhaps the strongest proof of his old-time understanding of politics is that he later contacted the Congress to ask that his honour and dignity be defended from attacks in the news organs. (By 1996, holding a responsible position in sport involved danger to life and limb, perhaps not least owing to a provision for tax-free importation of alcohol by the ministry.)

Ryzhkov was correct in calling the procedure of review 'not very pleasant'.[21] L. Rozenova, the government's nominee to chair the State Prices Committee, broke down under the strain of being grilled in committee and was subsequently refused approval (duly reported in the phrase 'the result was distressing to the candidate'[22]). In calling for the press not to over-dramatise events, Ryzhkov none the less confirmed that it was necessary for all members of the government to go through this 'purgatory'.[23]

An article in the state news organ summed up the proceedings favourably and hinted at the difficulties presented by incumbency concerning responsibility for past mistakes. One thing, at any rate, 'was clear ... [A new aspirant to ministerial office] will have a firm knowledge of who is going to hold him accountable and for what.'[24] This was a strong claim for a new convention; more likely, as with review of ministerial appointments (or approval of Cabinet appointees) in Western democracies, the Soviet variant suffered mightily from caprice.[25] It is sufficiently noteworthy that the Supreme Soviet, a fledgling institution in an authoritarian shell, exercised an initial check on executive appointments. As Eugene Huskey notes in a lively and perceptive account of relations between Soviet executive and legislature,

> At the very moment when the Soviet parliament was beginning to assert its long dormant law-making power, the presidency appeared on the scene to challenge this traditional prerogative of the legislature.[26]

The President could try for the power of decree and bypass parliamentary law-making, but appointments offered a forum where the parliament was less easily deterred (although equally easily bypassed, initially, as will be shown below). The collapse of the Soviet Union left the Russian parliament and President to battle over new rules.

Pre- and Post-Constitutional Skirmishes Over Appointments

The many constitutional drafts circulating before the dissolution of parliament in 1993 all contained provision for approval by parliament of at least some ministerial appointments. Not surprisingly, the new Constitution put forward by the Yeltsin administration after the dissolution of parliament and adopted in December 1993 had the least generous terms for parliament's role when compared with all other prominent versions, including the much-amended Russian Constitution in place. The unsuccessful proposals mentioned here are generally dubbed the Sakharov, Rumyantsev and (early) presidential constitutions.[27]

Andrei Sakharov may have felt compelled to try his hand at constitution-writing before his death in 1989 in part because of the stonewalling tactics of Anatolii Lukyanov, head of the legislative Commission to Draft a New Constitution.[28] Sakharov's constitution, emphasising international law and human rights,[29] provided for the proposal of candidates by the Chairman of the Council of Ministers and then confirmation by the Congress of People's Deputies of 'all ministers, other than foreign minister and defence minister ... [and of] chairmen of Council of Ministers committees ...'. These were generous terms for the parliament, but the exclusion of two ministries reflected an understanding that the President needed to feel secure with a few allies in key positions as well.

Several parliamentary versions offered less balanced allocations of influence on appointments. The most important missed opportunity for these was the fourth draft of the Constitution of the Russian Federation presented in November 1992 and referred to as the 'Rumyantsev' constitution, after the articulate and opinionated executive secretary of the Russian Federation Constitutional Commission. Article 93 provided for appointment by the President, with the consent of the Supreme Soviet, of the Chairman and members of the government of the Russian Federation. Article 99 allowed the legislature sweeping powers of dismissal, essentially forcing the President to fire any official against whom a majority vote of deputies (in each chamber) could be raised.

An American analyst of the draft constitution expressed fundamental concern about the combination of Articles 93 and 99:

> ... while the structure has the appearance of a separation of powers between the legislative and executive branches of government, in practice the structure may allow the legislative branch to exercise extraordinary control of the administrative branch by withholding consent to the appointment of the chairman and other officials and forcing the resignation of these same officials at the whim of the legislature.[30]

It is unlikely that this potential crippling of executive power had been overlooked by the parliamentary commission.

In a similar vein, the proposed presidential amendments to the parliamentary draft constitution had a proprietary executive bent, but were more modest regarding the power of appointment than later presidential drafts. The President wished to specify which members of the government were subject to consent of the (then) Supreme Soviet, proposing that Article 93 should add to 'the Chairman and members of the government of the Russian Federation' the specification: '... in charge of issues of economics and finances, internal affairs, foreign affairs, defence, and security and also appoint other members of the government of the Russian Federation'. On ministerial appointments in Article 99, Amendment 14 required a two-thirds rather than a simple majority vote (in both required rounds) by the Supreme Soviet in order to dismiss members of the government or other specified officials. These qualifiers seemed reasonable, especially when compared with later developments, and illustrate how extreme the pressure on the executive was to compromise on appointments, among other issues. Since there were some strong presidential provisions included among the proposed amendments[31] it is unlikely that the concessions on appointments were empty gestures to please an avid Western and restless domestic audience.

Also in September and November of 1992 the tussle over appointment powers featured strongly in the discussion of a draft Law on the Council of Ministers, with the September presidential version featuring presidential appointment and dismissal of the Prime Minister, the Deputy Prime Ministers, and other ministerial appointments, candidates having been vetted by a Supreme Soviet committee and approved by parliament as a whole. The November legislative response would have granted Congress control over the ministerial appointment process, ranging from nomination to supervision.

By April 1993 the tension between executive and parliament had significantly worsened, and Yeltsin unveiled a relentlessly presidential draft Constitution allowing for parliamentary approval only of the proposed Prime Minister. All other ministerial appointments were to be made 'in consultation' with the higher chamber, vague language reminiscent of Soviet-ese which disappeared from the final version. Ultimately, even what might be called the prime ministerial concession in the December 1993 Russian Constitution was made hollow. The Duma has two rounds to acquiesce in the President's choice(s) for Prime Minister; should it deny approval, the President can dissolve parliament and call new elections. Since many legislators serve with the understanding that the public's perception of corruption and ineptitude in office dooms their chance for re-election, the President holds a powerful club on the sole ministerial appointment that is subject to constitutionally-granted parliamentary scrutiny.

Quarrels over the draft Constitutions themselves were mighty, but the struggles between President and parliament over actual appointments have been brutal when parliament is crossed. Although some of the high rate of turnover in the government is due to Yeltsin's personal displeasure, more often the baying of parliament has brought reluctant presidential dismissal and served to make the tenure of even favoured presidential appointees uncertain.[32] Several examples will serve to illustrate the informal influence of parliament – as well as other constituencies – *vis-à-vis* the President on ministerial appointments.

Promptly upon reassembling after the 1991 coup, the Supreme Soviet sharply criticised Yeltsin's ministerial appointments. At least two high-stakes deals appear to have been brokered between Yeltsin and the Speaker of the parliament (at the time called the Chairman of the Supreme Soviet), Ruslan Khasbulatov, involving powers of appointment: in September 1992 Yeltsin retained the power to appoint heads of administration in the localities by promising not to dissolve parliament before the sitting deputies' terms expired; and in November 1992 he granted parliament's right to confirm his choice of Prime Minister and important Cabinet ministers in order to retain his emergency powers of naming the Cabinet and ruling by decree.[33]

As for change in ministerial personnel under parliamentary pressure, in April 1992 Yeltsin himself was forced to resign as Prime Minister at the insistence of the Sixth Congress (and in line with post-Khrushchevian practice in the USSR of separating chief executive from head of the government). Yeltsin indirectly acknowledged parliament's role in his abandonment in December 1992 of previous favourites and economic reformers Yegor Gaidar (who had been appointed 'acting' Prime Minister so as to avoid an increasingly certain refusal by the Supreme Soviet) and Gennadii Burbulis after one year of service; in his memoirs, Yeltsin essentially substantiated charges brought against Gaidar and Burbulis by powerful deputies (and in a rather Soviet vein: Gaidar was 'out of touch' and needed to travel around the country more; Burbulis was power-hungry and too visibly relished the trappings of office).[34] It was during this year that Ruslan Khasbulatov famously declared that the Cabinet of Ministers should be accountable to the Congress and not to the 'collective Rasputin' surrounding the President.

Indeed, Yeltsin had taken to padding the layer of Deputy Prime Ministers in the apparatus so as to avoid having them subjected to parliamentary approval, but not without drawing wry press commentary: 'The post of Deputy Prime Minister is becoming a widespread occupation in our country.'[35] Yeltsin's seven Deputy Prime Ministers, two of whom were designated First Deputy Prime Ministers, formed a seething cauldron of intrigue, with responsibilities shifting nearly as frequently as blame. The art of kremlinology became useful once again, generally in the assessment of influence according to office location.[36]

As we have seen, 1993 brought continued struggle over constitutional reform and increasing ill will on both sides. Parliamentary pressure on the executive, which had included a narrow defeat for a vote of no confidence in April 1992, took the form of a narrow defeat for a vote for impeachment of the President in March 1993.[37] Further struggles between President and parliament resumed in 1994, following the eventual literal battle between presidential and parliamentary forces and subsequently the adoption of the Constitution by referendum.

The new parliamentary elections did not yield a more quiescent parliament, especially on the issue of appointments. Nor did it lessen the real chief executive's efforts to dominate appointments at the expense of the formal head of government. While everyone understood that the Prime Minister was likely to propose ministers who had in fact been selected by the President, Yeltsin frequently abandoned even the pretence of a prime ministerial role and appointed ministers by presidential decree.[38] It is no wonder that commentators trying to follow the wild swings with appointments became a little snappy:

> Boris Yeltsin's idea of a government reshuffle seems to be to knock back a few vodkas, dump the cards on the floor and let the winner of the resulting brawl pick up the best hand.[39]

It was as much the resulting mix of officials as the style of appointment that made Yeltsin's administration quixotic. Yeltsin kept in place Prime Minister Viktor Chernomyrdin, a sufficiently orthodox figure to satisfy parliament, but in 1994 and again in post-election 1996 he empowered the free-market reformer Anatolii Chubais. Giving up Foreign Minister Andrei Kozyrev for the more conservative Yevgenii Primakov early in the presidential election year was motivated in part by the need to mute parliamentary criticism.

Yet on several occasions when his formally prescribed powers might have made him impervious to opposition, Yeltsin has abandoned key ministers. The Interior Minister Viktor Yerin, the Federal Security Service Chief Sergei Stepashin and the Nationalities Minister Nikolai Yegorov were sacked by Yeltsin in June 1995 with his admission that '...[the deputies] promised to vote in favour of the government, but the price was high – sacking the power ministers'.[40] The crafty President held on to his unpopular Defence Minister Pavel Grachev through this crisis (and until 1996), however, seeing whether three heads would suffice to placate parliament.

The upheaval of June 1995 is most significant in that much of parliament's displeasure with its own powerlessness focused on review of appointments. The Duma voted by an overwhelming majority to adopt several constitutional amendments. These three draft amendments included two on appointments: consent of the State Duma would be required for the appointments of the Prime Minister, Deputy Prime Ministers, and the Ministers of Foreign Affairs, Defence and Internal Affairs, and also the Directors of the Foreign Intelligence Service and the Federal Security Service; and votes of no confidence from the Duma in individual government ministers would force the President to act within two weeks. These measures would have had to garner a 75 per cent majority vote in the upper chamber and be approved by two-thirds of the legislatures of the subjects of the Federation to come into effect, but the failure for this support to materialise does not make the attempt less important.

Thus, even a much weakened parliament continues to hector the President; even with a hand-crafted Constitution in place, Yeltsin has contravened its procedures for ministerial appointment and, more surprisingly, made concessions on appointments in favour of parliament well beyond the few that are constitutionally required. And the demands for openness in procedure of appointment[41] and for further accountability to parliament[42] continue to pour in.

Sources of Executive Responsiveness

From the very first days of the reforms, the Gaidar government was operating under terrible mental duress as the press and the parliament let loose a hailstorm of criticism and kept up an incessant drumbeat of protest. Gaidar and his people were cut virtually no slack and were never given even a modicum of freedom to maneuver.[43]

This moan from Yeltsin's memoirs testifies to the kind of power that the parliament in Russia, considerably aided by the press, retains: the power to frustrate. The State Duma since 1993 has behaved as a highly selective facilitator and a loudly cursing impediment to presidential initiatives as its deputies see fit.

The very nature of checks and balances deserves consideration here. It could be argued that legislative bodies are not and cannot be particularly skilled at 'checking' the executive or 'exposing' individuals or practices – they are, after all, intended to create legislation which *enables* other bodies to act.[44] And when a 'check' is exercised, in the form of review of ministerial appointments in this case, the goal is preferably to rebalance rather than to destabilise the government. The American political system is one indication that the relatively recent development of appointments as direct extensions of policy struggles between President and parliament corrupts both the procedure and inter-branch relations.[45]

The Russian parliament's great handicap is its inability to penetrate presidential armour by conventional means under the current constitutional regime. It is well recognised in Russia that the Constitution is hardly the last word on the Duma's power *vis-à-vis* the President,[46] but even those who take comfort in the Constitution as a stable base for more positive change[47] concede that political institutions have by no means solidified into a democratic framework. It will be difficult to characterise the present situation in appointments as potentially democratic until clearer lines of accountability develop and the President ceases to monitor the proceedings from just above the fray. No wonder that by 1996 an ailing Yeltsin stacked up his Cabinet as a balancing act rather than as a unified, like-minded group: in unity there is responsibility, with disarray there is always someone else to blame. And keeping the disarray *within* a branch rather than *between* branches of government allows for more executive management, if not perhaps control.

In a climate of weak party organization – compounded especially by the chief executive's ability so far to face elections without a party apparatus – institutionalised forces to keep the executive in line are few. Potentially great presidential independence is tempered by the need for a working relationship with parliament and by the relentless probing of the media, but the balance among these forces teeters in a sufficiently precarious fashion to favour executive resolution.

Yeltsin has clearly reacted to legislative, popular and international pressure on presidential appointments during his first five fraught years in office. As with Gorbachev towards the end of his rule, personnel issues became the easiest concessions, something a besieged leader can deliver when legitimacy is scarce and authority correspondingly difficult to wield. The neat half of this equation is that making the executive more responsive begins with the introduction of broader accountability of its principal decision-makers. An accumulation of petty, personal conflict can be a major – perhaps the most important – factor in establishing meaningful checks and balances.

In short, the Russian President, like executive authority elsewhere, is likely to *try* to dodge checks on his power before undertaking major initiatives. The cost of this dodging has been raised by the events of the past ten years to the point that Yeltsin had to shed blood to do it in 1993. He has since moved more gingerly than his tailored Constitution would appear to permit, and parliament is distinctly unsubdued. What has made Russian executive authority most notable over the past century is its relative success in avoiding accountability to parliament despite revolutionary regime change. The current political scene, while still disappointingly dominated by the executive, suggests that the cost of avoiding checks and thus hindering balance in Russian politics has increased.

Notes

1. Diana Woodhouse, 'Back to Basics: Matters Constitutional', *Parliamentary Affairs* **47**, no.3 (July 1994), p.491.
2. M. Steven Fish, 'Democracy Begins to Emerge', *Current History* **94** (October 1995), pp.317–21. Fish's recent book, *Democracy from Scratch: Opposition and Regime in the New Russian Revolution* (Princeton, NJ: Princeton University Press, 1995), is similarly hopeful about at least the aspirations of democrats in Russia.
3. Margot Light, 'Democracy Russian-style', *The World Today* **49**, no.12 (December 1993), p.231.
4. One of the harshest critics in Russia of presidential power and the conflict in Chechnya is the ousted chairman of the human rights commission, Sergei Kovalev: see his 'On the New Russia', *The New York Review of Books*, 18 April 1996, pp.10 and 12.
5. *Segodnya*, 26 July 1996, for example, could not resist noting the irony of parliament recessing for the summer just as the new government was being formed after the presidential election.
6. This is part of the definition provided by Clayton Roberts, *The Growth of Responsible Government in Stuart England* (Cambridge: Cambridge University Press, 1966), p.viii. The other aspect of responsible government he discusses is individual responsibility for ministers, rather than collective responsibility accruing to executive authority (the King).
7. The following accounts are based on the official record of the proceedings (*Pervaya sessiya Verkhovnogo Soveta SSSR. Stenograficheskii otchet*) and the author's viewing of the sessions on television. Of particular interest is the confirmation hearing of Defence Minister Dmitrii Yazov, *Pervaya sessiya ... Byulleten' 9*, 3 July 1989, pp.71–103.
8. This was decided only after considerable discussion during the first session of the Congress of People's Deputies in 1989. The arguments centred on the possibility of putting in sufficient time as a deputy while also heading a ministerial branch or, in

Ryzhkov's case, the entire ministerial structure.

9. *Izvestiya*, 9 June 1989.

10. He is less restrained in his opinions in a querulous 1995 biography: N.I. Ryzhkov, *Desyat' let velikikh potryasenii* (Moscow: Kniga. Prosveshchenie. Miloserdie, 1995). On pp.294 and 447, Ryzhkov presents the Supreme Soviet as one of the many obstacles to his professed – and prototypical ministerial – desire to get the job done.

11. Nine candidates were formally rejected; a tenth withdrew from the confirmation process in order to avoid certain defeat.

12. As with all personnel votes in the USSR, a victorious candidate had to receive over 50 per cent of the vote. The negotiable part is whether that is 50 per cent of votes cast or 50 per cent of votes eligible.

13. *Izvestiya*, 5 July 1989.

14. Vladimir Kontorovich, 'Discipline and Growth in the USSR', *Problems of Communism*, **XXXIV**, no.6 (November–December 1985), pp.27–8.

15. *Izvestiya*, 6 July 1989.

16. *Pravda*, 11 July 1989.

17. *Izvestiya*, 5 August 1989.

18. *Pravda*, 11 July 1989.

19. Polad-zade was particularly vulnerable because of his record as First Deputy Minister for the same bureau. He was a proponent of the controversial Siberian rivers diversion scheme, which was ultimately defeated by a powerful coalition of the environmentally-minded: see Sergei Zalygin, 'Povorot: Uroki odnoi diskussii', *Novyi mir*, 1987, no.1, pp.3–18.

20. *Izvestiya*, 3 July 1989.

21. *Pravda*, 28 June 1989.

22. *Izvestiya*, 24 June 1989.

23. *Pravda*, 28 June 1989.

24. *Izvestiya*, 6 July 1989.

25. For a chronicle of the quirks of British ministerial review in the post-war period, see Geoffrey Marshall (ed.), *Ministerial Responsibility* (Oxford: Oxford University Press, 1989).

26. Eugene Huskey, 'Legislative–Executive Relations in the New Soviet Political Order', Robert T. Huber and Donald R. Kelley (eds), *Perestroika-Era Politics: The New Soviet Legislature and Gorbachev's Political Reforms* (Armonk, NY: M.E. Sharpe, 1991), p.160.

27. Oleg Rumyantsev provides a useful comparison of six constitutions as an appendix to *Osnovy konstitutsionnogo stroya Rossii* (Moscow: Yurist, 1994), pp.224–53, but he does not include the provisions for ministerial appointments.

28. See Sakharov's account in *Moscow and Beyond: 1986 to 1989* (New York: Vintage Books, 1992), pp.156–8.

29. Article 33, Constitution of the Union of Soviet Republics of Europe and Asia, Komsomolskaya pravda, (Vilnius), 12 December 1989 (JPRS-UPA-90-003, 19 January 1990, pp.1–5). For a discussion of the Sakharov Constitution as a whole, see A.A. Mishin, 'Nekotorye mysli o Konstitutsii A.D. Sakharova', *Pravo i vlast'* (Moscow: Progress, 1990), pp.231–40.

30. From the comments of James W. Benton, Jr, Court of Appeals of Virginia, in The American Bar Association Central and East European Law Initiative, 'Analysis of the Draft Constitution of the Russian Federation', 21 January 1993, Appendix B, p.8.

31. For example, a mightier amendment to Article 93 would have given the President the

power to appoint unspecified 'federal officials who shall act within the bounds of the authority of the President of the RF in accordance with federal law to republics, regions, *oblasts*, autonomous *oblasts*, and autonomous districts'.

32. One foreign intelligence officer, in commending the appointment of Primakov as Foreign Minister, mentioned especially his unusual ability to have stayed in his previous post for five years: *The New York Times*, 21 March 1996.

33. The best discussion of this troubled period is Richard Sakwa, *Russian Politics and Society* (London: Routledge & Kegan Paul, 1993), pp.56–73.

34. Boris Yeltsin, *The View from the Kremlin* (London: Harper Collins, 1994), pp.155–60.

35. *Izvestiya*, 3 June 1992.

36. This particular marker of status continues to be commented upon and, as with the sequence of parade reviewers on top of Lenin's mausoleum in Red Square, signifies an executive branch where the chief's favour is a more important indicator of power than is title.

37. Once the Constitution was adopted, parliament could afford a successful vote of no confidence once before consequences began to pile up, so they exercised their prerogative in autumn 1994, March 1995 and June 1995. These votes of no confidence differ dramatically from British parliamentary norms, where the proceedings at least pretend to hinge upon the ability of government-backed initiatives to muster enough votes to pass.

38. For a perceptive discussion of this and other presidential transgressions, see Vera Tolz, 'Problems of Building Democratic Institutions in Russia', *RFE/RL Research Report* 3, no.9 (4 March 1994), pp.1–7.

39. *The Economist*, 12 November 1994, p.18.

40. *The Moscow Tribune*, 28 June 1995.

41. 'The degree of secrecy over the process of Cabinet formation has exceeded all reasonable limits' snapped *Nezavisimaya gazeta*, 31 July 1996, as the swirl of speculation over post-election appointments reached its height.

42. Following the presidential election in 1996, Communist Party leader Gennadii Zyuganov demanded that any candidate for Prime Minister present an outline of the new government programme to the Duma so that deputies could conduct a more informed approval process.

43. Yeltsin, *The View From the Kremlin*, p.154.

44. L. Peter Schultz, 'Congress and the Separation of Powers Today: Practice in Search of a Theory', in Bradford P. Wilson and Peter W. Schramm (eds), *Separation of Powers and Good Government* (Lanham, MD: Rowman & Littlefield, 1994), pp.193–4.

45. For a discussion of this problem, see James D. King and James W. Riddlesperger, Jr, 'Senate Confirmation of Appointments to the Cabinet and Executive Office of the President', *The Social Science Journal* 28, no.2 (1991), pp.189–202.

46. Eduard Batalov has written two penetrating essays regarding the limitations of the law in determining legislative practice: 'Bez kontrolya nad vlast'yu net demokratii', *Rossiiskaya federatsiya*, 1994, no.12, pp.2–3, and 'Vybiraya Gosdumu, vybiraem i Pravitel'stvo', *Rossiiskaya federatsiya*, 1995, no.20, pp.17–18.

47. Fish, 'Democracy Begins to Emerge', especially p.321.

3 Presidential Prefects in the Russian Provinces: Yeltsin's Regional Cadres Policy

William A. Clark

Increasingly since the collapse of Soviet power in Russia, critics of Boris Yeltsin's regional cadres policy have pointed to what they consider to be the Russian President's re-creation in a different guise of the old centrally controlled Communist Party apparatus in the provinces and localities.[1] Specifically, the development of a policy whereby the centre is ultimately responsible for the naming of regional and local Heads of Administration (*glavy administratsii*, or GAs) and Presidential Representatives (*predstaviteli prezidenta*, or PPs) in Russian provinces, municipalities and districts, in almost all cases without the input of the local electorate and often without the support of the relevant elected soviet, has been negatively evaluated in the light of the practice of the erstwhile Soviet leadership of naming *obkom*, *gubkom*, and *raikom* secretaries throughout the republics of the USSR. Such was the sentiment, for example, of Leonid Smirnyagin, a member of the President's Council, who in 1994 remarked that

> I would consider the most important of the new tendencies to be the sharp intensification of the executive authority in the outlying areas. The governor became, almost everywhere, the indisputable leader of the region, and his administration became the key, and practically the sole, agency of administration and not only state administration, but also largely economic. Outwardly it would seem that the times of the oblast committees are returning.[2]

It is in the sense articulated by Smirnyagin that this chapter utilises admittedly anachronistic language in its title. When Soviet power collapsed in Russia in 1991, scholars in the West foresaw a general

24

empowerment of the elected assemblies at all levels, assemblies that had, of course, remained almost universally powerless during the preceding seventy years.[3] To the degree that such predictions carried with them an air of positive expectation, the idea that in 1995 Russia should have Presidentially appointed governors, mayors and 'vice regents', and that locally elected soviets would remain in a secondary decision-making position, might be considered by some to be surprising and disappointing.[4]

This study seeks to describe and evaluate the nature of this regional cadres policy and to predict future developments in this area. As will become clear below, it would be shortsighted to investigate the question of Yeltsin's regional cadres policy as if it were divorced from more macro-political issues that have developed in Russia since 1991. Issues of institutional infighting at the national level (horizontal power distribution) and within the confines of the question of federalism itself (vertical power distribution) have helped shape the nature of this regional policy. Moreover, in evaluating comparisons between the Soviet and post-Soviet institutional arrangements, it is important not to reify either set of institutional practices.

National Contests and Regional Variations

One of the defining characteristics of the process that led to the collapse of the USSR was the breakdown of centralised power as the constituent republics of the USSR in the years leading up to 1991 were ever more able to defy Moscow's rule and create greater areas of local policy autonomy. After the demise of the USSR in December 1991, many observers have chronicled a similar process within Russia itself, as the equilibrium of decision-making power between the central government in Moscow and the provincial authorities in the 89 territorial–administrative regions of Russia[5] has been the focus of considerable political struggle. President Yeltsin, in an attempt to enhance the power of the Russian presidency *vis-à-vis* regional authorities, has instituted a number of policies aimed at maintaining a high degree of central authority in Russia's regions.

A second defining characteristic of the final period of the USSR and the early years of post-Soviet Russia has been the process by which the division of power between organs of representative government (soviets and dumas) and organs of executive power evolved in a generally confrontational manner. While the details of the executive-legislative competition at the national level in Russia, culminating in the storming of the Russian parliament on 4 October 1993, is well known and has been the focus of numerous analyses over the past few years, the regional variation on this competition has attracted much less attention. Regional soviets during the events of October 1993 frequently sided with Ruslan Khasbulatov and adopted a pro-parliament stance in opposition to Yeltsin and his policies. Interested as they were in maximising their own regional prerogatives, many regional soviets had adopted for at least the year prior to October 1993 a confrontational stance opposed to Yeltsin's attempts to control events in the provinces. With the 'defeat' of parliament in October, Yeltsin availed himself of the opportunity to order the disbanding of the local soviets[6] and to rely on his own representatives in the provinces.

Examination of the centre–periphery issue necessitates attention to both the strict issue of the degree of geographic centralisation of power within Russia, and the nature of executive–legislative relations. Clearly, Yeltsin has adopted a policy that seeks to maximise the power of the centre and the power of the executive President. In the regions, this has manifested itself in Yeltsin's attempts to have local power adhere to his own two appointed representatives: the Heads of Administration and the Presidential Representatives. Legislative forces have, of course, sought to counter these measures by enhancing the prerogatives of the State Duma at the national level. Regionally, local forces have sought both to empower local soviets and to weaken the President's control over regional Heads of Administration.[7] This chapter examines the dynamic elements of this interplay between central authority and local government.

As might be expected, the institutional and political contests at the national level in Russia over the past half-decade or so have had substantial sub-national variations that have further complicated Russia's transition from communism. Specifically, the questions of constitutional design, federalism and executive–legislative relations, to say nothing of the substantive economic and other public policy issues of individual governments, have become a complex web of competition, displaying both a national and the regional character. Russia is probably one of the most ethnically and politically heterogeneous states in the world. This trait, combined with the fact that, unlike most post-authoritarian transitions in Latin America or Southern Europe, Russia has had simultaneously to undergo fundamental political as well as economic restructuring, has made the Russian case particularly difficult. As will be seen, Yeltsin's attempts to exercise central authority in Russia's localities must be viewed in the context of these myriad political forces.

A major pole around which politics has revolved in Russia has been the determination of a proper horizontal distribution of political power between executive institutions and parliamentary bodies at the national level. The revolutionary slogan 'all power to the soviets' maintained some sort of political appeal throughout the life of the USSR, in part, one supposes, because these parliamentary bodies were ubiquitous (numbering in the early 1980s over 50,000 in total[8], and entailed great, although largely untapped, potential for representative government (bringing in, as they did, over two-and-a-quarter million citizens into parliamentary roles). Given that parliamentary bodies in the USSR, from the USSR Supreme Soviet down to the more than 40,000 village soviets, had been politically emasculated, many observers drew the conclusion that their very emasculation was a key to the USSR's decline into party autocracy. This logic assumed that the reinvigoration of these parliamentary bodies would be a key to the escape from party autocracy. Indeed, much of the talk of the Gorbachev period encouraged those political forces that sought to centre Russian political power in parliamentary bodies.[9] Indeed, one of the hallmarks of the past decade in the USSR and Russia (until recently) has been the rise in power of parliaments.

Politically, and especially from the perspective of pro-reform democrats, the effectiveness of these soviets as vehicles for positive change in the country has been called into question. Unlike a few of its East European allies that had throughout the late 1970s and 1980s exhibited sufficient political and social 'space' to permit the slow development of social movements that could be converted into political parties after the fall of communism,[10] such was not the case in Russia. Because sound and stable party systems are crucial to parliamentary affairs, Russia's immature party system rendered its parliament relatively ineffectual. In addition, President Yeltsin missed a fine opportunity in the autumn of 1991 to disband the Russian parliament and call for new elections.[11] What he and his reformist government were left with was a Russian parliament, elected in 1990 under less than fully democratic procedures, that had become in many ways a political anachronism which served as a fetter on the reform agenda. The 'cohabitation' of such a parliament and such a President, who differed not only on the merits of political reform but also on the proper relative balance of power between the executive and the legislature, made the events of 1992–93 almost inevitable.

The details of the Yeltsin–Khasbulatov confrontations are well known and need not be reiterated here. For present purposes, it is worth noting that the executive–legislative battle in Russia may be viewed as a case study of a similar paradox existing in many countries experiencing post-authoritarian or post-communist transitions. Students of such transitions have noted the dilemma posed by the demands of transition that seems to require strong executive leadership so as to be able to push through the often unpopular measures that comprise democratisation and marketisation.[12] Michael McFaul, for example, has argued that radical economic reform, even one predicated on liberalising society, has often required authoritarian controls, coercion, and even violent repression.[13] More generally, speaking about the connection between political and economic reform in post-communist states, Tsuyoshi Hasegawa has stated that 'to ensure the success of marketisation, "iron hands" may be needed to silence the opposition'.[14] It seems clear in retrospect that Yeltsin distrusted the Russian parliament with respect to its commitment to democratic reforms and was willing, in the name of such reforms, to call for and utilise less-than-democratic powers against the parliament. Likewise, throughout the year leading up to the events of October 1993, parliament tried several times to impeach the President. In some measure, the implicit understanding that such 'iron hands' may be needed in transitions from post-communist authoritarianism may explain the relatively benign reaction to Yeltsin's autumn 1993 destruction of the Russian parliament.

The institutional contests at the national level certainly displayed their regional variations. There, too, horizontal battles over political dominance in the localities have been fought between executive and parliamentary bodies. Unlike at the national level where a strong President was already on the scene, however, the executive organs of local government in Russia seemed likely to benefit from the collapse of local Communist Party dominance. Executive powers were already technically in the domain of the local soviet's executive committee (*ispolkom*). While this arrangement was, of course, subject to the right of verification by the erstwhile corresponding Party committees, with the collapse of Communist Party power, and in the potential absence of a suitable substitute, local councils looked to exercise very much expanded power. Such a proposition challenged both Yeltsin's substantive political reform agenda (because local soviets were often perceived as much less democratically inclined than Yeltsin desired) and the effective prerogatives of the office of President. Not surprisingly, to the degree that Yeltsin was interested in separating local soviets from the exercise of executive power throughout Russia, and to the degree that he wanted a greater degree of centralised executive authority to reside in his office, he was compelled to create an executive substitute for the Communist Party committee secretariats that he had done so much to destroy. It is this dual motive – to ensure Presidential predominance by defeating a recalcitrant parliament at the national level and to maximise the President's control of events in the regions – that helps explain the vital connection between the horizontal and vertical components of Yeltsin's policies. Yeltsin's 'suitable substitutes' for the Communist Party *obkoms, raikoms* and *gorkoms*, substitutes that, like the old local Party organs, enhanced both the likelihood of the centre's political policies being implemented in the localities and the maintenance of centralised leadership in Moscow, took the form of two new institutions manned by what one observer has term Yeltsin's 'vice regents and governors'.[15]

Heads of Administration

The institution of local Heads of Administration (GAs) can be traced back to the very election of Boris Yeltsin to the post of President of the Russian Federation on 12 June 1991, although the actual legislation dealing with the GAs did not come until later in the year. As Yeltsin campaigned for the presidency, he came out in favour of transferring local power to Presidentially appointed GAs, thereby usurping the power of conservative, communist-dominated local soviets that had been elected earlier. Upon Yeltsin's election it was announced that three other individuals elected that day were to be Heads of Administration of cities where pro-reform democrats had won solid majorities in elections to the city soviet. The new 'mayors' were to be Gavriil Popov (Moscow), Anatolii Sobchak (St. Petersburg) and the lesser known Valerii Lyskov (Severodvinsk, Arkhangel *oblast*). Appointing these men municipal GAs was termed an 'experiment', but within a few months momentum had developed around the idea that a Head of Administration would be appointed in all localities in Russia. Very often those designated by Yeltsin to serve as the GA were individuals other than the incumbent head of the local government.

Ever since the initiation of discussions about the institution of the role of GA, there has been debate over the manner of selection of these individuals. Specifically, at least four variations in the selection process have been discussed at various times: (1) appointment by the Russian President; (2) nomination by the Russian President, with local soviets approving or disapproving of the nominees; (3) local soviets presenting to the President a short list of acceptable nominees to the position, from which list the President would select the GA; and (4) a multi-candidate slate of nominees, with the vote of the local electorate filling the GA slot. This debate was essentially resolved with the October 1993 events helping the Russian President gain most of the discretion in the naming of the GAs, although in many cases the third alternative was adopted.[16] The nature of this contest over the selection of local Heads of Administration has helped define the struggle between the Moscow centre and the local soviet authorities over the past few years.

On 22 August 1991, in the immediate aftermath of the attempted coup in Moscow, President Yeltsin issued Decree No. 75, which defined the position of Head of Administration and gave the President the right to nominate to the position. The decree makes clear that the GAs were to be 'appointed by the President of the RSFSR and be accountable to him'. The decree goes on to specify the responsibilities and authorities of the GAs. Briefly, as originally conceived, GAs: (1) exercise executive command functions in the localities; (2) can issue resolutions and orders which are compulsory for subordinate executives in the regions; (3) ensure interaction with the corresponding soviets of people's deputies; (4) report annually to the corresponding soviets on the executive budget; (5) may override the decisions of the corresponding soviet;[17] (6) may repeal the administrative actions of subordinate executive organs if they are deemed to be in violation of extant legislation; and (7) create and organise subordinate executive structures, including the appointing and firing of relevant executive officials. Heads of Administration (8) are not permitted to carry out other duties in state, commercial or public organs. Given these wide powers, the GAs are the most important political figures in the Russian regions and localities.

Functionally, Heads of Administration are responsible for running the day-to-day affairs of government at their respective level of administration. Heads of Administration name their own executive government teams, although it is not unusual for the local soviets again to influence certain choices. Typically, the oblast GA will name a First Deputy Head of Administration and five–seven additional deputies, with differing substantive executive responsibilities. A look at Moscow city administration may provide an indication of the functional responsibilities of these oblast deputy GAs. The five Moscow city deputy GAs are responsible for (1) territorial administration, (2) economic reform, (3) the municipal economy, (4) long-term city development, and (5) social security.

Each of these deputy GAs would head a number of specialised departments that combine to constitute the leadership of the executive branch of government. More minor department heads are also named, but do not usually carry the title of deputy GA. Frequently, administration activities are organised by a Chief of Staff.[18] Structurally, at least, such an arrangement does not look strikingly different from a Soviet-era *oblast* Party committee (*obkom*) secretariat.[19] In Moscow city, there is also a structure whereby the prefects of the city's ten *raions* meet in executive session to co-ordinate municipal policy. What is more, as of September 1992, *oblast* GAs have been given the responsibility by means of a Presidential decree of naming and supervising these city-level GAs themselves.[20]

In the month following the decree, on 6 September, it was further stipulated by the President that popular elections to fill the GA posts would take place on 24 November 1991. One may assume that the large number of GAs appointed by Yeltsin were to be nominated to run in these elections. In October, relevant legislation had emerged from the Russian parliament on this matter, but it stipulated that Heads of Administration were to be nominated by the President and elected by the local constituency, not approved by the corresponding soviets, as had been expected. Furthermore, the law stated that the GA at the *oblast* level was to be called 'governor' (*gubernator*), at the city level 'mayor' (*meyr*). Finally, the law designated that the soviets would function in policy-making and representative roles, but would not be involved in executive politics. Hence, *raiispolkomy*, *gorispolkomy*, and *oblispolkomy* would have their executive functions transferred to the GAs, who would be empowered to create their own executive officers and staff. In October 1991, parliament passed and Yeltsin signed this 'Law on Elections of Heads of Administration',[21] although, as will be seen, some elements of this law never came into force.

In late October 1991, Yeltsin petitioned the Russian parliament to declare a one-year moratorium on the election of the GAs scheduled for later that year. This specific petition was granted on 1 November 1991 by the parliament as part of a larger package of enhanced Presidential powers, under the title 'On the Organisation of Executive Power in the Period of Radical Economic Reform'.[22] This resolution granted Yeltsin the authority to appoint GAs until such time as elections to the posts could be held. As part of the emergency powers granted to the President, parliament stipulated that no elections could be held until 1 December 1992. At that time, the resolution stated, local soviets would be assigned the right to nominate the GAs, with the President being reserved the right to have the final say in all matters affecting the removal of any GA he felt was not acting legally. This change in the method of filling the GA positions, which evidently weakened the President's prerogatives in this sphere, seems to have been a *quid pro quo* agreed to by Yeltsin in return for the granting of the larger set of emergency powers. As with the October 1991 law on elections, this law of 1 November 1991 requiring eventual elections of GAs after December 1992 never came into effect. In the four years following this agreement, Yeltsin maintained his role as the predominant determiner of regional and local executive authority throughout Russia. However, a more careful reading of the political forces at work over this period reveals a more complex dynamic.

The President's administration in Moscow has since attempted to exercise control over the local election of GAs. In the autumn of 1994 Yeltsin issued a decree banning gubernatorial elections in the provinces without Moscow's consent.[23] This having been said, however, Yeltsin has been forced to relent and permit elections in certain cases. For example, in his old *oblast*, Sverdlovsk, Eduard Rossel, the speaker of the *oblast* soviet, successfully pressured Moscow to permit GA elections there.[24] In any event, the nature of the selection process for regional GAs is still under debate. State Duma legislation looks to GA elections once the regions are successful in adopting their own charters.[25]

It is important to resist the conclusion that no nation-wide election of GAs has taken place purely because Yeltsin did not want them held, although he clearly did not.[26] Throughout 1993, despite its confrontation with the President, the Russian parliament did not push to have the October 1991 law on GA elections enforced. As part of this executive–legislative stand-off in Moscow, parliament was depending in good part on local support for its position. The parliament understood that in an environment where it was not at all clear who would emerge victorious from the confrontation, it needed as much support as it could garner. If it demanded immediate election of GAs in conformity with the October 1991 law, the incumbent GAs, fearful of losing their positions, would almost assuredly side with President Yeltsin who, after all, had appointed them in the first place. By permitting the incumbent GAs to keep their posts, the national parliament was hoping to have them at least remain neutral in the national executive–legislative conflict. Parliament stipulated that GAs were to remain in office so long as the relevant local soviet deemed it appropriate. While it is true that in two instances Yeltsin had successfully overridden local soviets' calls for GA elections (Moscow city in March 1993 and Chelyabinsk *oblast* in April 1993) and appointed his own GAs, several provincial GAs were replaced via local elections in April 1993 (with Yeltsin's nominees losing to more conservative candidates). In sum, no national GA elections were held because, for different reasons, neither parliament nor the President pushed for them. At the time, parliament and the GAs seemed likely to agree that GA elections should coincide with the next scheduled normal parliamentary elections (that is, in March 1995). The prospects for such a deal, however, were scuttled by the events of October 1993 and the dissolution of local soviets by Yeltsin's Decree No.1617 of 9 October 1993 .

The political nature of the genesis of these posts is obvious from the mechanics and timing of Yeltsin's appointment of GAs. In the aftermath of the August 1991 *putsch*, Yeltsin focused his immediate attention on those regions where support for the attempted coup had been most evident. His initial appointments to the post of GA were loyal pro-Yeltsin figures named to fill executive positions in 'disloyal' regions. Within five weeks of the failure of the *putsch*, Yeltsin had named nine *oblast* GAs, in Arkhangel, Astrakhan, Irkutsk, Kaliningrad, Kaluga, Kemerovo, Riazan, Volgograd (Tsaritsyn) and Vladimir. Inasmuch as the GAs have tended to be named via a Presidential decree, it is easy to track the pace at which Yeltsin filled these posts. Simply put, Yeltsin acted very quickly to get these regional and local executives in place, and by the middle of December 1991 (that is, within four months of the *putsch*) he had named GAs to 64 of the 68 regional units of Russia.[27] Given that Yeltsin's power was at its peak in the initial post-*putsch* months, he was able in many cases to name allies to these posts even in the face of some local opposition.[28] In other instances, however, Yeltsin was forced to accede to the wishes of the relevant local soviets, which in many localities were able greatly to influence the appointment of GAs. In fact, according to Darrell Slider, most of the GA appointments in the aftermath of the initial post-coup appointments simply 'redesignated' the incumbent soviet chairmen as Heads of Administration.[29]

Background information on the Yeltsin GAs is generally available, and the following conclusions seem warranted. First, there has been very little tendency, and certainly less than the system operating during the Soviet period, to 'parachute' individual GAs into the regions from outside areas. Scholars who studied the Soviet *obkom* first secretaries, for example, will be struck by the fact that the vast majority of those named as regional and local GAs have emerged locally, and are far less likely to be moved administratively from one *oblast* to another.[30] Indeed, Peter Rutland has shown that during the 1980s, the tendency of RSFSR *obkom* first secretaries to be parachuted into outside *oblasts* increased from 28 per cent of all cases in the 1981 sample to 41 per cent in that of 1988.[31] Very few GAs in the current cohort have been parachuted in from other regions of the country. Indeed, the general practice has been to name to the GA position a local official, in many cases the sitting head of the local soviet. To be sure, however, President Yeltsin attempted to appoint reformist local officials as Heads of Administration, sometimes dipping into the middle ranks of the local political elite to do so. In such cases, local opposition to the GA has been more intense, often emanating from the caste of political supporters of the 'higher ranking' officials who may have been passed over by Yeltsin.

Second, by and large, GAs exhibit a much less 'scripted' previous career than did *obkom* first secretaries. Much was made of the 'generalist' training of the Soviet-era party prefects, with relatively routinised training in Komsomol, soviet and party posts prior to being named *obkom* first secretary. While there does remain a sizeable element of this legacy in the current GAs (and in Yeltsin himself, of course), the likelihood of such non-traditional figures as mining executives (Primorskii *krai*), economics instructors (Kaliningrad *oblast*), civil engineers (Moscow *oblast*), radio physicists (Nizhnii Novgorod) and joint venture directors (Sakhalin) being named to important executive political positions has certainly increased. This having been said, however, the current GAs have a good sprinkling of former *oblispolkom* chairmen (for example, Astrakhan, Irkutsk, Moscow and Ulyanovsk) and deputy chairmen (for example, Kostroma), common 'feeder posts' to the *obkom* leadership under Communist Party rule.

Third, this traditionalism with respect to career training and background of regional GAs is likely to increase with the incidence of local direct elections of new GAs. In the few cases where regional and local GAs have been directly elected, old-fashioned communist-style *apparatchiki* have frequently won election despite Yeltsin's opposition. Specifically, in April 1993 the direct election of the GA resulted in the political resurrection in Orel *oblast* of Yegor Stroev, the Gorbachev-era *obkom* first secretary (1985–89) and voting member of the all-Union Politburo (1990–91) who had been languishing out of politics as Director of the All-Russian Institute of Horticultural Plant-Breeding. Likewise in the same month, the electorate of Penza *oblast* elected as regional GA Anatolii Kovlyagin. Kovlyagin had been Penza *obkom* second secretary (1986–89) and chairman of the *oblispolkom* (1989–91). It seems as though a number of regional and local communist-era officials have made successful transitions to the post-communist period, although in not a few cases they have done so with a decidedly nostalgic political message. Until time and the actuarial tables deplete the stock of Soviet-era regional *apparatchiki*, one should expect additional instances of political resurrection, especially if the economy recovers slowly and Yeltsin's ability to appoint GAs gives way to a greater incidence of their popular election.

Finally, the initial cohort of late 1991–early 1992 GAs seems to have achieved some degree of longevity in these posts. No fewer than fifty GAs named by Yeltsin during the initial eight-month period after the August 1991 *putsch* were still in the same post at the end of summer 1994. Two interpretations combine to explain this phenomenon. First, it may be assumed that in the post-*putsch* months, Yeltsin had sufficient political power to name individuals with whom he shared a political agenda, even if at times those individuals were confronted by regional or local opposition. If this were the case, there would be very little need for the Russian President to replace his own GAs. Again, students of regional party affairs in the Soviet era will immediately call to mind the Brezhnev policy of 'trust in cadres' whereby *obkom* secretaries acquired what one scholar referred to as a 'near-life peerage' in these posts. From this perspective, and even in the face of rather high degrees of political instability, Yeltsin's 'trust' in his GAs is neither surprising nor a break from tradition. A second interpretation, however, makes the current situation clearer. Inasmuch as Yeltsin was able to avoid the national direct popular election of GAs – and judging by the few local instances where such elections produced anti-Yeltsin GAs he would wish to maintain this position – the longevity of his original GA cohort may also be partially explained by his hesitancy to create GA vacancies. Thus in a different political environment marked by better electoral prospects for pro-Yeltsin regional and local officials, a greater degree of turnover in GA positions may have been evident.

One of the ironies that revolves around the controversy of the Presidentially-appointed local Heads of Administration is that the institution itself represents something of a reversal of political trends that started with Gorbachev. As is well known, through the mid-to-late 1980s local power in the USSR resided in party officials appointed by Moscow, and this characteristic of political power at the *oblast*, city and district levels was very aptly captured by Hough's 'prefect' label. Gorbachev initiated a number of reforms in this area that sought to decentralise local party authority by tying local party secretaries to an electoral process that made them increasingly vulnerable to the electorate. In addition, local soviets were empowered and quickly shed the complacent rubber-stamp character of the Soviet period.[32] At the time of these changes, many students of Soviet politics applauded the increase in democratic and local authority that they entailed. It is, again, somewhat ironic that, four years after the demise of communist power in Russia, perhaps the most important individual in this process should seek to rule Russia's provinces in essentially the same manner as the communists: with unelected 'governors' and 'mayors' appointed by Moscow authorities presiding over regions and cities, dominating the local councils of representative government. Like the communist party first secretaries in *krais, oblasts* cities and districts, Heads of Administration have become the most significant actors in local politics, and have, by and large, been political supporters of the President who named them to these posts.[33] It is perhaps a testament to the difficulty of the post-communist transition that such developments have occurred.

Presidential Representative

The idea of Presidential Representatives being sent off to the regions to serve as a political liaison officer of the Moscow executive, ensuring the enforcement of central legislation, especially with respect to the reform agenda of the President, can be traced back to the late Gorbachev era.[34] At the XXVIII Congress of the CPSU, held in June–July 1990, Boris Gidaspov, then first secretary of the Leningrad *gorkom*, encouraged Soviet President Gorbachev to name Presidential Representatives to the Soviet federal units in an attempt to counter the centrifugal political tendencies associated with the so-called 'war of laws' that defined centre–periphery relations at that time.[35] Gorbachev was in favour of the development of such a set of posts, but at the Congress a bloc of liberal reform democrats scuttled the proposal.

Despite initial democratic opposition to the idea of Presidential Representatives being named to the regions, by the middle of 1991 Yeltsin and his camp had come to support the idea. Indeed, Yeltsin's campaign for the Russian presidency in the spring and early summer of 1991 explicitly called for the introduction of the post. About two months after his election to the Presidency, Yeltsin followed up on this idea and created a Chief State Inspectorate to supervise the naming of the PPs. As stated above, the August 1991 *putsch* galvanised Yeltsin's resolve with respect to the regions as a result of many local officials' support for the Committee for the State of Emergency. It is important to avoid the conclusion that Yeltsin's desire to appoint GAs and PPs to the regions of Russia originated in the August 1991 coup. As Valerii Makharadze, then first Chief State Inspector of the Russian Federation and, by virtue of that post, the man responsible for oversight of these Presidential Representatives, stated in a September 1991 interview, it was something of a coincidence that the reform of the executive structures in the localities and the August 1991 coup attempt occurred at roughly the same time.[36]

In any event, in order 'to enhance the co-ordinating activities of the RSFSR, *krai* and *oblast* bodies of executive power', on 24 August 1991 Yeltsin issued Decree No. 87, entitled 'On Representatives of the President of the RSFSR in *Krais* and *Oblasts* of the RSFSR'.[37] The decree named the first wave of fourteen PPs to be sent to the regions. At that time, it was not clear whether the creation of PP posts would be a permanent or only temporary addition to the structure of Russian government. As was the case with Yeltsin's GAs, his first appointments of Presidential Representatives were targeted at those regions that seemed especially untrustworthy from the President's perspective.[38] While the initial decree went so far as to name these PPs, it was not until one week later that a temporary regulation *(polozhenie)* actually defined the powers and responsibilities of the positions. More formal enunciation of the nature of the positions would have to wait until July 1992.

While there was at the outset a great deal of speculation about the local role of the Presidential Representatives, it seems clear that from the start they were to have significantly less political authority than their parallel Heads of Administration. One PP described his role as follows: it 'does not involve executive power, ... is not a procurator, not a governor-general and not a Pontius Pilate ... [it does not involve] removing anyone from his post, allocating money or obtaining pipe.' Rather, the main function of the Presidential Representatives is 'monitoring fulfilment of the President's decrees and Russian laws, engaging in constructive interaction with local bodies of power, analysing the state of affairs and maintaining constant contact with the RSFSR President, so that he will be aware of situations developing locally.'[39] In effect, then, PPs saw themselves as the President's eyes and ears in the regions. Critics, in fact, have referred to them as little more than 'squealers'.[40] Presidential Representatives themselves acknowledge the nature of their role. Gennadii Veretennikov, the PP of Moscow *oblast*, admits, 'to be sure, we President's representatives do not have any levers of power', but serve primarily as watchdogs for the Moscow executive.[41] This functional role often placed the PP at odds with the respective wishes of the relevant Head of Administration and the local soviet.

In a more formal sense, however, the Presidential Representatives' duties were defined carefully in July 1992 in a series of decrees and statutes. Presidential Decree No. 765 described the positions as permanent, and placed the responsibility for their upkeep (office space, telephone, living space and so on) on the offices of the Heads of Administration.[42] The statute that was issued simultaneously spells out in detail the nature of these positions.[43] Of note among the general provisions of the statute are the fact that the Presidential Representatives: (1) are personally responsible to the Russian President; (2) are appointed by the President through the Chief State Inspector of the Russian Federation; (3) may not be members of any political party or other political association; (4) may not hold any positions in state organs or local organs of self-government, in enterprises, institutions and other organisations; and (5) may not engage in any entrepreneurial activities. The statute goes on to list a series of powers that inhere in the position. Specifically, the Presidential Representatives in the Russian regions represent the President locally, promote the observance of federal laws, decrees and orders of the Russian President, present to the President analytical information on political, social, and economic activities taking place in the region, co-ordinate the activities of territorial services of the federal organs of executive authority in the respective regions, organise inspections of executive and parliamentary organs, enterprises and other local institutions, and make proposals to the Russian President concerning local developments. These powers describe the authorities of what has been called the President's 'vice-regents' in the regions of Russia.[44]

As was the case with the regional Heads of Administration, Yeltsin acted quickly to fill the great majority of Presidential Representative slots. Close to 60 of the 68 regional positions were named within six months of the original decree of 24 August 1991. That is, roughly 90 per cent of the regional Presidential Representatives were in place prior to the July 1992 statutes legally defining their roles. Moreover, as has been the case with the GAs, Presidential Representatives as a whole have enjoyed rather stable 'terms' in office. Fifty-three of the 61 slots for which data are available were still filled in mid-1994 by the original members of the initial PP cohort. In a word, low turnover has marked both the regional Heads of Administration and the Presidential Representatives.

Thanks to the analysis of Boris Bogatov, we have a substantially complete picture of the types of individuals named by Yeltsin to be his Presidential Representatives in the regions.[45] According to this analysis, Yeltsin's Presidential Representatives have come overwhelmingly from the liberal, pro-reform wings of executive and legislative organs, at both the all-Union and the RSFSR levels. In terms of their previous positions, fourteen were members of committees and commissions of either the USSR (n=2) or RSFSR (n=12) Supreme Soviets, nine were either chairmen or deputy chairmen of *oblispolkoms* (n=2), *gorispolkoms* (n=5), or *raiispolkoms* (n=2). An additional 12 PPs came from the technical (n=7) or scientific (n=5) intelligentsia. The remaining Presidential Representatives included in Bogatov's study included three elected officials, two economic managers, two journalists, two medical personnel, and two members of the Democratic Russia organisation. Twenty-seven of the PPs named in the initial phase in 1991 were at one point people's deputies during the first five congresses, with the overwhelming majority of this number, not surprisingly, coming from the democratic wing of the parliament. In a word, Yeltsin named as his representatives in Russia's regions individuals with experience in public organs who shared his vision of Russia's future. This picture of the political leanings of the Presidential Representatives is bolstered further by Gennadii Vladimirov.[46] From his analysis, of the 68 PPs named by the end of 1991, 42 were either deputies of the Russian Congress of People's Deputies or its Soviet national equivalent. An additional fifteen were deputies of *oblast* or city soviets. Almost all the PPs appointed at that time were members of the Democratic Russia pro-reform faction.

Governors, Vice-Regents and Local Power

While it is fair to say that Yeltsin has at least in the short term successfully instituted both the Heads of Administration and the Presidential Representatives as legitimate authorities at the regional level, the battle to do so has revealed aspects of both the executive–parliament and centre–periphery competition. Superimposed in many cases on these two institutional fault lines has been the added variable of public policy debates. This combination of institutional in-fighting and policy differences has made the task of untangling the motivations of actors in the centre–periphery debate much more difficult.

One obvious general statement that can be made at the outset concerning the institutional competition at the local level in Russia is that by and large the local soviets have tended to side with the national parliament in its confrontations with the President, while the Heads of Administration and Presidential Representatives have tended to be political allies of the President. The myriad reasons for this split, again, lie both in the institutional and in political struggles. While it might be tempting to assume that the root cause of these debates is overwhelmingly concerned with policy, such a view cannot account for every instance of conflict. For example, a number of even the more liberal, pro-reform soviets that have captured power in municipalities have come into conflict with both the

GAs and PPs owing to a lack of clear articulation of the exact jurisdictions of these bodies.[47] Moreover, inasmuch as Yeltsin's Presidential Representatives have as part of their duties the oversight of the corresponding Heads of Administration, these two local authorities have often come into conflict, even in cases where on substantive political grounds the two individuals may be like-minded.[48] Many GAs resent the lack of responsibility of the Presidential Representatives over local policy results, even as they interfere in the work of the GAs. What is more, there have even been instances (for example, in Novosibirsk and Irkutsk) when Yeltsin's attempts to remove the local Head of Administration have been blocked by the united resolve of the local Presidential Representative and soviet.[49] Such examples speak to the difficulty in presenting a simple generic view of the political situation in question.

The above caveat notwithstanding, however, it is clear that the competition between the executive and parliament has been a significant feature in Russia's regions. Many key figures within the more radical reform movement identified the soviets themselves as the root cause of the problem in reforming Russia. The mayors of St. Petersburg (Anatolii Sobchak) and Moscow (Gavriil Popov) called openly in the early 1990s for the 'de-sovietisation' of Russia, and Popov's claim that the attempt to preserve for the soviets a viable role in post-communist Russia was the key to the country's problems set the tenor of the politics of the day.[50] At even higher levels, Yeltsin himself made clear his disdain for the soviets and, in addition to his attempts to restructure the soviets and to render them superfluous at the regional and local levels by introducing his GAs and PPs, he stated in June 1993 that to his mind 'the soviets and democracy are not compatible'.[51] Thus, throughout the period between the August 1991 *putsch* and the October 1993 dissolution of the soviets, parliamentary forces in Russia found themselves in direct opposition to Yeltsin on both institutional and political grounds, and at both the national and the local levels.

With the help of the national legislature, local soviets attempted to resist or counteract the encroachment entailed in the creation of the two new local posts by President Yeltsin. First, in January 1992 the Russian parliament attempted to designate its own parliamentary representatives in the regions as a way of countering Yeltsin's envoys there.[52] As described above, Yeltsin responded by strengthening the post of Presidential Representative via Decree No. 765. Second, in a number of separate sessions in 1992 and 1993, the Congress of People's Deputies attempted to abolish Yeltsin's ability to name Presidential Representatives to the regions, but in each instance Yeltsin simply ignored the parliament. For example, on 5 December 1992 the Russian Congress of People's Deputies passed a resolution that stripped Yeltsin of his authority to appoint regional Heads of Administration, and called for the abolition within one month of the Presidential Representatives in Russia. Yeltsin's response was his Decree no.186, of 5 February 1993 making the PP position permanent and under the supervisory jurisdiction of his chief of staff. Ruslan Khasbulatov, the speaker of the Russian parliament, responded to this act two weeks later by calling on local soviet authorities to deprive all Presidential Representatives of office space. Finally, as has been shown, parliament succeeded in facilitating a number of local elections to fill GA positions. Despite Yeltsin's opposition to the idea of elections to these posts, a small number of vacancies were filled by means of local election. As noted above, these elections took place in April 1993 in several regions. The results of these elections, especially in Bryansk, Chelyabinsk, Lipetsk, Orel, Penza and Smolensk *oblasts*, were reversals for Yeltsin, as they resulted in the election of former Communist Party officials or pro-communist hardliners.[53]

In the aftermath of the October 1993 defeat of the parliamentary forces and the passage of the new Russian Constitution in December 1993, Yeltsin may again have the upper hand in this executive–legislative battle. On the latter development, the new Constitution is rather vague with respect to the issue of how the regional GAs and PPs are to be assigned. Article 83 states, *inter alia,* that 'The President of the Russian Federation appoints authorised representatives of the President of the Russian Federation and relieves them of their duties'. As regards local Heads of Administration, they are not mentioned explicitly in the Constitution. Article 78 comes closest to touching on these posts, stating that 'In order to exercise their powers, the federal bodies of executive power may create their own territorial agencies and appoint appropriate officials'. In neither case is mention made of any 'advise and consent' role for either local or other national organs. Since both PPs and GAs have until now been appointed in the main by Presidential decree, Article 90 of the Constitution, which defines decree power, also comes into play. This article simply states that the President may issue decrees and directives, that these decrees and directives are binding throughout the Russian Federation, and that the decrees and directives may not violate the Constitution or federal law. One measure of his continued supremacy on these issues, then, would be his ability to avoid further popular elections of GAs in Russia's regions.

Future Developments

It seems clear that the trend under-way in Russia is for greater powers to be located at the local level, less in the centre. Local officials, for better or worse, have long since come to the conclusion that, at least with respect to the resolution of local political, social, and economic problems, Moscow does not provide the immediate answer. Heads of Administration at the regional level and below are staking out a more independent position *vis-à-vis* the Russian President, especially as Yeltsin's policies appeared to have hurt his political prospects. Even as far back as 1992, one pro-Yeltsin GA, Vladimir Yelagin of Orenburg *oblast*, argued that 'we have the same policy [as the centre], but this does not mean we have to do everything they tell us. A division of authority between the centre and the territory is not done by whimsy ... We need reasonable freedom of action.'[54] In the following three years, this 'reasonable freedom of action' certainly expanded.

Aiding and abetting this vertical decentralisation of power will be the eventual local popular election of the Heads of Administration. As stated above, even the threat of such an electoral mechanism to decide on the GAs made incumbent GAs more sensitive to local pressure. The implications of such a mechanism for the selection of leadership personnel for the vertical concentration of power in Moscow is obvious: local Heads of Administration would be beholden to a local constituency rather than to the Kremlin. The independence of such a political cohort would obviously be expanded, at least *vis-à-vis* the centre.

Less obvious, perhaps, are the implications of directly elected regional Heads of Administration on the horizontal institutional battles at the national level. One might expect a general increase in the effective power of the national upper chamber, the Federation Council. In mid-1995, roughly 47 of the 55 (85 per cent) Russian *oblast* and *krai* Heads of Administration were members of the Federation Council, representing their respective regions. In six cases,[55] moreover, the other member of the region's two-person delegation to the Federation Council was either a regional Deputy GA or the GA of the region's capital city (that is, in either case named by the regional GA). Such representation of a cohort that has, in effect, been named by the Russian President in the upper chamber of the Russian parliament has given Yeltsin a great deal of potential strength in the parliament. Should these regional Heads of Administration, by virtue of their election locally, become a great deal more independent in their political behaviour, and should they continue to be the logical choices for one of the region's seats in the Federation

Council, then one might expect this upper chamber to gain independence and power *vis-à-vis* the national executive. Such a development would make the Russian legislature a great deal more effectively bicameral than it has been to date.

Before drawing the conclusion that the Russian bicameral parliament will necessarily become a more powerful institution *vis-à-vis* the national executive, one should remember that strong bicameral legislatures are not necessarily more powerful legislatures than effectively unicameral ones.[56] In other words, if the Federation Council comes to exercise greater power, it may very well slow down the legislative process of the parliament as a whole, compete with the State Duma over legislative authority (say, by stressing regional issues and prerogatives over national ones[57]), and otherwise divide the parliamentary check on the national executive.

It must be stated that the political elites of Russia's republics and regions attempted to take advantage of the fact that Russia was until December 1993 operating without a new Constitution. More precisely, it was operating with the awkwardly cut-and-pasted 1978 Brezhnev Constitution. In such a political environment where the constitutional rules of politics are in constant debate, where the results of the political contests at the centre are very much in doubt, and where republic and regional elites have identified their own specific political goals to pursue, a natural tendency towards political decentralisation obtains. Such a centrifugal tendency may be considered more likely in a state where almost all serious politicians agree that one of the major faults of the Soviet *ancien régime* was its excessive concentration of power in Moscow.

This feeling among politicians notwithstanding, however, the maintenance of the Russian state required the re-establishment of some measure of centralising authority. Yeltsin has been willing, and to date able, to supply such authority. The irony of the situation revolves around the fact that Yeltsin was himself a Soviet-era regional party leader and served in that capacity as a part of the communist cadres system that ensured central control over regional policy making and implementation. It was precisely the destruction of the regional and local Communist Party structures (thanks in no small measure to Yeltsin himself) that threatened a loss of such control over post-Soviet regional policy. From one perspective, then, Yeltsin has been seeking a suitable substitute for these party committees to ensure his major goals of keeping Russia united, allowing for the local implementation of his own policy agenda, disenfranchising what were considered the last vestiges of Soviet-era power (the soviets), and enhancing the power of the central President *vis-à-vis* parliamentary authority. Perhaps it should not be surprising that the creation of some sort of institutional arrangement that would supply the central Russian leadership with the same potential for controlling events outside Moscow was inevitable.

Moreover, from this perspective, it should not be surprising that those forces that are seeking to expand regional and local prerogatives *vis-à-vis* the Moscow centre have been criticising Yeltsin's regional policy as tantamount to the re-creation of the old Soviet-style regional Communist Party leadership structure. Indeed, these criticisms are in some ways on target. While Yeltsin's Heads of Administration and Presidential Representatives are not the substantive equivalents of the old *obkom*, *gorkom*, and *raikom* secretariats, it may not be too far off the mark to argue that these new posts do at the moment represent their functional analogues. The second irony, though, is that just as the *obkom*, *gorkom*, and *raikom* secretariats pushed the soviets to the margins of decision making in the USSR, Yeltsin's Heads of Administration may be doing a similar thing to Russia's local dumas.

Conclusion

This chapter opened with a quotation from Leonid Smirnyagin suggesting the parallels between the Soviet-era local Communist Party organs and the contemporary cadre of Heads of Administration and their staffs. Much of the paper has addressed these parallels. Revisiting Smirnyagin, then, may be an appropriate way of concluding. In that same article, he argues that

> the chief cause of the headlong increase in the influence of the executive authority in the outlying areas lies in the fact that it is effective. These directors not only of state plants, but even of joint stock plants, bow down to it because in their 'White House' it is actually possible to resolve very acute economic questions that are beyond the capability of an individual enterprise director.[58]

Such a conclusion highlights a key theoretical component of contemporary debates. Post-communist transitions are characterised by tremendous changes in both politics and economics. That is, post-communist transitions are dual transitions: from authoritarian to democratic politics, and from centrally-planned to market economies. In the general literature that confronts the problem of creating markets out of planned economies, there is clearly the suggestion that democracy and marketisation may in fact be incompatible. Because popular forces will resist the kind of austerity programmes and social dislocation that are inevitable in post-communist marketisation processes, even pro-democracy reformers may find themselves inexplicably supporting the partial suspension of democratic procedures so as to keep the reforms on track. As one observer of the Russian transition has expressed this dilemma, it may be that 'former communist countries can sustain the appropriate economic policies only by depriving their citizens of the power to change them'.[59] This dilemma, between the requirements of political democratisation on the one hand and economic marketisation on the other, is reflected in a number of analyses, and is captured by the economist Richard Portes's comment that one of Chile's 'clear advantages' during its economic transition in the 1970s (and one not at present enjoyed in East Central Europe) was 'a dictatorial government to enforce unpopular measures'.[60] Another student of these processes takes an even more direct stance on this issue. Claus Offe has argued that the process of creating capitalist markets in the West was not accomplished under democratic conditions and that such conditions would have retarded marketisation.[61] Finally, Tsuyoshi Hasegawa has argued that 'to ensure the success of marketisation, "iron hands" may be needed to silence the opposition'.[62] What all four of these Western analysts are pointing to is the fact that transition issues are controversial and painful, and may benefit from strong executive leadership that is, relative to the assembly, immune to popular disapprobation. The question of Yeltsin's regional cadres policy, in both its horizontal and its vertical characteristics, should also be seen in this light.

Thus, while many of the Western states that introduced markets first may have done so in essentially pre-democratic social settings, post-communist market reformers may not be afforded the same privilege. For our present concerns, then, even political reformers may look for ways to mitigate the political leverage of the more democratically-conceived political institutions (namely, elected assemblies). From this perspective, the prevalence of Presidential regimes in post-communist Europe, and the rather ubiquitous murmurings about the need for neo-authoritarian leadership with 'iron hands' or 'benign dictators' to lead reform, makes sense.[63] Such a democratic dilemma may not only explain the allure of the neo-authoritarian models of economic reform (China, Taiwan, Singapore, Korea) felt by many Russian democrats, but may make the standard arguments against strong executive leadership in post-communist states somewhat less convincing.

It must be stated in closing, however, that the adoption by Russia of a new constitutional scheme that, like such regimes elsewhere, encourages powerful Presidents to ignore or by-pass elected assemblies, remains a politically risky reform strategy. Even the sceptic who has concluded that a parliament-based political system is too indecisive and incapable of making and defending the hard choices inherent in post-communist economic marketisation and that, as a result, strong Presidential leadership of the Russian type is the only viable option, must admit to two problems with the present system. First, a neo-authoritarian Presidential institutional structure may be acceptable so long as that office is held by Boris Yeltsin. But a political system that was created in a sense by Yeltsin so as to maximise his own Presidential prerogatives may become a liability when Yeltsin is no longer in power. The institutional powers of the President as stipulated in the Russian Constitution will outlive Yeltsin. While his personal authority may keep the confused nature of the current presidential–parliamentary regime from contributing to a breakdown of democracy, the next Russian President may not be so talented (or so inclined).

Second, by marginalising the parliament, the Constitution makes the President the sole focus of what Edward Walker has referred to as the 'politics of blame'. 'Rather than creating an institutional order in which power, and hence responsibility and blame, are well-distributed,' he writes, 'the President will come to embody "democracy", and all that it brings with it, in the minds of the people. When the inevitable occurs, and the popularity of that President declines, the popularity of democracy will decline with it.'[64] Regardless of one's view of Presidentialism, the present Constitution or Yeltsin himself, the risks to democratic stability that inhere in this strategy are sizeable indeed. From an institutional perspective, these risks are likely to increase when Yeltsin leaves the political scene. Stephen Holmes and Christian Lucky have written that 'constitutions are usually retrospective documents, not prospective ones. They are designed to solve the most pressing problems of the past, not of the future.'[65] The new Russian Constitution may indeed have solved much of the problem of legislative–executive confrontation that existed during 1991–93 in Russia. The issue becomes whether, as Holmes and Lucky suggest, the Constitution is well crafted to deal with the problems of the future.

Susan L. Clark and David R. Graham have argued convincingly that 'the main challenge facing Russian leaders today is to find a proper balance of power and authority between Moscow and the other components of the country'.[66] Thus, the struggle by Yeltsin to create and maintain these regional executive authorities has been, of course, a decidedly political one. One's views of Yeltsin as an individual leader, of

Russia's post-communist parliaments, of the relative desirability of government based on a strong executive rather than a viable parliament, and of the question of the proper level of the centralisation of power, all filtered through the necessities of a political and economic transition, are a few of the obvious considerations that contribute to an overall evaluation of Yeltsin's tactics in these political battles. Perhaps like many other things that are constitutive of the post-communist transition in Russia, a final determination of the issues may require time and events to continue apace.

Notes

1. For example, see *Rossiiskaya gazeta*, 13 May 1992 (FBIS USR-92-063, 29 May 1992, pp.56-7); *Peterburgskie vedomosti*, 17 September 1992 (FBIS-USR-92-133, 18 October 1992, p.78); *Segodnya*, 2 August 1994 (FBIS-USR-94-091, 21 August 1994, pp.32-5); and *Segodnya*, 13 January 1995 (*Current Digest of the Post-Soviet Press* **XLVII**, 2, 1995, p.22).
2. *Segodnya*, 2 August 1994 (FBIS-USR-94-091, 21 August 1994, p.32).
3. See, for example, Michael E. Urban, *More Power to the Soviets: The Democratic Revolution in the USSR* (Aldershot: Edward Elgar, 1990), and Thomas F. Remington (ed.), *Parliaments in Transition: The New Legislative Politics in the Former USSR and Eastern Europe* (Boulder, CO: Westview, 1994).
4. To students of Soviet communist party affairs, the term 'prefects' is, of course, well known. Jerry F. Hough's *The Soviet Prefects: The Local Party Organs in Industrial Decision Making* (Cambridge, MA: Harvard University Press, 1969) likened the *obkom* first secretaries to the French prefects. While Hough was using the term to refer specifically to what in the present set of arrangements would be the Heads of Administration, or GAs, some recent Russian commentators have used the same label to refer to Presidential Representatives, or PPs. For example, in a 1993 *Literaturnaya gazeta* article on the role of the PPs, entitled 'Who Needs the Squealers?', the author directly parallels the French prefects with the Russian PPs: see *Literaturnaya gazeta*, 10 February 1993 (FBIS-USR-93-023, 3 March 1993, p.4). In the title of this chapter, I use the term to refer generically to both GAs and PPs.
5. Russia is at present divided into 21 republics, six *krais* (territories), 49 *oblasts* (regions or provinces), ten autonomous *okrugs* (districts), one autonomous *oblast*, and two cities (Moscow and St. Petersburg) that have the status of *oblasts*. In Russian parlance, any administrative level at the *oblast* and below is considered 'local'.
6. On 9 October 1993, five days after the military storming of the Russian parliament, President Yeltsin signed Presidential Decree No. 1617, dissolving city, *raion* (district) and village soviets; *oblast* and *krai* soviets were also instructed to disband, and did so throughout the autumn of 1993: see 'O reforme predstavitel'nykh organov vlasti i organov mestnogo samoupravleniya v Rossiiskoi Federatsii', *Rossiiskaya gazeta*, 12 October 1993.
7. For a good summary of this confrontation, see 'Nastuplenie provintsii na Kreml'', *Moskovskie novosti*, 3 October 1993.

48 *William A. Clark*

8. Everett M. Jacobs cites the total number of soviets as 50,991 at the time of the February 1980 elections; his source was *Pravda*, 1 March 1980: see Everett M. Jacobs (ed.), *Soviet Local Politics and Government* (London, Allen & Unwin, 1983), p.10, Table I.1.

9. For more on this trend, see Urban, *More Power to the Soviets*.

10. The case of Solidarity in Poland comes immediately to mind as perhaps the most significant movement in the region at the time.

11. One could argue that one of Yeltsin's mistakes was his failure to dissolve the Russian parliament in the immediate aftermath of the August 1991 *putsch*. In suspending the activities of the Communist Party throughout Russia, Yeltsin took only one of two necessary steps. He could easily have dissolved the assembly and called for new elections. It could be argued that, in the euphoria of the period, the odds that the electorate would have returned an assembly more in line with Yeltsin's political goals were at their highest.

12. On the institutional battles of post-authoritarian transitions more generally, see Matthew Soberg Shugart and John M. Carey, *Presidents and Assemblies: Constitutional Design and Electoral Dynamics* (Cambridge: Cambridge University Press, 1992); Juan J. Linz, 'The Perils of Presidentialism', *Journal of Democracy* 1, no.1 (1990), pp.51–69; Scott Mainwaring, 'Presidentialism, Multipartism, and Democracy: The Difficult Combination', *Comparative Political Studies* 26, no.2 (1993), pp.198–228; and Juan J. Linz and Arturo Valenzuela (eds), *The Failure of Presidential Democracy* (Baltimore, MD: Johns Hopkins University Press, 1994).

13. Michael McFaul, *Post-Communist Politics: Democratic Prospects in Russia and Eastern Europe* (Washington, DC: Center for Strategic and International Studies, 1993), p.85.

14. Tsuyoshi Hasegawa, 'The Connection Between Political and Economic Reforms in Communist Regimes', in Gilbert Rozman (ed.), *Dismantling Communism: Common Causes and Regional Variations* (Baltimore, MD: Johns Hopkins University Press, 1992), pp.83–4.

15. Valerii Vyzhutovich, 'Vitse-Regenty i Gubernatory', *Vek*, 1994, no.15, p.10.

16. For an interesting description of the nominating process of the Omsk *oblast* GA, see John F. Young, 'Institutions, Elites, and Local Politics in Russia: The Case of Omsk', in Theodore H. Friedgut and Jeffrey W. Hahn (eds), *Local Power and Post-Soviet Politics* (Armonk, NY: M.E. Sharpe, 1994), pp.142–5.

17. The soviets could, however, override the decision of the GA with a vote equal to the majority of seats in the soviet.

18. *Oblast* administration Chiefs of Staff existed in 47 of 55 Russian *oblast* and *krai* structures in 1994; Astrakhan, Belgorod, Ivanovo, Kemerovo, Moscow, Novosibirsk, Samara and Tyumen organisations lacked this position.

19. One difference of note has been the influence in many cases of the local soviets in the President's selection of the GA. Such leverage did not exist in the cadre process that placed *obkom* first secretaries in the regions during the Soviet period.

20. Decree No. 1070, signed 10 September 1992: 'O vnesenii izmenenii v Ukaz Prezidenta RSFSR ot 25 Noyabrya 1991g. No.239 "O poryadke naznacheniya glav administratsii"', *Rossiiskaya gazeta*, 15 September 1992.

21. *Vedomosti Verkhovnogo Soveta*, 1991, No.41, pp.1718–66.

22. *Izvestiya*, 2 November 1991.

23. The decree 'On Measures to Strengthen the Unified System of Executive Power in the Russian Federation' is discussed in *Segodnya*, 5 October 1994 (*CDPSP* XLVI, no.40

(1994), p.17). This decree was prompted by the events in the Maritime *krai* where the GA, Yevgenii Nazdratenko, engaged in a confrontation with both the *krai* PP and the soviet, sought to re-establish his right to hold the GA position.

24. *Kommersant-Daily*, 13 May 1995 (*CDPSP* **XLVII**, no.19 (1995), p.13).
25. See *Moskovskie novosti*, 9–16 April 1995 (*CDPSP*, **XLVII** no.16 (1995), pp.17–18).
26. On this and related issues, see Julia Wishnevsky's fine analysis, 'Problems of Russian Regional Leadership', *RFE/RL Research Report* 3, no.19 (13 May 1994), p.8.
27. The 21 ethno-territorially-based republics of the Russian Federation, comprising 28.6 per cent of Russia's territory and 15.2 per cent of its population, are outside the domain of the central GA system. They have been given the right to determine their own systems of government, and to elect their own leading officials, including their Presidents: see Ann Sheehy, 'Russia's Republics: A Threat to Its Territorial Integrity?', *RFE/RL Research Report* 2, no.20 (14 May 1993), pp.34–40.
28. There are exceptions to this general trend. Yurii Goryachev was named regional Head of Administration in Ulyanovsk in January 1992, and has frequently butted heads with Yeltsin over various aspects of the latter's regional policy. In like fashion, Belgorod *oblast* GA Viktor Berestovoi, a former *obkom* second secretary, appointed GA in November 1991, has in effect re-created his old *obkom* organisation. Three-quarters of his former *obkom* colleagues – first secretaries, secretaries, party department heads – have been placed in responsible positions in the *oblast* administration: see *Rossiiskaya gazeta*, 13 May 1993 (FBIS-USR-92-063, 29 May 1992, p.56).
29. Darrell Slider, 'Federalism, Discord, and Accommodation: Intergovernmental Relations in Post-Soviet Russia', in Friedgut and Hahn (eds), *Local Power and Post-Soviet Politics*, p.257.
30. An exception to this general trend occurred in October 1991 when Yevgenii Kuznetsov, the incumbent Presidential Representative in Volgograd *oblast*, was named Head of Administration in Stavropol *krai*.
31. Peter Rutland, *The Politics of Economic Stagnation in the Soviet Union: The Role of the Local Party Organs in Economic Management* (Cambridge: Cambridge University Press, 1993), p.191.
32. See Urban, *More Power to the Soviets*.
33. See *Segodnya*, 13 January 1995 (*CDPSP*, **XLVII**, no.2, 1995, pp.22–3).
34. One can also point to Stalin's Central Committee representatives in the regions, a post that was dissolved in the mid-1950s.
35. See comments by Jeffrey Hahn in Peter Reddaway *et al.*, 'Two Years After the Collapse of the USSR: A Panel of Specialists', *Post-Soviet Affairs* 9, no.4, (October–December 1993), p.290.
36. *Izvestiya*, 12 September 1991.
37. Ibid., 26 August 1991.
38. According to the *Izvestiya* article on the decree, 'the lists of such [i.e., disloyal] regions and the appointments of Presidential representatives coincide almost completely'. Specifically, the regions cited are Krasnoyarsk and Khabarovsk *krais*, and Astrakhan, Volgograd, Vladimir, Ivanovo, Kemerovo, Novosibirsk, Orenburg, Ryazan, Saratov, Tambov, Tyumen, and Yaroslavl *oblasts*: see G. Shipitko, 'Yeltsin Appoints His Own Representatives in Territories and Provinces', *Izvestiya*, 26 August 1991 (*CDSP* **LXIII**, no.35 (1991), p.21).
39. *Izvestiya*, 26 August 1991 (*CDSP* **LXIII**, no.35 (1991), p.21).
40. 'Who Needs the Squealers?', p.4.
41. *Rossiiskaya gazeta*, 14 April 1992 (FBIS-USR-92-046, 24 April 1992, p.64).

42. See 'Ob utverzhdenii polozheniya o predstavitele Prezidenta Rossiiskoi Federatsii v krae, oblasti, avtonomnoi oblasti, avtonomnom okruge, gorodakh Moskve i Sankt-Peterburge', *Vedomosti S"ezda Deputatov Rossiiskoi Federatsii i Verkhovnogo Soveta Rossiiskoi Federatsii*, 1992, no.29 (23 July), p.2163, Item 1767.

43. 'O predstavitele Prezidenta Rossiiskoi Federatsii v krae, oblasti, avtononmoi oblasti, avtonomnon okruge, gorodakh Moskve i Sankt-Peterburge', *Rossiiskaya gazeta*, 24 July 1992.

44. Vyzhutovich, 'Vitse-Regenty i Gubernatory', p.10.

45. Boris Bogatov, 'Kto ty – "Oko Gosudarevo"', *Nezavisimaya gazeta*, 6 November 1991.

46. Gennadii Vladimirov, 'Rossiiskii tsentr i mestnaya vlast': opyt instituta predstavitelei prezidenta', *Politicheskii monitoring*, 1993, no.4, pp.5–22.

47. See, for example, Wendy Slater, 'Moscow City Politics Reflects National Issues', *RFE/RL Research Report* 2, no.10 (5 March 1993), pp.5–10.

48. Most observers have concluded that in the aftermath of the appointment of the more centrist Viktor Chernomyrdin as Prime Minister and the December 1993 elections, the balance of power locally between the Heads of Administration and Presidential Representatives swung decidedly in favour of the former. Interestingly, while part of the responsibility of the Presidential Representative is to report on the activities of the local Head of Administration, there has been one instance where a single individual has simultaneously held both posts: in Nizhnii Novgorod, Boris Nemtsov was named the region's PP in August 1991 and appointed its GA in December 1991; on 19 April 1994 President Yeltsin accepted Nemtsov's resignation from the post of regional PP; Nemtsov retained the governorship.

49. Vera Tolz, 'Power Struggle in Russia: The Role of the Republics and Regions', *RFE/RL Research Report* 2, no.15 (9 April 1993), p.12.

50. Elizabeth Teague, 'Yeltsin Disbands the Soviets', *RFE/RL Research Report* 2, no.43 (29 October 1993), p.3.

51. Ibid., p.4.

52. 'O polnomochnom predstavitele v respublike v sostave Rossiiskoi Federatsii, krae, oblasti, avtononmoi oblasti, avtononmom okruge Rossiiskoi Federatsii, gorodakh Moskve i Sankt-Peterburge', *Vedomosti S"ezda Deputatov Rossiiskoi Federatsii i Verkhovnogo Soveta Rossiiskoi Federatsii*, 1992, no.4 (23 January), pp.213–14, Item 157. For analysis of this measure, see *Izvestiya*, 11 January 1992.

53. See Teague, 'Yeltsin Disbands the Soviets', pp.4–5, for the confusing situation in Chelyabinsk. At the time of the April 1993 election to the post of head of administration there, the original and incumbent GA, Vadim Solov'ev, then a 46-year-old former city party secretary and city soviet chairman, but one who was obviously pro-reform, refused to consider the election legitimate and declined to stand for election. The election was held in any event, and Petr Sumin, the former Chelyabinsk *obkom* second secretary with less democratic credentials but with better support in the local soviet, won the election. The Yeltsin government considered Solov'ev the GA, and the odd situation existed where the region had two competing GAs, one appointed by Yeltsin in October 1991 and one elected in April 1993, competing for influence over local events. For additional information, see also Wishnevsky, 'Problems of Russian Regional Leadership', pp.8–9.

54. *Rossiiskie vesti*, 15 October 1992 (FBIS-USR-92-1:52, 27 November 1992, p.49).

55. Volgograd, Kostroma, Moscow, Penza, Saratov and Ulyanovsk.

56. The difference between 'bicameral' and 'effectively bicameral' is revealed quite

nicely in the British system. The analogy is not lost on Russian observers, one of whom, at least, has referred to the Federation Council as 'Russia's House of Lords': see *Moscow Times*, 14 April 1995.

57. According to a recent article in *Izvestiya*, two-thirds of the members of the Federation Council are drawn from 'the regional power elite' – heads of administration, Presidential representatives, and heads of legislative assemblies: *Izvestiya*, 31 January 1995.

58. *Segodnya*, 2 August 1994 (FBIS-USR-94-091, 21 August 1994, p.32).

59. Michael Mandelbaum, 'Introduction', in Shafiqul Islam and Michael Mandelbaum (eds), *Making Markets: Economic Transformation in Eastern Europe and the Post-Soviet States* (New York: Council on Foreign Relations Press, 1993), p.12.

60. Richard Portes, 'From Central Planning to a Market Economy', in Islam and Mandelbaum (eds), *Making Markets*, p.38. In the same volume, Shafiqul Islam speaks of the allure of the 'iron-fist-in-the-golden-glove' approach to economic policy: ibid., p.194.

61. Claus Offe, 'Capitalism by Democratic Design?: Democratic Theory Facing the Triple Transition in East Central Europe', *Social Research* 58, no.4 (1993), p.881.

62. Hasegawa, 'The Connection Between Political and Economic Reforms', pp.83–4.

63. Shigei Hakamada and Gilbert Rozman, 'The Soviet Union and China: Coping with Modernity', in Rozman (ed.), *Dismantling Communism*, pp.152–81.

64. Edward R. Walker, 'Politics of Blame and Presidential Powers in Russia's New Constitution', *East European Constitutional Review* 2, No. 4 – 3, No. 1 (double issue, 1993–94), p.118.

65. Stephen Holmes and Christian Lucky, 'Storm Over Compatibility', ibid., pp.121–2.

66. Susan L. Clark and David R. Graham, 'The Russian Federation's Fight for Survival', *Orbis* 39, no.3 (Summer 1995), p.331.

4 Post-Soviet Clientelist Norms at the Russian Federal Level

John P. Willerton

Post-Soviet transition and efforts at democratisation have not lessened the importance of informal connections and extra legal arrangements to Russian political life. Indeed, the institutional and political confusion of the past half-decade has encouraged much informal manoeuvring among political elites. Political patronage continues to be a significant facet of post-Soviet reality. But the continuing transformation of the political system has altered the ways by which career connections and political networks function in the policy process. A Yeltsin patronage network, composed of long-term Sverdlovsk protégés and more recently recruited clients, has been influential in the post-Soviet Russian federal executive. Institutional sectoral interests have also become important actors in the negotiations over budgetary and other policy issues, and in contrast with the Soviet past, these actors can openly aggregate and articulate their own parochial interests. Indeed, as I will argue, established and resource-rich institutional actors now constitute important channels for mobility within the political elite.

During the past seven years, the most fundamental principles underlying Russian policy making and governance have been subject to debate. Important struggles have revolved around new divisions of power and authority and the delineation of new formal and informal rules governing the behaviour of decision-makers. Since the collapse of the USSR in 1991, federal-level political power has been increasingly concentrated in executive branch institutions. The Russian presidency and the institutions directly linked with it now enjoy hegemonic power.[1] The former Soviet leader Mikhail Gorbachev has commented that the office of the Russian President has amassed a level of power greater than that of the former CPSU General Secretary.[2] Meanwhile, the legislative branch has been significantly weakened from its more influential position in 1990–93. Uncertainties continue to surround the potential of the post-Soviet judiciary.

The Russian federal political scene remains highly dynamic. This is due in large measure to the wide gap between President Boris Yeltsin's formal institutional power and his actual political standing. While Yeltsin's institutional prerogatives have been unrivalled, his personal political standing has steadily eroded and he has become increasingly isolated politically. As a consequence, important questions remain as to the durability of the political arrangements which emerged through the 1993 Russian Federation Constitution and under Yeltsin's leadership. Meanwhile, the past half-decade has entailed a wholesale turnover in the ranks of the governing political elite. Few prominent federal officials from the Soviet period survived the events of 1991 to maintain power in the newly independent Russian Federation. In the wake of the coup attempt of August 1991, the Russian Federation executive and legislature co-opted the powers of disgraced Soviet federal institutions. During the past five years increasing numbers of younger politicians who had been outside the Soviet party–state mobility hierarchy were recruited into the executive or won election to the legislature. The Russian political opportunity structure was open to a different, wider and more varied group of aspiring politicians.[3]

Given this chaotic political transformation, patron–client relations and informal politics have assumed an important role in elite mobility, regime formation and governance. The mobility norms of the hierarchical Soviet *nomenklatura* system have been succeeded by a less formal but extensive cultivation of protégés, clients and allies by higher-level officials. In this chapter I consider emergent post-Soviet mobility norms through an examination of the composition and recruitment patterns of the Yeltsin federal executive. A Yeltsin 'network' or 'team', composed of longer-term protégés and shorter-term cultivated clients, and augmented by political allies drawn from powerful sectoral interests, has dominated the post-1991 Russian decision-making process. Notwithstanding tremendous political and social pressures and policy setbacks, Yeltsin and this network have maintained and even expanded their formal power position.

Critical to the functioning of the Yeltsin government has been the forging of working relations with influential politicians who did not have past (pre-1992) career linkages to the President. In addition, powerful bureaucratic lobbies – grounded in sectors of the economy with considerable material resources and political clout – have played a growing role both in the composition of the Yeltsin government and in the formulation and evolution of the government's policy programme. Top-level sectoral officials with strong ties to these institutional lobbies have assumed leading positions in Yeltsin's government. Meanwhile, nascent political parties and elite factions have emerged as often highly visible springboards by which aspiring politicians make their career and issue interests known. While faction leaders generally influence the political process through their membership of the legislature, they are actors with whom Yeltsin and the executive have worked, during the emergence of a broader governing coalition embracing the executive and the legislature.

The politics of lobbies, factions and political personalities continue to be important as governing elite coalitions are formed. Although we have only five years of post-Soviet Russian experience to assess, we can begin to identify emergent patterns of patronage and informal politics at the federal level.

Political Patronage and the Soviet Russian Past

Patronage and other types of informal extra-legal politics were pervasive and influential for elite mobility and regime formation in pre-Soviet and Soviet Russia.[4] Patronage networks are centred upon a guiding leader or patron. Generally reliant upon pre-existing personal relationships among members, patronage networks are vehicles uniting politicians' career interests. I understand the patron–client tie to be a personal, reciprocal, asymmetrical and interdependent relationship in which each member gains from the other through transactions to which each is a contributor. Patrons recruit politicians who are loyal and reliable, where loyalty and reliability help in bringing the patron's (and the client's) political ambitions to fruition. The careers of patrons and clients are interdependent, as network members help one another climb the political ladder. The power and influence of each depends on that of the other. While there can be risks linked with such career associations, patron–client ties can provide security and direction to network members' career ambitions.

The Soviet political system, with its centralised, stratified and interconnected set of bureaucratic hierarchies, was very conducive to patronage politics. A relatively narrow set of institutional interests structured political elite mobility. Soviet leaders had the ability to transfer political status and influence to subordinates. Given the absence of formal checks on the manipulation of power by the top elite, high-level officials were in a strong position to cultivate trusted associates. The

Soviet experience reveals that leaders could build governing teams on the basis of coalitions across institutional and sectoral interests. They could build alliances with those already in power while bringing in their own personnel.

A patronage network includes two types of members whose rise to power is grounded in different preconditions: first, 'protégés', who are politicians with past common experience with the patron and who experience mobility under that patron; and second, 'clients', who are politicians who experience significant career mobility under a patron, even though there is little or no past common experience with that patron. In addition, a broader – or 'extended' – network could build a bridge to other politicians whose recent and past career mobility was not dependent on a patron's actions. Such political alliances involve a congruence of career and policy interests which bring politicians together. Alliances, however, are highly dynamic relationships, and they are vulnerable to the exigencies of a given moment and may be short-lived.

Soviet history revealed the success of Stalin, Khrushchev and Brezhnev in using patron–client relations to recruit loyal subordinates and to build and maintain governing coalitions. In the later Soviet period, Leonid Brezhnev developed an extensive patronage network, including several especially powerful protégés with their own groups of clients. Brezhnev's 'extended network' spanned diverse political institutions, economic sectors and regions. Other patronage networks also thrived during this period, serving as an informal check on the extended Brezhnev network. The broader governing coalition under Brezhnev included political alliances bridging these networks.

The importance of changed institutional arrangements and mobility norms for patronage politics was demonstrated by developments in the Gorbachev period.[5] The decentralisation of decision-making and the democratisation of the political process resulted in the emergence of an increasingly open and diversified structure of political opportunities. An important consequence was that the means by which Gorbachev and other politicians could cultivate lower-level officials were increasingly circumscribed. Gorbachev's network was more limited in size and more narrow in scope when compared with those of his predecessors. Thus, while Gorbachev relied upon a few select long-term protégé for key posts, his network primarily included upwardly-mobile politicians who were recruited under his sponsorship. As the *perestroika* period evolved, the Gorbachev regime increasingly reflected dynamic political alliances in which members brought together short-term common policy and career interests. These alliances included experienced officials who were already institutionally well-situated and who were not beholden to Gorbachev for their career success.

Gorbachevian institutional and policy reforms would have transformed the manifestations and norms of informal politics and patronage in the Soviet system. They were already doing so by 1991, when the USSR collapsed. Those changes and that collapse concomitantly removed one political opportunity structure, grounded in the Soviet federal party–state apparatus, and contributed to the enhanced importance of others. Bottom-up popular electoral and social pressures had been unleashed which significantly influenced the motivations and behaviour of politicians operating within the Russian federal legislature and the Russian executive. Rather than a unified, centralised set of hierarchical institutions, separate and competing institutions increasingly influenced politicians' mobility aspirations. Moreover, there was a growing range of non-institutionalised political actors, including emergent political parties and factions, which provided avenues for career mobility. All these developments would hasten the institutional, personnel and policy changes we now associate with the Yeltsin period.

The Post-Soviet Political Context

With the collapse of the Soviet system, political power at the Russian federal level was divided among a growing number of political actors, including executive branch institutions, the legislature and nascent political parties, interest groups and smaller factions. The formal arrangements of the late Soviet period had suggested the pre-eminence of the popularly-elected legislature. But political realities diverged from formal legal and institutional arrangements: policy momentum lay with the executive branch and the leading figure in the anti-Soviet opposition, President Boris Yeltsin. Developments of the period September 1991–October 1993 revealed an aggrandisement of power by the executive, with the events of autumn 1993 and the approval of the Yeltsin Constitution only confirming the hegemonic position of the Russian President.

President Yeltsin has been the central figure – the 'patron' – in the evolving post-Soviet Russian polity. His policy legacy has been mixed, with contradictory tendencies simultaneously enhancing and undercutting his political power. The decisive victory of the executive in the 1993 showdown between the executive and the legislature left the President as the primary policy initiator and co-ordinator.[6] The executive is now the primary arbiter among competing political interests. The executive is powerful not only because the President's political position is now legally superior to that of all other institutions, but because the President enjoys considerable institutional freedom of manoeuvre. He has an almost unrestrained ability to direct the decision-making process. He can appoint and remove government officials with ease as well as dismiss the entire government. His decrees have the force of law and permit him to set policy almost unilaterally.[7] Formal constraints on the presidency are minimal: other branches assume an essentially advisory or reactive function.

But the executive branch's aggrandisement of power occurred while Yeltsin's personal standing, with both the political elite and the wider society, fell precipitously.[8] His style of leadership and fluctuating policy preferences alienated many supporters. Executive actions suggested the unpredictable application of institutional prerogatives. Yeltsin could be assertive in countering opponents, but he sometimes appeared remote and even indecisive. His occasional reliance on authoritarian means – said to be necessary to safeguard the fragile democratisation process – helped to alienate the very supporters who had helped bring him to power.

In this setting, building and maintaining effective political coalitions is a more difficult yet constant priority. Yeltsin must contend with a post-Soviet political elite which includes a widening array of politicians. Even in the wake of the events of autumn 1993 and the introduction of the 1993 Constitution, their career ambitions are only partially influenced by Yeltsin and other members of the top federal leadership. As we shall see, the career backgrounds and recruitment tracks of these politicians are increasingly varied. Just as varied are politicians' policy preferences. These preferences have been quite diverse, ranging from those of extremist reformers drawn to Western economic and political experience to those of chauvinistic nationalists inspired by Russia's past. Although organising this spectrum of views is increasingly difficult and risky as the post-Soviet reform process evolves, I identify three major attitudinal groupings which have influenced the post-1991 Russian policy agenda: (1) radical reformers, (2) conservatives and nationalists, and (3) centrists who have adopted selected positions favoured by reformers or conservatives. Each of these categories encompasses politicians with various policy preferences. Indeed, there has been a continuing division of these categories, reflecting the fragmentation of political parties and the dynamic politics of political personalities. But coalitions have been at least partially grounded in these policy distinctions, with Yeltsin-led coalitions having tended to draw members with particular policy orientations.

'Radical reformers' include political figures who have supported a rapid shift to a market economy, the rapid privatisation of trade and services, the freeing-up of prices, the limiting of government involvement in economic management, and the opening-up of the economy to domestic and foreign entrepreneurs. These reformers have supported a foreign policy line favouring close political and economic relations with the West, full-scale disarmament, and Russia's rapid integration into the global economy. They have championed a free press which illuminates both systemic problems and relevant domestic and foreign policy responses. Many leading radical reformers emerged from outside the traditional communist-bureaucratic apparatus, and from academia.

Counterpoised to radical reformers are a diversity of conservatives and nationalists. Although difficult to generalise across all groups, most have emphasised a unified and indivisible Russia, with their economic proposals favouring the traditional military–industrial and agricultural sectors. They have attempted to retard privatisation, stabilise prices, and maintain a high profile for the government in economic management. Sceptical about international economic and political connections, they prefer Russia to rely on its own resources as it addresses its economic woes. They are especially hostile to the westernisation of the country's culture.[9]

Situated between the radical reform and conservative and nationalist groups are various centrist elements whose political orientations entail selected aspects of reformers' and conservatives' policy preferences. In general, centrists have supported more modest economic reform programmes, wanting to avoid the excesses and trauma of the shock therapy strategy. Likewise, they have been committed to a stronger and unified Russia, but they do not favour arrangements that threaten the independence of former Soviet states. Centrists have stressed reliance on Russian domestic resources, preferring a reduced Western role in providing investment and assistance.

Given the policy differences among these groups, the accelerating political cleavages of 1992–93, which revolved around an executive–legislative struggle, were predictable. President Yeltsin's policy preferences, as set out both when he chaired the Russian parliament and as Russian President, placed him squarely in the ranks of radical reformers. His supporters within the parliament generally adopted centrist to radical reformist political stances. Centrist and conservative opponents, comprising a majority of the parliament's membership, rallied around the parliamentary speaker Ruslan Khasbulatov. Much of the political manoeuvring of 1992–93 involved efforts by both sides to construct alliances with cautious centrist elements, including those representing powerful sectoral interests (for example, the military–industrial sector). Such manoeuvring entailed a nearly constant rotation of radical reformer and centrist elements within the Yeltsin executive. Without retracing the complex manoeuvrings of both the executive and the legislative branches, suffice it to note that the executive branch's victory of autumn 1993 temporarily emboldened reformist elements. The radical reformer Yegor Gaidar's brief return to the executive branch signalled as much. But these developments, combined with the conservatives' successes in the December 1993 parliamentary elections, lent momentum to the forging of a loose consensus on social and political stability among reformist, centrist and even some conservative elements in 1994. One formal outcome was the near-universal signing of the Pact on Social Accord in spring 1994. The Yeltsin government adopted more conciliatory positions, while the Prime Minister and government leadership developed a working relationship with the parliamentary leadership which yielded some significant legislation.[10]

There were powerful incentives for most politicians and interests to work with the federal executive even when they opposed the government's broad political orientation or particular policy initiatives. Most conservative opponents, aware of the fate of the 1990–93 parliament when the executive was less powerful, attempted to safeguard their own parochial interests through political accommodation. Meanwhile, the Yeltsin government reframed its policy programme and adopted more moderate policy stances. As we shall see, the evolution of the government's composition yielded an increasingly more centrist political team.

While the institutional foundations of a post-communist political system were solidified by 1994, the renewed concentration of power in executive organisations was reminiscent of the decision-making realities of the Soviet past. Arguably the single most important policy decision taken by the Yeltsin government, the application of force against Chechnya, reflected this: Yeltsin and his presidential apparatus unilaterally took the decision with no outside consultation and by orchestrating the Security Council deliberations.[11] The subsequent public debate and prosecution of the war revealed the inherent weakness of the legislature and other actors in halting executive action.[12] Thus, under Yeltsin, the executive branch reclaimed the decision-making initiative. But the governing coalition that he and his associates constructed spans a diversity of institutional interests which are centrist and which favour policy solutions at variance with those set out by Yeltsin and the radical reformers just a few years earlier.

John P. Willerton

The Political Elite and the Yeltsin Team: A 1994 'Snapshot'

First through his personal political standing and then through extensive formal prerogatives, President Yeltsin was in a strong position to influence the recruitment and mobility of politicians aspiring to federal-level executive posts. Those greatly opposed to Yeltsin and his policies, whether from a conservative or a rival reformist perspective, looked to the legislature, political parties or sub-federal political institutions for career mobility opportunities. In this setting, Boris Yeltsin was able to construct a governing coalition based in part upon a cohort of trusted career associates. Yeltsin's extended network spanned longer-term protégés and more recent clients, with its decision-making position significantly bolstered by the forging of alliances with other politicians and institutional interests.

By Yeltsin *protégés* I mean politicians who worked with Yeltsin since before his election in 1991 as Russian Federation President. This includes his years of work in the Sverdlovsk (1968–85) and the Moscow party apparatus (1985–87) and in the USSR federal government (1987–89). These protégés linked their careers with that of Yeltsin *before* he became the top decision-maker in post-Soviet Russia, and at a time when the political risks made their relationships especially interdependent. While they experienced career mobility – or career stagnation – along with their patron, there was a personal dimension to their relationships with Yeltsin, and their careers exhibit a level of interdependence not necessarily characteristic of more recent Yeltsin clients.[13]

By Yeltsin *clients* I mean politicians who enjoyed rapid career mobility under the Russian President. For purposes of systematic identification, a client is a politician who experienced at least two career promotions under Yeltsin after he was elected Russian President in June 1991. This measurement means that trusted subordinates who experienced only one promotion are not identified as Yeltsin clients (for example, Foreign Minister Andrei Kozyrev). Such politicians, especially if they have served under Yeltsin for some time, are probably Yeltsin supporters and could be viewed as allies. This measurement of clients also precludes the identification of possible patronage relations between Yeltsin and members of the legislature, though the assumption of this study is to view such pro-Yeltsin legislators as potential allies (for example, the Chairman of the Council of the Federation, Vladimir Shumeiko). By definition, the conferring of political elite standing through popular election signifies political mobility independent of a patron's powers.[15]

Table 4.1 provides a 'snapshot' view of the composition of the

Table 4.1. Selected Characteristics of Leading Russian Federation Executive Branch Members, March 1994.

	No.	Average age	Per cent former	Per cent higher education	Pre-August 1991 federal officials*	Per cent elected to representative body**
Yeltsin Network	19	51	95	100	32	16
Protégés	5	56	100	100	40	0
Clients	14	49	93	100	29	21
Others	55	52	87	96	27	25
Sectoral specialists	22	52	86	100	36	14
Outside specialists	14	52	77	92	7	21
Soviet period independents	6	61	100	100	100	50
Post-Soviet independents	13	49	92	92	0	38

* Percentage of politicians in a given category who held a Soviet federal level position before the August 1991 coup attempt.

** This refers to a legislative, or parliamentary, body.

top Russian executive as of March 1994, suggesting the size of the Yeltsin network as set against other categories of regime members. This population of executive branch members includes all senior-level officials serving in agencies comprising the Russian presidency for whom biographical and career details were available.[15] Senior-level executive branch members refer to members of the Security Council, heads and chairs of commissions, committees and councils under the jurisdiction of the presidency, presidential counsellors, and government ministers. I have chosen spring 1994 because of the greater availability of biographical and career details for top officials and because that particular Yeltsin government reflects Russian political realities of the period after the autumn 1993 executive–legislative showdown and the approval of the 1993 Yeltsin Constitution. Since there was a considerable turnover of high-level government personnel throughout the Yeltsin period, this population excludes many prominent members of the early Yeltsin regime (for example, Gennadii Burbulis and Yegor Gaidar). But the result is a more complete representative sample of government officials, enhancing our confidence in the reliability of the findings presented.

Table 4.1 reveals few long-term Yeltsin protégés within the executive leadership as of spring 1994: compared with the experience of CPSU

General Secretaries, the number of Yeltsin protégés is limited. Of the five identified protégés, only two – Viktor Ilyushin and Oleg Lobov – had influential decision-making positions. Ilyushin, who had served as a top assistant to Yeltsin for over a dozen years, headed the President's Secretariat and was his top assistant.[16] Lobov also served as a deputy to Yeltsin, being appointed to high executive positions (for example, deputy prime minister) before eventually becoming secretary to the powerful Security Council. The other three identified Yeltsin protégés held second-tier positions, with more narrowly-focused policy responsibilities.[17] What is striking about the political standing of all of these protégés is that their power is highly dependent on Yeltsin. A review of their careers reveals their political mobility. The shift from Sverdlovsk to high positions in Moscow was never legitimated by popular election or by strong standing in a powerful institution or a party: their standing derived from that of the patron. It is unlikely these officials would be able to maintain their high elite standing in Yeltsin's absence.[18]

Fourteen high-level executive branch officials are identified as Yeltsin clients. Compared with patron–client relationships of the Soviet period, when career linkages were cultivated over the course of decades, these relationships are short-term, having arisen only since 1991. Most of these clients were either lower-echelon politicians from the late Soviet period, or specialists drawn from outside the Soviet bureaucratic establishment. A number of these clients were holdovers from the original Yegor Gaidar reform team of late 1991–92.[19] Some clients had supported Yeltsin in the legislature and were recruited into the executive as advisers.[20] Many had expertise and extensive formal training in economics and related areas that were critical to the government's reform programme.[21] Finally, there were a number of middle-tier Soviet officials with specialised competence, especially in the areas of security and internal affairs, who enjoyed rapid mobility under Yeltsin.[22]

While the length of association between Yeltsin and these clients was shorter than that for protégés, the responsibilities delegated to these politicians often exceeded those extended to protégés. It is difficult to evaluate from public information the rationale for this, but many clients assumed a 'trouble-shooting' or 'point-man' role for the Yeltsin programme. Sergei Filatov, Pavel Grachev and Viktor Yerin, for example, assumed important roles in the transition of political responsibilities from Soviet to Russian Federation institutions. All three were top members of the Yeltsin regime from late 1991 to at least mid-1995 heading some of the most powerful ministries and executive institutions. Sergei Shakhrai, another Yeltsin client who has been on the Russian federal political scene only since 1990, has been a presidential adviser and troubleshooter on several important issues, especially inter-ethnic relations.[23]

Combining protégés and clients, the Yeltsin network had a significant presence within the executive branch, but in fact most politicians in this population of top-level executive branch officials (74 per cent) fell outside the network. A review of their career details reveals that their inclusion in top executive positions reflected technical expertise or a political standing that pre-dated and was independent of Yeltsin's powers. As Table 4.1 indicates, I organise these identified 'others' into four groups which reflect different career backgrounds and political credentials: (1) sectoral specialists, (2) outside specialists, (3) Soviet-period independents, and (4) post-Soviet independents.

Approximately two-thirds of the officials not identified as Yeltsin associates were 'specialists': that is individuals with academic credentials and considerable career experience in focused domains of responsibility. Specialists' career tracks generally entailed mobility through non-political or lower-level academic and research institute positions to posts in related government ministries. The subgroup 'sectoral specialists' had professional credentials and work experience in Moscow-based federal-level institutions. Such sectoral specialists spanned a range of institutional sectors, including military–industrial, agricultural and security. For most, the politically-relevant component of their careers had begun in the Brezhnev era. During that period, most were working in government or academic research institutes, though approximately one-third held high federal government positions.[24] Their formal institutional standing revealed them as accomplished technicians rather than as leading 'generalist' politicians.[25] Some were competent in technical areas critical to Yeltsin's policy programme.[26] Others combined considerable experience with public positions compatible with those of Yeltsin.[27]

In addition to Moscow-based sectoral specialists, there were specialists recruited from outside the federal state institutional hierarchy of the Soviet period. These officials were pulled into the Russian government sometime after Yeltsin had been selected as Russian Supreme Soviet Chairman (May 1990). Again, the careers of these 'outside specialists' generally originated in the Brezhnev period. Most were academics recruited from research settings to more narrowly-focused technical government posts.[28] A number of them had gained prominence at the federal level by first running for and winning parliamentary seats.

However, the more powerful politicians within the category identified as 'others' are what I term 'independents': politicians whose political standing was independent of that of Yeltsin and whose federal elite status transcended focused technical competence. As Table 4.1 reveals, there were relatively few such Soviet-period independents in the Yeltsin government of 1994. These Soviet-period independents were usually policy generalists with a diverse career background. A number became prominent reformers in the Gorbachev period and continued along reformist lines after the collapse of the Soviet Union.[29] A few prominent Soviet-period government officials with at least moderate (in other words, post-Soviet 'centrist') stances proved able to work with reformers in the Yeltsin period (for example, Viktor Chernomyrdin). All such individuals had to adjust to post-Soviet realities; it is not an accident that half of them had won popular election to representative bodies sometime in the previous five years.

There was also a significant number of 'independents' who did not get involved in federal politics until after the collapse of the USSR. Their political activism had generally begun in the *perestroika* period, during which they were drawn into local or regional reform efforts.[30] Their political experience was outside the traditional Soviet party–government apparatus. As was generally true of the executive in the Yeltsin period, their expertise was in economics or related technical areas.[31] Over one-third of these post-Soviet independents came to federal-level political power through popular election to parliamentary bodies.[32] But over half of these politicians had political ties with already-prominent figures when they ascended to federal government positions.[33]

A significant number of politicians who had long-term career ties to Yeltsin or who experienced rapid mobility under him constituted the nucleus for a governing coalition. However, they were not a monolithic group: as we shall see, there were significant policy differences among these officials. When we compare these Yeltsin network members with all other politicians, we find few systematic differences in key background attributes. As Table 4.1 indicates, the more significant background differences are found across the identified groups *within* both the Yeltsin network (that is, protégés versus clients) and the 'others' (that is, sectoral versus outside specialists; Soviet versus post-Soviet independents). This reflects differences between identifiable political generational cohorts: in particular, differences between Soviet politicians of the pre-*perestroika* era and those from the *perestroika* and post-*perestroika* eras.

Comparing Yeltsin's associates with all other politicians, there is little difference in age: with the exception of Soviet-period independents, all network and other groups averaged in age from their late forties to mid-fifties. But there is an identifiable cohort of post-Soviet officials, who were generally born in the Khrushchev period and whose careers began in the Gorbachev and Yeltsin periods. This cohort is split across the career categories, and it is found both in and out of the Yeltsin network. In the Yeltsin network, protégés tend to be older (average age, 56) than clients, reflecting that their careers generally originated along with Yeltsin's in the Khrushchev period. As for clients, a number became politically active only in the *perestroika* period, and hence had little or no career experience with the Soviet party–state hierarchy.

Turning to CPSU membership and higher education – measures reflecting past political loyalties and expertise – there is little difference between Yeltsin's associates and other politicians. Nearly all politicians had been CPSU members at one time, and nearly all had higher education. Only the 'outside specialists' group exhibited a somewhat lower rate of CPSU membership, but as a group these individuals were arguably the most removed from the power hierarchy and politics of the Soviet past. Meanwhile, the near-universal presence of higher education for all politicians revealed that the days of poorly educated political hacks holding high office were over.

As for previous high-level Soviet political experience, there was little difference between Yeltsin associates and other politicians: only 32 per cent of Yeltsin associates and 27 per cent of all other politicians had held federal-level (all-Union) posts before 1992. The positions held were generally second- or third-tier: with the exceptions of Aleksandr Yakovlev and Viktor Chernomyrdin, no senior member of the Gorbachev or earlier Soviet leaderships survived politically to hold high office in the post-Soviet regime. The more telling differences are between the older and younger cohorts within both the Yeltsin network and the 'others' category. Yeltsin protégés, similar to sectoral specialists and Soviet-period independents, were more likely to have held influential federal-level posts in the Soviet system; Yeltsin clients, outside specialists and post-Soviet independents generally had not had such power. In their formative political experiences, the clients, outside specialists, and post-Soviet independents were more subject to such late- and post-Soviet influences as contested elections and regional political pressures. And this is important when considering the mobility calculations of these politicians.

Unlike the traditional Soviet hierarchical system, in which top-down pressures were strong and rewarded bureaucratic–administrative prowess, the emergent post-Soviet system has increasingly rewarded politicians who are attentive to public pressures. An important way to enhance one's position has been to secure public support through popular election to representative bodies. But such bottom-up political pressures on aspiring politicians separate those politicians' long-term career interests from those of powerful politicians such as Yeltsin. Even though my population of cases is composed of executive branch officials, during the past five years a growing number ran for and won elective office. We have already noted that half of the Soviet-period independents who survived politically had done so, but so had 38 per cent of post-Soviet independents. Yeltsin clients (21 per cent) and outside specialists (21 per cent) were also more likely to have been elected to representative bodies than their older counterparts.

Thus, we find a well-positioned Yeltsin network in the federal executive in spring of 1994. Its membership is diverse, with politicians linked to Yeltsin for varying lengths of time and in more and less durable ways. A number of network members are among the key officials responsible for the development of Yeltsin's policy programme. But that network is not monolithic: there is career background evidence of differences in generation and experience among network members. Indeed, background differences among network members are comparable to those separating the network from other politicians. Meanwhile, the relative power of trusted long-term protégés is lessened by their minimal presence and by the significantly larger number of sponsored clients in the network. Few key executive posts are held by long-time protégés of Yeltsin.

The Yeltsin regime has evolved, in both its composition and its policy programme. That evolution has reflected different – generally declining – reformist proclivities. As we turn to the evolution of the Yeltsin 'team' and regime, we shall find the President's power position increasingly reliant upon sponsored clients and allies whose long-term reliability is much less certain.

Evolution of the Yeltsin 'Team' and Regime

This study focuses on the Russian federal executive and the role of the extended Yeltsin network in that institutional setting. I have not included the post-Soviet legislature, in part because the definition and measures for patron–client relations are not appropriate to the popularly-elected parliamentary setting. Moreover, factional politics within the State Duma and the Council of the Federation are more tied to constantly changing short-term issue and career concerns than to long-term career network considerations. Major gaps in the availability of career details for all parliamentary members also preclude a more systematic analysis of career links.[34] Yet the parliament has constituted the major formal institutional constraint on the president and the executive branch, both before and after the restructuring of the executive–legislative relationship in autumn 1993. With its membership decidedly more conservative in orientation than the members of the Yeltsin government, the parliament has influenced the composition and policy line of the executive. Thus, while characterising the President's powers as hegemonic, the composition of his team has evolved since 1992. I survey that evolution, looking beyond the population of spring 1994 executive branch officials, to consider the major figures and stages in that team's development.

Yeltsin began creating a presidential system even before the collapse of the USSR,[35] and he was especially able in the first year of his regime to recruit politicians with reformist perspectives congruent with his own. During late 1991–92, there was a higher degree of congruence in attitudes among regime members than at any time after the collapse of the USSR. This gave way to a widening diversity of views from late 1992 to the present, but throughout the entire post-Soviet period trusted Yeltsin loyalists guided the major executive agencies. At the outset of the Yeltsin regime, Gennadii Burbulis, a reformist co-founder of the Democratic Russia movement, directed the State Council, while Yurii Petrov, a more centrist former Sverdlovsk party First Secretary, oversaw the presidential administration.[36] Yurii Skokov, who served with Yeltsin in the USSR parliament (1989–91) and in Yeltsin's first government (as first deputy chairman, 1990–91), assumed responsibility for the Council of the Federation and Territories. Subsequent events would point to the complexities in the Yeltsin–Skokov relationship, but until spring 1993 Skokov was a trusted associate, and he maintained a working relationship with leading members of the Yeltsin regime even after his departure from the government.[37] Outside conservative pressures ultimately forced the removal of Burbulis[38] while an internal reorganisation led to the departure of Petrov[39] from the Yeltsin administration. However, their successors, Viktor Ilyushin and Sergei Filatov, were also close associates of Yeltsin.[40] Again, both men had been supporters of Yeltsin during critical moments of his past career, either in Sverdlovsk or in Moscow; both were experienced in late Soviet-period organisational politics. These politicians ensured the political reliability of presidential appointees and the efficient functioning of presidential agencies. They were joined by Yeltsin's security service director, Major General Aleksandr Korzhakov, who assumed a comparable role as key aide and even policy adviser. Korzhakov's influence expanded to personnel matters (for example, the composition of staff accompanying Yeltsin on trips) and to his apparent input on policy issues.[41]

It is not surprising that institutions comprising the post-Soviet presidency were guided by Yeltsin's associates. But given that political power was so concentrated in the executive, this recruitment pattern had decision-making significance. Most top-level decisions were taken by the president operating unilaterally. The agencies comprising the presidency structured most federal-level policy initiatives and discussions. Thus, associates of Yeltsin in immediate supporting positions possessed a good deal of political clout. Their own and Yeltsin's political interests were interdependent. Moreover, these associates' standing was entirely derived from that of Yeltsin. They were vulnerable to outside political pressures and in all likelihood they would have no career future in Yeltsin's absence.

The development and implementation of a radical reformist policy programme required the recruitment of a new cohort of officials into top government positions. Senior advisers of Yeltsin publicly complained about the conservative nature of the Russian federal government at the time of the demise of the Soviet Union.[42] At the opening of the Russian Congress of People's Deputies on 28 October 1991, Yeltsin had committed himself to putting together a *unified* team of reformers.[43] Yegor Gaidar, then Director of the USSR Academy of Economic Management's Economic Policy Institute, was named Deputy Prime Minister for the economy in November 1991. A group of economists and *perestroika*-generation politicians from outside the traditional political establishment was recruited by Gaidar, Burbulis and Yeltsin to fill key government slots; they assumed the cutting-edge role in constructing the radical reform programme of 1991–92.[44] Other reformers recruited to key posts augmented this group surrounding Gaidar.[45] With profound changes affecting all components of the government's policy programme, decision-making responsibilities were divided among the senior politicians. During his tenure as Yeltsin's chief economic policy-maker, Gaidar oversaw the all-important economic ministries, while Burbulis oversaw the ministries dealing with foreign policy, the press and mass media, and legal issues, and Aleksandr Shokhin oversaw ministries dealing with social policies. All these officials constituted the core group of reformist clients cultivated by Yeltsin. I view them as Yeltsin clients because they were recruited from outside the political establishment and experienced rapid mobility into top posts under him. While many did not survive Gaidar's departure from the prime ministership in late 1992, most did remain as influential federal-level figures (for example through emergent political parties and legislative factions).

This extended team of protégés and clients spanned the range of critical positions within the federal executive only for the first year of the Yeltsin regime. It was immediately confronted by a hostile parliament, with mounting conservative pressures leading to almost immediate personnel and policy changes. By mid-1992 there was a growing need for a more dynamic balancing of radical reformist interests, generally championed by network members, with more centrist and even conservative interests, especially as grounded in the traditionally favoured ministries and economic sectors. At the time, most key members of the Yeltsin network came from outside established institutions. It was necessary to build bridges to those institutions and sectors in order to fashion a larger and more effective governing coalition. An immediate result of such bridging efforts was the selective rotation of personnel and the inclusion of more sectoral representatives, who tended to hold more centrist policy perspectives.

The most important leadership change involved the selection of the centrist Viktor Chernomyrdin to serve as Prime Minister. Drawn from the Soviet fuel and energy sector, Chernomyrdin was known to favour a more cautious reform programme with greater state controls. His selection signalled the beginning of a period of accommodation with established bureaucracies and sectoral interests. The man almost simultaneously selected to serve as Chernomyrdin's Deputy Prime Minister, Boris Fedorov, described the Prime Minister as 'a prominent product of the economic-branch *nomenklatura*'.[46] Given that Fedorov was a radical reformist, his appointment balanced that of Chernomyrdin.[47] The subsequent recomposition of the government in 1993–94 reflected an awkward rebalancing of reform and centrist elements. Under Chernomyrdin, the recruitment of centrists and establishment technocrats broadened the governing coalition's political base. Chernomyrdin favoured industrialists who, in comparison with anti-inflation market economists, wanted larger government subsidies and higher employment. He occasionally relied on associates from the Russian Gazprom to serve in his government.[48] A number of his associates assumed ministerial positions.[49] The public posturing of both Chernomyrdin and Yeltsin in 1993–94 suggested that the personnel changes were endorsed, if not initiated, by the President himself. Indeed, Yeltsin's efforts at balancing reformers with centrists more tied to established institutional interests had begun as early as summer 1992, when Vladimir Shumeiko (associated with the military–industrial complex) had been selected for a deputy prime ministership. Under Chernomyrdin's stewardship, this tendency in recruitment accelerated.[50]

This dynamic balancing of reformist and centrist politicians continued

well into 1995. It was evident in the constantly changing political portfolio of the influential Yeltsin client and troubleshooter Sergei Shakhrai.[51]
Also, the selection of the centrist Yeltsin protégé, Oleg Lobov, to replace
Yurii Skokov as secretary of the increasingly powerful Security Council,
offset the position of more reformist advisers such as Sergei Filatov.
Such continuing efforts at dynamic balance were especially evident in the
rapid rise and fluctuating political portfolios of the two most influential
government officials serving under Chernomyrdin, Oleg Soskovets and
Anatolii Chubais. Soskovets was a centrist with strong ties to the military–industrial and machine-building sectors who was selected as First
Deputy Prime Minister in April 1993.[52] While a relative moderate on
price liberalisation, he tended to protect a large government role in
economic management. Over time, his portfolio of responsibilities widened and he served as a troubleshooter on a number of high-priority
issues, including the Chechen crisis.[53] In contrast, Chubais was a reformer who had overseen the early stage of the Yeltsin government's
privatisation programme. His administrative portfolio also grew dramatically in 1994–95 as he ascended to a first deputy prime ministership.[54]
He also served as a troubleshooter, especially in the implementation of
the government's austere 1995 budget.[55] Both men saw their policy-
making positions expand even as they represented alternative sets of
policy perspectives within the Yeltsin team. They were widely viewed as
the leading centrist and reformist candidates to replace Chernomyrdin as
the next head of government.

Between 1992 and 1995, the rotation of personnel tended towards the
displacement of Gaidar-style reformers with more moderate reformers.[56]
And as one prominent observer noted, there was a strong tendency to
recruit individuals who took their political cues directly from the President.[57] With a few notable exceptions, the changes in the government's
composition also pointed to the forging of alliances with centrist and
establishment elements. In my population of senior executive branch
members in 1994, there are numerous allies of Yeltsin, but it is difficult
to measure and deal with the notion of an 'ally' in a systematic way. I
understand allies as having bases of power independent from those of
Yeltsin and his associates. They did not come to federal-level elite status
on the basis of career ties to the Yeltsin network, yet they joined forces
with it in the forging of a policy programme. In general, these allies
were linked with powerful economic sectors (for example, the military–industrial complex). Among the more prominent examples in the
Yeltsin – Chernomyrdin government were Deputy Prime Ministers Shumeiko, Aleksandr Zaveryukha and Yurii Yarov. All these officials were

tied to powerful sectoral interests and they articulated those sectoral concerns before being recruited into the government. Since early 1994 and the formation of the new parliament, bridges were also built to centrist–conservative parliamentary elements through the recruitment into the government of influential party leaders such as Aleksandr Nazarchuk (Agrarian Party), Vladimir Panskov (Women of Russia) and Valentin Kovalev and Vladimir Isakov (Communist Party of Russia).[58] Once again we are referring to politicians with important connections to established sectoral interests.

Post-Soviet Russian norms of elite mobility and regime formation involve the augmenting, if not replacement, of traditional patron–client networks with institutionalised lobby groups more able to promote their sectoral interests openly. The recruitment of what I term 'allies' has in fact entailed the Yeltsin regime building coalitions with the most influential sectoral interests in Russia. This recruitment and coalition-building strategy can be seen as corporatist, if we understand corporatism to constitute the inclusion and balanced representation of sectoral interests in the governing elite coalition.[59] Rather than finding a more established Yeltsin regime composed of a large and growing extended patronage network in the style of Leonid Brezhnev, we see the emergence of a Yeltsin-led coalition of often-competing institutional lobbies.

Lobbies and the Yeltsin Team

The collapse of the Soviet system has entailed the open aggregation and articulation of more parochial economic and other interests. Institutionalised sectoral interests continue to be among the most influential in both public and behind-the-scenes negotiations over policy and budgetary issues. Those sectoral interests now constitute major political lobbies and they possess considerable material and organisational resources as they promote their parochial interests. The Yeltsin government has been increasingly dominated by what one observer termed 'undisciplined lobbying'.[60] The radical reformers who were the prime policy shapers of the Yeltsin–Gaidar government had generally been drawn from research and academic settings not connected with such lobbies. But centrists and more conservative politicians recruited into the Yeltsin government, especially since 1992, often had such connections.

I am unable to address the issue of outright corruption by such institutional interests.[61] Indeed, this study does not analyse the actions or lobbying strategies of these sectoral interests. It is difficult from outside the decision-making process to assess how institutional lobbies influence government decisions. But a review of past work experience and career mobility patterns permits an identification of politicians with sectoral linkages and preferences. An examination of the composition of the Yeltsin regime reveals the unmistakable inclusion of politicians linked with the most resource-wealthy and institutionally well-ensconced economic sectors.

The traditionally favoured economic sectors of the Soviet system have continued to be the most influential after 1991: the military– industrial complex, the agricultural sector, and the fuel and energy sector. It is understandable that a major concern for all these sectors has been the character and specifics of the government privatisation programme. Representatives of these economic interests have focused their lobbying activities not only on government allocations, but also on price (where applicable) and tax structures, and on quotas and licences influencing production. Pressure has been brought to bear on both the executive and the legislative branches as lobbies attempt to influence the content of legislation and its application. It is hardly coincidental that representatives from these sectors have become prominent members of the government.

In Table 4.2 I re-examine the composition of the executive as of Spring 1994, identifying those politicians connected with one of the three major institutionalised economic sectors which have been especially active in lobbying government policies. Identifications were made on the basis of a politician's overall career, and not simply the position he or she held in March 1994. I find that a significant proportion of the entire elite population (21 of 74, or 28 per cent) had past careers grounded in institutions associated with one of these three sectors. Especially telling is the fact that 46 per cent (6 of 13) of the 'post-Soviet independent' politicians had careers based in these sectors. Thus, nearly half of the generalist newcomers were representatives of particular sector interests. This contrasts with the absence of sectoral representatives among Yeltsin protégés and the relatively lower level of such representatives among Yeltsin clients (29 per cent).

Turning briefly to each of the three sectors, we find representatives who were key members of the Yeltsin team who advanced the interests of their sectors. Vladimir Shumeiko, once the First Deputy Prime Minister and subsequently head of the Federation Council, actively supported allocations for the military–industrial sector. When he pushed for the creation of the state-operated Rosvooruzhenie corporation, he selected a former adviser to head it.[62] Another heavy industry representative,

Table 4.2. Representation of Selected Economic Sectors in Top Russian Federation Executive, March 1994.

	No.	Military industrial	Agriculture	Energy	Sectors combined	Sectors as per cent of number
Yeltsin Network						
Protégés	5	–	–	–	–	–
Clients	14	3	1	–	4	29
Others						
Sectoral specialists	22	6	–	2	8	36
Outside specialists	14	1	1	–	2	14
Soviet period specialists	6	–	–	1	1	17
Post–Soviet independents	13	3	1	2	6	46

Viktor Glukhikh, was appointed Chairman of the State Committee for Defence Branches of Industry, and he actively promoted sectoral interests in budgetary struggles.

In agriculture, early radical reformist efforts to transform the Soviet system rapidly were dealt a serious blow when Aleksandr Nazarchuk was appointed Agriculture Minister in autumn 1994. A leading member of the conservative Agrarian Party, Nazarchuk was described as a 'lobbyist minister' for the traditionally powerful collective farm element.[63] He replaced the more reformist Minister, Viktor Khlystun, and his appointment helped to shore up what had been an antagonistic government relationship with the more traditional agricultural establishment and its parliamentary group. What has been characterised as 'an underground agriculture department of the Central Committee', with links to all major government bodies (including the Ministries of Agriculture, Economics and Finance), survived from the Soviet period.[64] Given an Agriculture Minister such as Nazarchuk and an influential Deputy Prime Minister (Aleksandr Zaveryukha) with similar associations, the agricultural establishment continued to possess significant lobbying potential in the Yeltsin government.

Finally, no sector brought more material resources to its lobbying than did the energy and fuel sector. Moreover, its leading political survivor from the Soviet period, Viktor Chernomyrdin, came to head the government. Chernomyrdin's protégé, Yurii Shafranik, served as Minister of Fuel and Power, and he proved to be an active advocate for this sector. It is no surprise that the Chernomyrdin government officially identified the fuel and energy complex as 'a top-priority branch in which investments are to be financed by the state'.[65]

Beyond senior executive branch officials, many deputies in the legislature also had strong connections with established sectoral interests. A number of political parties and legislative factions (for example, the Agrarian Party) were directly tied to such interests. There has been considerable evidence of the ability of sectoral representatives in the executive and legislative branches to work together. In the agricultural domain, for instance, one observer wrote of 'a politburo of the agro-industrial complex', composed of top government officials (for example, Deputy Prime Minister Zaveryukha), legislative leaders (Duma Chairman Ivan Rybkin), and party leaders (for example, the Communist Party leader, Gennadii Zyuganov, and the Agrarian Party leader, Mikhail Lapshin).[66] Through their common efforts, these politicians were able to find trillions of extra rubles in the 1994 budget for agriculture.

Since the public approval of the 1993 Constitution and the election of a new parliament, the executive branch has developed its own institutional means by which to lobby for its interests in the parliament.[67] With lobbyist ministers and their subordinates working with legislative counterparts, the informal institutional arrangements have emerged which should enhance the ability of sectoral interests to influence the policy process. Thus, we find the more open manifestation of the Soviet-period sectoral 'complexes' or 'whirlpools' to which so much policy-making power had been informally delegated.[68] In this setting, aspiring politicians may find sectoral affiliations much more critical to their upward mobility than loyalty to particular political superiors. These established and well-ensconced institutional actors will represent major avenues for upward political elite mobility long after Yeltsin's departure from the Russian political scene.

Rethinking Patron–Client Issues

Informal and extra-legal political arrangements are important in post-Soviet Russian political life. But institutional and rule changes of the past half-decade have altered the norms of patron–client relations. The ability of high-level politicians to transfer political power to trusted subordinates unilaterally has been curtailed. A more open and diversified political opportunity structure has resulted in a more varied political elite. An important new reality of the post-Soviet transition period is that shorter-term political alliances, based on common power interests and policy agreement, have become central to elite coalition building. In addition, the cartelisation of Russian politics has reshaped the mobility calculations of aspiring politicians.[69] Traditionally favoured and powerful economic sectors bring the resources and institutional connections which constitute an effective springboard for aspiring politicians to achieve political elite status.

Focusing on the Yeltsin network and the top Russian federal executive, this study reveals a more limited presence and role of Yeltsin associates in regime formation and decision making. In comparison with past Soviet experience, the recruitment of long-term protégés into the executive was modest. While a significant number of Sverdlovsk associates assisted Yeltsin in his early years as Russian President, many failed to survive even the first year of the post-Soviet transition. Those who did survive tended to hold administrative support positions for Yeltsin rather than wielding major decision-making power in the government. The departure of prominent associates reflected the changing political needs of the patron and the inability of even the closest associates to help meet those needs. Thus, Yeltsin could ill-afford Burbulis's alienation of more conservative institutional interests, while he was less in need of Petrov's Soviet-period organisational prowess. The politically more self-reliant Burbulis and Petrov continued to be influential figures after they were jettisoned by Yeltsin, but they manoeuvred from the political sidelines and were independent of him.

As for Yeltsin's clients, a considerable number were to be found in the executive, but their relationships with the patron were more limited and of shorter duration. Serious questions could be raised about their long-term political reliability and loyalty to Yeltsin. Between 1991 and 1995 a good number of clients came and went. As a consequence of this, Yeltsin's governing coalition was especially dependent upon alliances with sectoral representatives and with politicians who brought an independent career base to their government positions. Such relationships are more dynamic than those in the Soviet period because these politicians no longer operated within a centralised, unified hierarchical system. Post-Soviet politicians are now objects of diverse and often counterpoised pressures, with those pressures coming from below as well as from above.

Given these new political conditions, how are we to view a patron's clients? How, for instance, are we to view the members of the Gaidar team who were treated here as Yeltsin clients? A good number of these clients were specialist colleagues of Gaidar drawn into government service. Were they Yeltsin clients or in fact short-term Yeltsin supporters? After leaving the Yeltsin government and becoming an influential party leader in the legislature, Yegor Gaidar continued to provide general support for the Yeltsin government.[70] But in a number of other cases, clients' support for Yeltsin waned as his government was reorganised and the policy programme evolved away from its initial radical reformist character. Indeed, numerous prominent reformers who had supported Yeltsin in the early days of his regime publicly broke with him. The most prominent reformist critic of the government, Grigorii Yavlinskii, was once a Deputy Prime Minister in the Silaev government, while another critic of Yeltsin's (and now an ally of Yavlinskii), Yurii Boldyrev, was once the chief state inspector of the Control Department in Yeltsin's chancellery.

How are we to view Yeltsin's relationship with a political ally such as Viktor Chernomyrdin? Their relationship was described by one observer as constituting a 'cohabitation'.[71] As argued here, Yeltsin and Chernomyrdin were the two leading members of a governing coalition. But their relationship was a relatively short-term one: there was no long-term past career interdependence, so diverging future political needs could lead the two men to part ways. We have already seen how this has occurred with other past allies of Yeltsin.

As we consider post-Soviet informal and extra-legal arrangements, we must shift our attention to institutionally well-ensconced sectoral interests and lobbies. Many Russian politicians can be associated with particular sectoral lobbies; we may find common career ties among such politicians which are grounded in those sectors. Care must be taken, however, not to assume monolithic sectoral interests. Career rivalries and issue debates can divide sectors.[72] Patronage networks have been beset with similar divisions.[73]

There is every indication that sectoral lobbies will continue to be critical actors in the post-Soviet Russian decision-making process. Boris Fedorov contends that the only way to reverse the political power of informal lobbies in the government is to recruit what he terms 'people from the outside'.[74] But there is little likelihood of this occurring in the immediate future. What is clear is that informal politics, including patronage networks and sectoral lobbies, will be of continuing importance when a post-Yeltsin regime and governing coalition emerges. What is also clear is that those informal politics will be structured by a more decentralised post-Soviet reality in which career ambitions are shaped by *both* top-down and bottom-up political forces.

Notes

1. For a discussion of the post-Soviet Russian hegemonic presidency, see John P. Willerton and Aleksei A. Shulus, 'Constructing a New Political Process: The Hegemonic Presidency and the Legislature', *The John Marshall Law Review* **28**, no.4 (Summer 1995), pp.787–825.
2. *Nezavisimaya gazeta*, 23 April 1994.
3. On political opportunity structures, see Joseph A. Schlesinger, *Ambition and Politics* (Chicago: Rand McNally, 1966), Chapter 1.
4. This background information on political patronage and its relevance to Soviet politics of the period from Brezhnev through Gorbachev draws upon John P. Willerton, *Patronage and Politics in the USSR* (Cambridge: Cambridge University Press, 1992).
5. For an overview of Gorbachevian reforms, see Stephen White, *After Gorbachev* (Cambridge: Cambridge University Press, 1993), especially Chapters 1–4 and 7.
6. These presidential powers are identified in Articles 80–93 of the 1993 Russian Federation Constitution.
7. Presidential decrees do lose their force once a federal statute has been passed by the parliament. The president has a powerful veto over such statutes, but the executive's power is not unrestricted. I want to thank William Reisinger for this important qualification and for other critical reactions to this chapter.
8. For example, see the survey results in the wake of the invasion of Chechnya, *Segodnya*, 17 and 19 January 1995.
9. The 'conservatives and nationalists' category can be further broken down into a 'left' and a 'right opposition'. The left opposition has encompassed communists, elements of the *nomenklatura* and technocratic elite, the old agricultural establishment, and those with social welfare policy preferences (for example, Gennadii Zyuganov). The right opposition has stressed the reassertion of Russian regional might through the strengthening of the country's military. More extreme members have tended to adopt strongly anti-Western and anti-Semitic positions, pointing to a global Zionist conspiracy said to be undermining Russia's socio-economic and political transformation (for example, Vladimir Zhirinovskii).
10. See Chernomyrdin's comments about this in *Segodnya*, 22 September 1994, and Yeltsin's and State Duma Chairman Ivan Rybkin's comments in *Segodnya*, 6 October 1994.
11. According to the then Justice Minister Yurii Kalmykov: *Komsomol'skaya pravda*, 20 December 1994.
12. See Petr Zhuravlev and Sergei Parkhomenko, *Segodnya*, 14 January 1995.
13. For instance, Viktor Ilyushin worked with Yeltsin in the Sverdlovsk and Moscow party organisations and in the Central Committee apparatus, held no responsible political posts during Yeltsin's political exile, and returned to head Yeltsin's secretariat when Yeltsin became the Russian Supreme Soviet Chairman in 1990.
14. This is not to deny the potential for political party bosses to operate as patrons in the mobility of elected legislators. But the underdeveloped state of Russia's political parties makes this a moot point. Indeed, the constant splits and rivalries among members of parliament and parliamentary factions reveal the contemporary difficulties for party leaders attempting to direct others' career choices.
15. Political elite biographical and career data used in this study are drawn from Russian newspaper summaries and *Kto est' kto v Rossii* (Moscow: Novoe vremya, 1993); *Kto*

est' chto (Moscow: Catallaxy, 1993); and *Politicheskaya Rossiya segodnya* (Moscow: Moskovskii rabochii, 1993), Volumes 1 and 2.

16. He was described by one employee of the President's staff as 'sitting at the centre of the information–organisational network': see Valerii Vyzhutovich in *Moscow News*, 1994, no.28 (15–21 July).

17. Yevgenii Sukhanov (a presidential assistant for relations with parliament and public movements), and Yevgenii Tkachenko (Minister of Education).

18. Note should be made of the role of Yeltsin protégé Gennadii Burbulis in further helping such politicians (for example, Yevgenii Tkachenko). Burbulis was forced out of a formal government post long before spring 1994 and hence is not included in this 1994 population of elite members.

19. For example, Vasilii Barchuk and Aleksandr Shokhin.

20. For example, Sergei Filatov, Mikhail Malei and Sergei Shakhrai.

21. For example, Konstantin Kagalovskii (foreign economic relations), Viktor Khlystun (agriculture), Mikhail Malei (economic conversion), Nikolai Malyshev (education and science) and Boris Sal'tykov (social policies).

22. For example, Pavel Grachev, Sergei Stepashin and Viktor Yerin.

23. For a biography of and extended interview with Shakhrai, see Lyudmila Telen in *Moscow News*, 1994, no.6 (11–17 February).

24. 'High' signifies a position at the level of a ministerial department head or higher.

25. For example, Gennadii Fadeev (in the rail transport area since 1961) and Yulii Vorontsov (in the Foreign Ministry since 1953).

26. For example, Oleg Davydov in the area of foreign economic relations.

27. Anatolii Krasikov, with 30 years' experience with TASS, came out against restrictive press practices in early 1991. To all intents and purposes, he guided TASS in the wake of the failed August 1991 coup, being appointed head of the president's press service a year later.

28. For example, Sergei Bezverkhii (standardisation and certification), Danilov Danil'yan (ecology), Rudol'f Pikhoya (archives), Vitalii Rassokhin (patents), and Tat'yana Regent (migration policy).

29. For example, Colonel General Dmitrii Volkogonov and Aleksandr Yakovlev. Such officials as Vitalii Ignatenko, Yevgenii Primakov and Aleksandr Yakovlev had a political acumen useful to both the late-Soviet and immediate post-Soviet regimes.

30. For example, Aleksandr Zaveryukha (Orenburg) and Georgii Khizha and Anatolii Chubais (Leningrad).

31. For example, Yurii Shafranik, Sergei Shoigu and Vladimir Shumeiko.

32. Including Sergei Kovalev, the prominent human rights activist who had been arrested and imprisoned on a number of occasions in the Soviet period.

33. For example, Vladimir Kvasov and Oleg Soskovets (with Viktor Chernomyrdin), Vyacheslav Kostikov (with Mikhail Poltoranin), and Anatolii Chubais and Georgii Khizha (with Anatolii Sobchak and Yegor Gaidar).

34. Information for top parliamentary leaders is much more readily available than that for other legislators. In addition, important pieces of information are missing (for example, the party affiliation of Council of Federation members).

35. See Alexander Rahr, 'El'tsin Sets Up New System for Governing Russia', *Report on the USSR* 3, no.34 (23 August 1991), pp.9–12.

36. Another Sverdlovsk associate of Yeltsin, Aleksei Tsaregorodtsev, headed the secretariat of the Russian Vice-President, Aleksandr Rutskoi.

37. See Vasilii Kononenko in *Izvestiya*, 27 September 1994.
38. While leaving his formal position within the Yeltsin government in November 1992, he continued to serve as an informal adviser, promoting radical reformist policies.
39. Selected to head the State Investment Corporation in early 1993, he worked for a more modest reform programme; he helped form a centrist party, Realists' Union, in spring 1995: see Gleb Cherkasov in *Segodnya*, 28 March 1995.
40. Filatov, among other activities, had played a key role in bolstering Yeltsin's position against the parliamentary chairman Ruslan Khasbulatov when Filatov served as parliamentary first deputy chairman, during 1991–93.
41. See Tamara Zamyatina in *Izvestiya*, 7 December 1994, and Korzhakov's interview with Andrei Uglanov in *Argumenty i fakty*, 1995, no.3.
42. See the interview with Gennadii Burbulis in *Izvestiya*, 26 October 1991.
43. For an overview, see Sergei Parkhomenko in *Segodnya*, 5 November 1995.
44. For example, Aleksandr Shokhin, Anatolii Chubais, Andrei Nechaev, Vladimir Lopukhin, Peter Aven, Konstantin Kagalovskii, Vladimir Mashchits and Aleksei Golovko.
45. For example, Mikhail Poltoranin, Sergei Shakhrai and Sergei Stankevich.
46. *Argumenty i fakty*, 1994, no.30.
47. Committed to fiscal responsibility and fundamental economic reform, Fedorov assumed a decisive role in maintaining the policy initiative *vis-à-vis* centrists.
48. For example, Vladimir Kvasov and Vladimir Babichev: see *Segodnya*, 15 and 16 November 1994.
49. For example, Yurii Shafranik, selected as Minister of Fuel and Energy, February 1993.
50. For a summary of the top personnel in the Chernomyrdin government at the end of 1994, see Kirill Aushkin in *Nezavisimaya gazeta*, 9 December 1994.
51. For example, see Leonid Nikitinskii's interview with Shakhrai in *Moscow News*, 1994, no.24 (17–24 June).
52. See Vladimir Petrov in *Novaya yezhednevnaya gazeta*, 6 July 1994.
53. See Irina Savvaleeva in *Izvestiya*, 19 January 1995.
54. See Vladislav Borodulin in *Kommersant-Daily*, 20 January 1995.
55. On Chubais's political staying power, see Ivan Krasnii in *Obshchaya gazeta*, 23–9 March 1995.
56. For a discussion of these changes as concessions to 'anti-market forces', see Vasilii Kononenko in *Izvestiya*, 5 November 1994.
57. For example, the Acting Chairman of the Russian State Bank, Tat'yana Paramonova, and Finance Minister Vladimir Panskov: see Sergei Chugaev in *Izvestiya*, 9 November 1994.
58. See Aleksei Kirpichnikov in *Segodnya*, 5 November 1994.
59. See Phillippe Schmitter, 'Still the Century of Corporatism', *Review of Politics* **XXXVI**, no.1 (1974), pp.85–131.
60. Valerii Vyzhutovich in *Izvestiya*, 6 December 1994.
61. For an overview, see the special issue, 'Organized Crime', edited by Louise Shelley, *Demokratizatsiya* **II**, no.3 (Summer 1994).
62. Viktor Samoilov.
63. Valerii Konovalov in *Izvestiya*, 29 October 1994.
64. See Aleksandra Lugovskaya in *Izvestiya*, 3 September 1994.
65. See Vyzhutovich, 6 December 1994.

66. See Lugovskaya (note 60).

67. A Presidential Department of Interaction with Deputies to the Federal Assembly was established to co-ordinate the activity of various government agencies attempting to lobby legislators: see Anna Ostapchuk in *Nezavisimaya gazeta*, 3 August 1994.

68. On the notion of interest 'complexes' and 'whirlpools', see Jerry F. Hough, 'The Brezhnev Era: The Man and the Regime', *Problems of Communism* **25**, no.2 (March–April 1976), pp.11–13.

69. I wish to thank Alex Pravda for his appropriate characterisation of the process of post-Soviet political change as involving a cartelisation of established institutional interests.

70. See Gleb Cherkasov in *Segodnya*, 13 March 1995.

71. Comment by Alla Yaroshenskaya, quoted in *The Wall Street Journal*, 23 March 1994, pp.1 and 8.

72. In the agricultural sector, for instance, there have been divisions between the two leading Yeltsin government ministers, Zaveryukha and Nazarchuk, and an open split between Zaveryukha and the Agrarian Party leader Mikhail Lapshin: see Gleb Cherkasov in *Segodnya*, 2 September 1994.

73. Within the Yeltsin network, for instance, there has been mounting evidence of a split between Viktor Ilyushin and more conservative elements and Sergei Filatov and more reformist elements: see Vasilii Kononenko in *Izvestiya*, 27 September 1994.

74. See Lugovskaya. Fedorov cites Chubais as an example of the kind of independent practical politician he has in mind.

5 From Power to Property: The *Nomenklatura* in Post-Communist Russia

Olga Kryshtanovskaya and Stephen White

For Pareto, revolutions were above all a matter of elite change.[1] And for many there was a revolution in this sense in Eastern Europe at the end of the 1980s, with changes in government and a shift towards pluralist and democratic politics throughout the region. Several years on, the change looks less decisive. Former communist parties returned to power in Hungary, in Poland, in Lithuania, and in Bulgaria. In Romania, there was a change of leadership but less clearly a change of political regime. Former communists maintained their position in Serbia and in Slovakia, and, with a change of nomenclature, in most of former Soviet Central Asia. In Russia itself the communist party left office, but it revived in early 1993, polled strongly in the elections in December of that year, and was by far the largest party in the Duma elections that took place in December 1995. The Russian public, for their part, remained committed to the concept of a USSR, they rated their political system less highly than the one they had experienced in the Soviet years, and in any case they thought the communists were still in power.[2]

There were differing views about the extent to which communists or former communists were still in power throughout the Central and East European countries. There was relatively little direct continuity in the Czech republic, where the communist party quickly became a marginal force,[3] and only a limited degree of continuity of leading personnel in Poland.[4] In Russia, some argued similarly, there was 'relatively little overlap between the Gorbachev and Yeltsin political elites'.[5] Others, by contrast, pointed to the very high degree of continuity at local level in the early post-Soviet period,[6] and went on to emphasise the continuities in post-communist government more generally.[7] If an observer had gone to sleep in Russia at the start of 1990 and then woken up to be shown a list of the current Russian government, as a commentator in *Nezavisi-maya gazeta* put it, he would be bound to conclude that the reformist wing of the communist party headed by Boris Yeltsin had finally come to power.[8]

The more considerable the changes at leadership level, clearly, the more readily we can consider the Russian and East European transition a revolution. But we need to differentiate at the same time between changes in central government and in the regions; between changes in different sections of the central government; and between rates of change in different sub-periods. We need to know if the elite has been changing in terms of age and gender, in terms of its social composition, its geographical origin, and its levels of education. And we need to know the extent to which the Russian elite has recruited its membership from the Soviet *nomenklatura* of the recent past. In the discussion that follows we consider, first, some of the operating principles of the former *nomen-klatura*, and then we examine the ways in which the *nomenklatura* attempted to protect their position – mostly through privileged access to the market – in the late 1980s. A final section considers the main financial and industrial groups through which the contemporary elite, many of them of *nomenklatura* origin, maintain their position in the post-communist 1990s.[9]

Defining and Measuring the Elite

By 'elite', we understand the ruling group in a society, consisting of the people who take decisions of national significance. We define the elite, in this chapter, in largely positional terms: in other words, on the basis of their occupancy of posts that involve the taking of decisions of national importance, including the deputies of the Russian Federal Assembly that was elected in December 1993, the government, the Russian President and his closest associates. We have not separately distinguished the leaders of the major political parties or the heads of regional administrations, as these two categories account for the bulk of the membership of the Russian parliament. A separate business elite is defined as a constituent part of the ruling elite, whose influence on public policy is defined by their position in the most important sectors of the economy and by the assets that they control.[10]

Our analysis is based upon a series of investigations conducted between 1989 and 1994 by the Sector on Elite Studies of the Institute of

Sociology of the Russian Academy of Sciences.[11] The main methods of study included informal in-depth interviews with elite members; formal interviews; surveys of expert opinion; observation; the study of official biographies; press analysis; and the study of official documents and statistics. The core of the study was based upon an examination of official biographical directories,[12] together with a series of interviews with elite members themselves conducted in association with the University of Glasgow. Altogether 3610 biographies were analysed, consisting of members of the Brezhnev elite (57 members of the government, 1500 deputies of the USSR Supreme Soviet, 282 members of the CPSU Central Committee, 26 Politburo and Secretariat members, and 131 *obkom* first secretaries); the Gorbachev elite, from 1985 to August 1991 (251 Russian Supreme Soviet deputies, 371 members of the CPSU Central Committee that was elected in 1990, 35 members of the Politburo and Secretariat, and 132 *obkom* first secretaries); and the Yeltsin elite, after September 1991 (based on 35 members of the Russian government, 44 members of the higher ranks of the Presidential Administration, 68 heads of regional administrations, 35 party leaders, 100 members of the business elite, and 543 members of the Federal Assembly).

The Soviet *Nomenklatura*

In order to understand how the elite changed in the post-Soviet period, we have to understand how it was formed over many decades of single-party communist rule. As this is a subject that has already been discussed in the scholarly literature[13] we will simply identify a number of its most distinctive features.

The elite, in the first instance, had a precise form as a result of its institutionalised character. Lists of leading positions were maintained in the Central Committee apparatus. Appointment to these leading positions was impossible without the agreement of the party hierarchy. The highest-placed members of the *nomenklatura* – that is, the holders of positions to which appointments required the approval of the Politburo or Secretariat of the CPSU Central Committee – were in effect the national elite. Equally, in spite of the varied character of the positions that were included in the upper *nomenklatura*, the Soviet elite was monolithic in nature, extending across all spheres of party, state and social life. Its monolithic character was assured by the fact that all its members were Communists, and by the manner in which all leading appointments had to be made or at least approved by higher-level party bodies. Elite members were accordingly obliged to espouse Marxism-Leninism and to observe the other conventions of Soviet public life.

The structure of the Soviet elite can be derived from the composition of the membership of the CPSU Central Committee. The following groups were always represented: the national leadership (the Politburo and Secretariat of the CPSU Central Committee, which were in effect the political executive); the leading officials of the Central Committee apparatus (in effect the national administration); the most important regional party first secretaries; the Prime Minister and other leading members of the government; the most important members of the armed and security services; leading diplomats; and the leaders of youth, trade union and cultural organisations. Formally, the Central Committee and Supreme Soviet also included workers, collective farmers, engineers and scholars. This group of 'ordinary Soviet people' had a purely decorative character: its function was to demonstrate that the USSR was a state run (as Lenin had put it) by cooks rather than professional politicians.[14]

Beyond this, the Soviet *nomenklatura* elite was strictly hierarchical. All *nomenklatura* positions as early as the Stalin era were divided into 14 ranks.[15] At the highest level was the General Secretary of the CPSU Central Committee, followed by members of the Politburo, Politburo candidate members and the Central Committee Secretaries. The next rank in the hierarchy consisted of the *nomenklatura* of the Politburo – that is, the list of positions to which appointments were made or approved at Politburo level. This list included the first and (sometimes) second secretaries of republican party organisations, the first secretaries of regional party committees and of the largest towns, All-Union ministers, the military hierarchy, ambassadors to all the socialist countries and to the largest capitalist countries, directors of the largest military–industrial enterprises, the leading officials of the creative unions, and the editors of central newspapers and journals. The level below this was the *nomenklatura* of the Central Committee Secretariat, including a more junior list of positions: deputy ministers, the second secretaries of regional party committees, the heads of regional soviet executives, and so forth. Then came positions that required the approval of the relevant Central Committee department, and after it positions that required the approval of regional, urban and district party committees, and even (at the lowest level) of local party branches.[16] The hierarchical principle required a steady progression through these stages, from level to level: it was similar in many ways to an army hierarchy, and (as in the armed forces) exceptions were rare.

The *nomenklatura* system had mechanisms that limited the tendency to self-recruitment or *semeistvennost'*. According to an informal convention, the children of higher-level officials never inherited positions with the same level of seniority as their fathers. Rather, 'elite children' had a series of special professional niches, often connected with work abroad. This was supported by a special system of *nomenklatura* education at elite institutions, particularly those that trained economists, diplomats and journalists specialising in international affairs. As a result of the restriction upon internal recruitment, the *nomenklatura* was replenished to a large extent by new members from other sections of society, including the intelligentsia, the working class and the collective-farm peasantry. The biographies of Central Committee members for the whole period of Soviet rule demonstrate how few (for instance) had a Moscow or big city background, and there were almost no members who had themselves been brought up in a *nomenklatura* household (this principle began to be violated only in 1986 when Brezhnev's son Yurii and son-in-law Yurii Churbanov joined the Central Committee; both had lost their jobs and been expelled by the following party congress, in 1990).

The *nomenklatura*, in addition, required of its members, and particularly of those who were likely to obtain advancement, that they serve in different parts of the country. The traditional *nomenklatura* career trajectory began with study in Moscow and then went on to the soviet, Komsomol, economic or party apparatus at district level, followed by recall to Moscow for a one- or two-year stint in the Central Committee headquarters and then a return to the provinces to a higher-level post (often an *obkom* first secretaryship). Apart from geographical mobility, another characteristic was a change in career specialisation. Over the Brezhnev period a number of typical *nomenklatura* career patterns developed, all of them under Central Committee auspices: party–economic, Komsomol–party, soviet–party, and party–diplomatic. The most typical was a career that moved upwards from Komsomol to party work, or from party to soviet work and back, or from economic to party work and back. There were also 'pure' career progressions, most often on the part of economic administrators. In cases of this kind, the people involved moved upwards at the same factory to the level of director, then into the relevant ministry and eventually to the rank of minister. The party–diplomatic career type, by contrast, was a feature of the decline of the *nomenklatura*, with ambassadorial posts in less important countries being filled by disgraced politicians as a form of honorable retirement.

The *nomenklatura* was served by a comprehensive and finely differentiated system of privileges. In Voslensky's words, it lived in 'Nomenklaturia, ... another, entirely different, and special country' from which ordinary citizens were 'carefully isolated'.[17] The existence of a system of this kind was related to the chronic deficits that existed throughout the Soviet period. Members of the *nomenklatura* were not rich in the conventional sense, but were removed by their position from the hardships of daily life and allowed to enjoy a better quality of life. Their money incomes were generally high, but their living standards were sustained more directly by a whole system of indirect payments or benefits. Prices in official restaurants, for instance, were significantly below their real cost; places in recreation homes were heavily subsidised; and so forth. *Nomenklatura* members were also accorded flats and dachas in the most fashionable areas, for rents that were symbolic.[18]

Apart from this, there was a well-developed distribution system that supported the special needs of *nomenklatura* members. At food processing plants, for instance, there was always a workshop producing higher quality foodstuffs for the elite. Special construction companies looked after their housing requirements at a level far above those of ordinary citizens. There were special ateliers, special shops, special polyclinics, and even (a labour veteran complained) special graveyards.[19] Privileges were strictly according to rank, and each rank in the *nomenklatura* ladder had its own list of benefits. In addition, there was a system of special *nomenklatura* education. It included the Higher Komsomol and Party Schools, the Academy of Social Sciences attached to the CPSU Central Committee, and the Academy of the National Economy. The Higher Schools were generally concerned with the training of local and regional-level nomenklaturists, and sometimes provided a local official with the educational qualifications that were felt to be appropriate. The Moscow Party School, the Academy of Social Sciences and Academy of the National Economy were, by contrast, institutions for raising the qualifications of *nomenklatura* members. A placement at any of these institutions meant, in practice, that the official concerned was being prepared for advancement to a still higher position.

From Power to Property

As the Soviet system began to change under the impact of the Gorbachev reforms, so too did the patterns of elite advantage that had become established over decades of Soviet rule. And as political position became a less secure guarantee of those advantages, the emphasis shifted to private property – as Trotsky, many years earlier, had predicted.[20] One of the most important forms through which this transition took place was the alternative or 'Komsomol' economy that began to develop in the late 1980s under the supervision of Yegor Ligachev.[21] Its focus was the Co-ordinating Council of Centres for Scientific and Technical Creativity of Youth (TsNTTM), established in 1987 and staffed by Komsomol officials, with a network of centres attached to every district party committee in Moscow. These were, in effect, the first commercial structures of any kind in the former USSR, and it was through these centres that many in the first wave of new Russian entrepreneurs became established: individuals such as Konstantin Borovoi, a computer scientist who moved into Komsomol business and thereafter established the country's leading raw materials exchange and his own political party; or Igor' Safaryan, who progressed from a Komsomol centre to a co-operative and then his own firm of brokers; or Konstantin Zatulin, a Moscow history graduate who gave up his dissertation to work for the economics secretary of the Komsomol Central Committee and then became chairman of 'Entrepreneurs for a New Russia'; or Mikhail Khodorkovskii, who graduated from a deputy Komsomol secretaryship at the Mendeleev Chemistry Institute to the chairmanship of Menatep Bank.[22]

The 'Komsomol economy' took its origin from a resolution adopted by the CPSU Central Committee on 25 July 1986 in which it approved a proposal from the Komsomol that it establish a network of scientific and technical centres for the benefit of its members. The new centres were supposed to operate on a commercial basis, basing themselves on agreements with enterprises and providing services that were not otherwise available.[23] A series of more formal agreements followed in the course of 1987, including one in March that established a Co-ordinating Council for the Scientific and Technical Creativity of Youth under the chairmanship of Deputy Premier Boris Tolstykh.[24] By the end of the year the term 'Komsomol economy' had come into regular use among Komsomol officials, and it was repeatedly employed by First Secretary Viktor Mironenko in his address to a Komsomol plenum in December 1987. He was able to report that co-ordinating councils had been established in most republics and regions, and that more than 60 centres were already operating in towns throughout the country.[25] The scope of the new centres was extended considerably during 1988, allowing them to engage in the manufacture of consumer goods and to establish economic relations with foreign firms and organisations;[26] they could set their own prices for the goods they imported from abroad, and were relieved of all customs duties.[27] The Law on Co-operatives, adopted in May 1988, was modified as a result of pressure from the Komsomol to cover 'other public organisations', and this allowed the new youth centres to broaden the basis of their activity.[28] Complaints soon began to reach government that youth organisations had been buying and reselling video recorders, computers and other forms of technology at inflated prices, and with 'crude violations of the law';[29] addressing the XXI Komsomol Congress in April 1990, Gorbachev warned that it was not appropriate for the party's youth movement to become involved in 'middleman activity' of this kind.[30] But the system was already developing under its own momentum; there was a youth bank, an import–export centre and a network of fashion shops, and by 1990 more than 17,000 youth co-operatives were in operation employing about a million staff.[31]

The Komsomol and its youth centres played a number of important functions in the establishment of an early Russian capitalism, including the conversion of paper assets into liquid cash. Not a single state enterprise, in the late 1980s, had the right to conduct a relatively simple operation of this kind. Armed with this concession, the new centres for scientific and technical creativity were able to charge a rate of up to 30 per cent on the profits that arose from such transactions; of these profits, 5 per cent were remitted to the CPSU Central Committee.[32] Formerly the privileges of the *nomenklatura* had been largely in kind, reflected in the granting of state property for private use, or in money and special services; now they began to acquire an increasingly 'monetary' character, with its members allowed to engage in activities that were prohibited for others and to make profits from such activities. Among the main privileges of this kind, in the *perestroika* period, were the following:

(i) The establishment of joint enterprises

The *nomenklatura* had always been distinguished by its special relationship with the outside world; and for many reasons, not necessarily connected with high politics. The difference between the official and unofficial exchange rates for the ruble, for instance, made any foreign economic activity profitable and gave opportunities for a speculative gain to anyone who was able to travel abroad. Contacts with the West were not simply agreeable and prestigious, they were also lucrative. In the broadest terms, the Soviet government was itself involved in commerce in the Brezhnev years of 'developed socialism'. Staff members of the Ministry of Foreign Trade, for instance, bought and sold commodities on the American stock exchange; and several grain deals in the 1960s and

1970s are still remembered in ministerial circles as enormously profitable.[33] From the very first stages of economic reform, the question of foreign dealings came under the close attention of the leadership. An association of joint enterprises was established in 1988, headed by Lev Vainberg, who joined a consultative council on entrepreneurship during the Gorbachev presidency in 1991 and was himself the director of a French–Italian–Soviet joint enterprise and Vice-President of the Scientific-Industrial Union (later the Russian Union of Industrialists and Entrepreneurs). The first joint enterprises to be registered by the USSR Ministry of Justice were directly linked with the CPSU; the very first Soviet–American joint enterprise, 'Dialog', was established in 1987 under the party's direct patronage. Through its 'authorised organisations' – the Main Computing Centre of VDNKh, VO Vneshtekhnika pri GKNT SSSR, PO KamAZ – the party invested 12 million rubles in the founding capital of the joint venture. After six months 'Dialog' in turn became the founder of another joint enterprise, 'Perestroika', whose president was Andrei Stroev, a relative of Yegor Stroev who was at that time a Central Committee Secretary.[34]

One of the first joint enterprises, 'Vneshkonsul't', founded in 1988, was established with the participation of a similar range of 'authorised representatives' of the CPSU: once again, Vneshtekhnika and the Main Computing Centre of VDNKh. The foreign participant was the Finnish concern Sarka-Sov Consulting (in practice, a foreign-based Soviet firm). Soon 'Vneshkonsul't' became a partner of one of the world's most important firms of business consultants, Ernst and Young: they jointly formed the joint enterprise Ernst and Young Vneshkonsul't. The 'authorised organisations' that took part in the establishment of joint concerns of this kind using the financial resources of the CPSU Central Committee included, in the agricultural sphere, RSFSR Gosagroprom and its affiliates; in the cultural sphere, the Bolshoi Theatre and the Kremlin Palace of Congresses; in computers, the Main Computing Centre of VDNKh and Vneshtekhnika; in various business spheres, the Znanie Society, the All-Union Trade Union Council, the Moscow and regional sections of Zhilsotsbank, the Komsomol Central Committee and others.

There were other less well-known organisations, which also became agencies through which the party began to adapt to a market environment. In a single day (11 January 1989), for instance, a specialised medical co-operative in Donetsk established three joint enterprises with a total capitalisation of $50 million. These were 'Rida' (with the Brazilian firm Brital), 'Koyana' (with the same Brazilian firm), and 'Valeo' (a joint venture with the Italian firm Imar). In no case did the foreign share exceed 25 per cent of the total investment, according to an analysis of the founding documents that were registered in the USSR Ministry of Justice; their role was rather to facilitate a process by which party-controlled assets could be converted into the more defensible form of an enterprise with foreign as well as Russian ownership and management.

(ii) The conversion of assets into cash

In the *perestroika* years only TsNTTM had the privilege of converting its nominal assets into cash. Money, at this time, was of two kinds: cash (*nalichnye*) and nominal (*beznalichnye*). Only cash was money in the real sense; bank credits were necessary for purely paper transactions between state organisations. An enterprise deducted what it needed for the pay of its employees, whose rates of remuneration were strictly regulated by the state, and no other source of income was possible than the one that arose from a regular salary or bonus payment. Ready cash, for its part, had to be limited, as otherwise there would be serious social tensions in circumstances of general shortage. The creation of the new centres, as a means of converting paper credits into cash, was not only a contribution to the emergence of a Soviet market; it was also one of the causes of a deepening problem of inflation. In Komsomol circles the scientific and technical centres began to be called the 'locomotive of inflation' for this reason; and the process by which money was processed in this way was itself a profitable and privileged one.

(iii) Advantageous credits

In order to obtain credit at low levels of interest (or sometimes without payment at all) it was necessary to belong to the *nomenklatura* or to have close links with highly placed officials. In the *perestroika* years it was particularly profitable to obtain a credit in foreign currency. There were three rates of exchange to the dollar at this time: the state one, the commercial one, and a special tourist rate of exchange. While the commercial and tourist rates gradually increased and moved closer to the level at which the currencies changed hands on the black market, the state exchange rate for a long time remained the same: 65 kopeks for a US dollar. It was this that made foreign currency credits so profitable. A firm might typically obtain a credit of a million dollars for a month, sell the dollars on the black market for (say) ten rubles each, and then return the credit to the state at the official rate of exchange, leaving a profit of more than nine million rubles. The first commercial banks, operating with the support of the state itself, were able to make profits in the same way.

(iv) Property dealings

In the early years of the economic reform only firms that were connected with the *nomenklatura* had the right to engage in property transactions. There were several reasons for this. In the first place, no one else owned any property. The mass population lived in state apartments, and enterprises were also based upon state ownership. Consequently, the officials who disposed of state property had enormous scope for their activities. While the first commercial firms were being established some of the best state property was sold at advantageous prices to firms that had been established with the participation of the *nomenklatura.* The *nomenklatura*, in this way, sold itself its own property – and at nominal prices. The MOST Group, for instance, which is now one of the most powerful financial and industrial associations in Russia, bought several buildings in the centre of Moscow for several tens of thousands of rubles, which was less than half their market value at the time.

In the Soviet period the CPSU had been the owner of a large number of buildings, in which its full-time officials, publishing houses, educational institutions, rest homes, living quarters and hotels were accommodated. These party buildings were, of their kind, the country's 'gold fund': they were the best buildings, in the most convenient and prestigious locations, and the best maintained. During the *perestroika* period the *nomenklatura* began to receive a profit from renting these establishments. The best rest homes, clinics, tourist bases and hotels were typically made available to foreign firms, and joint enterprises were actively established. A full-scale *nomenklatura* war developed over the right to make use of the Central Committee hotel '1 October'; the final victor was the administration of the Russian President himself. Similarly, offices in the best buildings in the centre of Moscow were rented out at low rates to firms that had *nomenklatura* contacts. Indeed in the mid-1990s it is still possible to judge how close a firm was to the party elite of the Soviet period by where it is located. The offices of a number of firms directed by Konstantin Zatulin, for instance, are in the complex of buildings on Old Square, where the Central Committee offices had been located: Zatulin, now a well-known politician and businessman, was (as we have noted) a former adviser to the Komsomol with special responsibility for the 'youth economy'.[35]

(v) Privileges in import–export operations

As in other spheres, the right to engage in foreign commercial operations in the *perestroika* years was a restricted one. Special firms were created by the *nomenklatura* to serve as a form of contact between domestic producers and their foreign clients. For other firms there was no means of access of this kind to the foreign market; and the profits that derived from the export of raw material and other competitive goods went directly into the pockets of these *nomenklatura* companies. A different procedure was followed in the case of imports. A system of state purchase prices for imported goods was still in operation, with a number of bodies that made the necessary arrangements. Commercial bodies were founded in their place whose function was the retail sale of imported goods; the difference between state and retail prices was considerable and it remained at the disposal of the owners of these new commercial importers.

(vi) 'Privatisation of the state by the state'

A process of this kind takes place when the public officials, using their formal powers, privatise those sections of the state for which they are themselves responsible. This began in 1987 and had largely concluded by the time a privatisation programme for the population at large was ready to be launched. Privatisation of this kind included wholesale changes in the system of economic management, banking and retail sale, and the sale of the most profitable enterprises. Ministries, for instance, were turned into concerns. The minister typically retired, or became a consultant to the concern that had succeeded the ministry. The president of the concern, as a rule, was a former deputy minister. The concern acquired the status of joint-stock company. The shareholders were typically the most senior management of the former ministry, together with the enterprises for which it had been responsible. The ministry's property, in this way, became the private property of its leading officials; and they themselves did not simply privatise the organisation for which they were responsible, but did so for their own benefit.

The privatisation of banking took place in a similar way. The reforms that were undertaken in 1988 and 1989 had led to the collapse of what had been a unitary and closely regulated system, which was no longer able to adapt to new requirements. Promstroibank and Zhilsotsbank, together with their regional affiliates, were dissolved entirely; and each part of this former system became a commercial bank. The buildings, the staff, the equipment, and often the management remained the same; what changed was the name and the means by which profits were distributed. The former Moscow Zhilsotsbank, for instance, became Mosbiznesbank, under the continued presidency of Viktor Bukato. Promstroibank retained its former name, simply adding the word 'commercial'; its president, as before, is Yakov Dubenetskii.[36]

A number of new commercial banks were created with the direct participation of officials of the Ministry of Finance. One of the main Russian banks, Imperial, was established under the auspices of the Ministry's department for relations with commercial banks, which was headed at that time by Sergei Rodionov; he duly became the new head of Imperial. Several other commercial banks were established on the basis of what was apparently a fresh initiative, but the history of their establishment, and the biographies of their directors, suggests a rather different interpretation. One of the first commercial banks, Menatep, for instance, began life in 1988 as a scientific and technical centre for youth creativity under the auspices of the Frunze district committee of the CPSU.[37] Gosbank officials and highly-placed staff in the Ministry of Finance did not receive a majority of shares in the banks of which they became directors; and their contribution to capital assets was generally insignificant. But their share was often sufficient to exercise a dominant influence, and that influence was exercised over what were often very profitable capital assets as well as over the circulation of currency.[38]

Retail trade was privatised in the same way. The Soviet trading system had two main forms: Gossnab, which was responsible for the allocation of the 'means of production', and various bureaux responsible for consumer goods. The USSR Ministry of Foreign Trade and its specialised administrations – 'Eksportkhleb', 'Eksportles' and so forth – was a particularly important part of this elaborate system. Gossnab duly became the basis upon which the first stock exchanges began to emerge. Major exchanges like the Russian Commodities and Raw Materials Exchange and the Moscow Commodities Exchange were headed by former Komsomol functionaries, and former specialists from Gossnab were invited to take over their management positions. Senior officials of the Ministry of Trade and of Foreign Trade moved quickly to establish commercial structures within the framework of their own organisations, which then monopolised the most profitable sections of the activities for which the former ministries had been responsible.

The most profitable enterprises were also privatised, becoming joint-stock companies long before a full-scale programme of privatisation had been instituted. Among the first to become commercially established were 'Butek', directed by Mikhail Bocharov; 'Mikrokhirurgiya glaza', directed by the surgeon and politician Svyatoslav Fedorov; and the KamAZ and AvtoVAZ automobile works, directed respectively by Nikolai Bekh and Vladimir Kadannikov (from 1996 a minister in the Russian government). The manner in which such firms had been privatised was unclear, as no legislation had yet been adopted to provide for such changes. Another form of 'privatisation before privatisation' was the creation of commercial structures based at the factories themselves, typically the creation of a more specialised agency involved in marketing and sales. The factory's production was first classified into competitive and non-competitive. Non-competitive output, either because it was of poor quality or because it was simply too expensive, was sold thereafter at state prices, while output for which there was a demand was sold through the factory-based firm. The difference between the state price and the retail price was converted in this way into profits for the factory directors, and a factory that had not yet been privatised became a source of material benefit for its management.

The outcome of all these changes was a substantial move towards the conversion of the power of the party–state *nomenklatura* into private property. The state, in effect, had privatised itself. Property, formerly, had been within the disposal of the *nomenklatura*, but not its private ownership; now it had moved from public into private hands, typically those of the factory administration. Ministers, by the same token, had become the owners of majority shareholdings in privatised companies, department heads at the Ministry of Finance had become presidents of commercial banks, and leading officials at Gossnab had become managers of exchanges. During this early, '*nomenklatura*' stage of privatisation, there were certainly some with no previous involvement in their new sphere of activity. Many of them, indeed, enjoyed a good deal of success. But taken as a whole, it is clear that the process of economic reform took place under the control of the *nomenklatura* and to its direct material benefit.

The New Russian Elite

As a result of all these changes, what had been a unitary Soviet elite divided into two broad sections: a political and an economic elite. Membership of the first was a consequence of position, and of one's standing within the political establishment; the second was made up of people whose influence was based upon their control of capital. The new

Russian elite, in other words, became a bifurcated one; its position now depended at least partly upon the ownership of property, and not simply on the temporary occupation of positions of influence.[39]

With the coming to power of Yeltsin the new elite began to consolidate itself. Yeltsin, as a rule, used officials who had been appointed by Gorbachev, or ones he had known himself in the Sverdlovsk party committee. And although the flow of new people into high-ranking positions continued, it was none the less clear that the revolutionary period of the transformation of the elite had ended. Structures of executive power had come into being – the administration of the President, and the government of the Russian Federation – and there was a functioning and freely elected assembly . The courts alone had not developed into an independent branch of government. The locus of authority was increasingly in the hands of executive bodies. The movement of officials from party to state that had begun under Gorbachev now showed its results. Throughout Russia administrations were being formed from the same source: the old *nomenklatura*. And a new pyramid of power arose above the former one.

The Yeltsin leadership took steps to 'close' the elite at this stage. The first step in this process was the dissolution of the Congress of People's Deputies and Supreme Soviet, which had up to this point resisted presidential control. The next step was the adoption of a new Constitution which made clear that the parliament of the future would consist in part of the heads of regional administrations that the President had himself appointed (they were represented in the upper house, the Council of the Federation), and in part of political leaders who also had their origins in the former *nomenklatura* and who were represented in the lower house, the State Duma. Ministers were allowed to combine their positions with seats in the Duma that was elected in 1993 (but not its successor, elected in 1995), strengthening the influence of the executive at least initially within the system of representative institutions.

While formally retaining the two branches of government, the Yeltsin leadership made great efforts to control the work of legislative bodies by methods that included increasing the presence within them of state officials, regulating the election of new deputies as closely as possible, and gradually absorbing the whole system of government within a *nomenklatura* framework. The Soviet tradition of 'selection and allocation of cadres' was in effect revived, and with it the 'table of ranks' – that is, the hierarchy of positions and corresponding rates of pay – that had given rise to the *nomenklatura* itself when it was established in the early 1920s.

The new system of appointment was as follows: at the apex of the pyramid were the supreme leaders, who occasionally lost their places as a result of high-level political intrigue. In their place a second and then a third stratum of the old *nomenklatura* rose to positions of power. Unlike the Soviet period, loss of position at the apex of the system was no longer equivalent to political death: a former leader, under these new conventions, soon found a position in a new power structure at a slightly lower point in the hierarchy. A process of replacement of this kind took place at different rates in the centre and in the localities: in Moscow the political process was more intensive and the top leadership was replaced more often, giving greater opportunities for lower levels of the former *nomenklatura* to advance their position. In many of the regions, on the other hand, there were only one or two cycles in the process of elite renewal. In Krasnodar *krai*, for instance, the former chairman of the territorial council, Nikolai Kondratenko, was dismissed for his support of the attempted 1991 coup and replaced by the democrat D'yakonov. D'yakonov resigned in turn and was replaced by his deputy Nikolai Yegorov, a representative of the 'third layer' of the *nomenklatura* who had not been discredited by his previous activity and who now declared himself an 'independent politician of centrist views'. Unlike the Soviet period, when resignation meant the end of a political career, both Kondratenko and D'yakonov remained active and influential members of the regional elite. Kondratenko, who became the leader of the local opposition, won a large majority at the polls in December 1993 and became a member of the Council of the Federation; and D'yakonov went on to head the territorial committee of 'Vybor Rossii'.[40]

There was a concentration, not only of political power, but also of economic resources. The period of economic reform from 1987 to 1992 was associated with a process of decentralisation and collapse of the formerly powerful 'vertical' links in the state system of economic management. Formerly, for instance, the banking system had been represented by Gosbank, Promstroibank, Zhilsotsbank and their local affiliates, and the whole system had been closely regulated by the Ministry of Finance. In the *perestroika* period this monolithic system collapsed and a whole series of commercial banks developed in its place, often by simply renaming themselves. A similar process took place in other sectors of the economy.

In 1992 a process of recentralisation began to assert itself, but based on horizontal rather than vertical links. Commercial banks were no longer united by their capital, but by a range of interrelated activities of other kinds. A variety of new forms of enterprise developed on this basis, including holding companies, groups of companies, and industrial-financial concerns. All of them, typically, were based upon a 'mother' firm, whose activities ranged from the sale of computers to building and construction. This mother firm, having accumulated sufficient resources, would then establish 'daughter' firms including its own bank and commodity exchange, its own insurance society, its own chamber of commerce and so forth. A logical development was the establishment of its own joint enterprises (to improve its contacts with the West and to allow its capital to be exported). Similarly, a philanthropic fund might be established, or an investment or pension fund; and the firm would also acquire its own newspapers, its own lobbyists, sometimes its own political parties, and eventually its own security services. Financial groups of this kind had every means thereafter of exercising influence on public policy and on mass opinion.

The new Russian elite, as it had developed by the mid-1990s, may be conceptualised as a three-layered pie. At the top level were politicians and their allies, who competed among themselves for power. The middle layer consisted of enterpreneurs, who financed the politicians' electoral campaigns, lobbying, newspapers and television. At the bottom level were the security services which not only maintained order but also acted as a means of influence and contract enforcement. Private security forces of this kind had been established very widely by the largest corporations or by their agencies, and had also been set up on an 'independent' basis. The periodic reforms of the KGB had a number of effects, one of which was to oblige many of its staff to leave and find alternative employment; and it was former KGB employees who formed the core of the security services of major banks and companies. The significance of a Moscow bank came to be reflected, not in its financial position, but in whether its security service was headed by a general or merely a colonel from the KGB. The new security services also employed athletes with a specialisation in unarmed combat; one of the forms of philanthropy in which the major financial groups engaged was precisely the support of clubs for children and young people, where karate and other combat sports were taught.

The heads of private security services of this kind were, as a rule, important and well-known figures in their own right. The president of the Lev Yashin fund, Otari Kvantrishvili, was regularly received at the highest levels of the Kremlin;[41] and the heads of the national associations of kick-boxing, field athletics and *kung fu* were, as a rule, of considerable political influence. In 1993 the first political party was formed in order to represent their interests – 'Sportivnaya Rossiya', with branches in local areas as well as in Moscow. The USSR was a major sporting power, and post-communist Russia is still home to a large number of outstanding athletes. These new 'sports parties' enjoyed a considerable public following, especially among young people, whose ideal in life was often to be able to shoot and fight professionally. The redistribution of power on this basis appears to have been completed and with it the 'second Russian revolution' has come to an end. It was a revolution in which a younger generation of the *nomenklatura* ousted its older rivals. In effect it was a bourgeois revolution, in that it led to a change in the sociopolitical system in the direction of private property and political pluralism. And it involved a redistribution of political power, towards a group of younger, more pragmatic nomenklaturists, some of whom became politicians and some businessmen. In the economy there was a corresponding shift of power into property, based upon the privatisation of the key sectors of the infrastructure: finance, retail trade, international economic relations, and the most profitable sectors of industry (especially the energy and extracting complexes).

Towards State Capitalism

The concentration of capital that has taken place in post-communist Russia has led to the formation of a number of dominant holding or financial–industrial groups.[42] Some of these were formed 'from above', on the basis of a group of industrial enterprises with a common technology or regional location. Banks then attached themselves to these groups as sponsors; but they remained artificial creations, poorly adapted to a real-life market environment and with few long-term prospects. A second kind of more genuine financial holding was one that established its own banks. The expansion of the major banks had a financial as well as an industrial aspect. In the first instance, the major banks established their branches in the regions, then, after the collapse of the ruble in October 1994 and changes in the wider banking environment, they absorbed other small and medium-sized banks and entered into larger consortiums. In industry they restricted their actions to the purchase of shares in their own companies, and shares in enterprises with a promising future – specialised exporters, or firms whose output could replace particular kinds of imports.

A third type, banks that have established their own holding companies (or 'empires'), represents a real force on the contemporary Russian market. They began to be established in 1992, when the largest Moscow banks began buying up the shares of industrial companies. This was not particularly advantageous, as investments of this kind were bound to lose value at the rate of inflation that prevailed at the time, and most of the banks bought with a view to selling at some future point. But a number of banks began to emerge that were seriously concerned with investment for its own sake. The most important of these banking and industrial 'empires', according to press reports, were the following:

  (i) the Promstroibank holding (more than 20 separate sections);
  (ii) the Vneshtorgbank empire;
  (iii) the Menatep empire (more than 60 separate sections);
  (iv) the United Export–Import Bank empire (more than 30 separate
     sections);
  (v) the Russian Credit Bank empire (more than 30 separate sections);
  (vi) the Inkombank empire (about 30 separate sections); and
(vii) the MOST empire (42 separate sections).

Of these seven groups, two – Vneshtorgbank and Promstroibank – represent the interests of the state itself; the remaining five are the most powerful of the interests that the state has authorised to act on their own behalf.

Of these five, the MOST group has a particular interest in trading and commercial capital in Moscow and is not directly involved in the struggle for influence that engages the others. The remaining four – the United Export–Import Bank, Menatep, Inkombank and Russian Credit – are the most powerful financial and industrial groups on the territory of the Russian Federation today. It is these banks, for instance, that occupy the upper ranks of the ratings of credit-worthiness[43] and that have been the main bidders at the auctions at which the most substantial blocs of state property have been sold. The clearest winners in this competition were the United Export–Import Bank and Menatep, and it was these banks, with the state itself, that formed the 'premier league' in financial markets. The others – Russian Credit, Inkombank and Alphabank – formed a powerful but subordinate division immediately below it.

The Russian economy by 1996 had accordingly the following features:

  – it consisted of a number of major industrial and financial groups;
  – it was co-ordinated by a class of 'agents', or major property owners,
    to whom the state had entrusted the development of the market;
  – it functioned in the absence of equal opportunities for all to 'make
    money'.

A system of this kind had at one time been called 'state capitalism' by Lenin. But the Leninist model had a crucial weakness: the proletarian state had been obliged to appoint bourgeois managers at the head of its commercial structures, who were then placed under strict control. This deprived them of any incentive and left the whole structure without the potential to survive and develop. State capitalism today has educated its own managers, a class of agents who can act on its behalf. Agents of this kind have a personal interest in profits; at the same time, 'agent business' is guaranteed from bankruptcy or other economic difficulties, and as a result it brings an element of stability into the anarchy of the post-communist market. And at the same time, the new economic elite that has emerged in this way provides a counterbalance to what would otherwise be the unrestricted plutocracy of the 'new Russians'.

In Russia today, the economic elite is a limited circle of people who control the major concentrations of finance capital and manufacturing industry with the sanction of the governing authorities. Self-made men have generally been forced out of this group into small and medium-scale business. The economic elite has come into existence at a time of the decline of industry but the rapid growth of financial institutions. The concentration of capital, in turn, is taking place under the guidance of the banks. As a result the oligarchy that is being formed is above all a financial one. And like every other social group, it is concerned to survive and develop. It is accordingly interested in maintaining its economic privileges as the basis on which it receives profits. This conditions its interest in political stability and its antipathy towards democracy: democracy, in its view, is a form of government whose main weakness is its inability to maintain public order.

The economic interests of the new Russian business elite determine its basic values. These are:

(i) Statehood (*gosudarstvennost'*), or the wish to establish a strong, centralised state. Finance capital, based in Moscow, is interested in a high degree of concentration, which is most readily achieved under a strong central government.
(ii) Patriotism, based on protectionism: in other words, a policy of privileges for domestic enterpreneurs. The economic elite can protect itself in this way from the competition of Western banks and companies.
(iii) Civic peace and consensus: as it is only with a calm and satisfied population that political – and, accordingly, economic – stability is possible. Big business, at the same time, is objectively interested in raising

living standards and reducing the level of crime. The better off the average citizen, the less likely he is to look for change; and this is another source of stability.

(iv) Monopolism was always a feature of the Russian economy, particularly in the Soviet period. In a big country, it seems, there is always a bias towards large-scale enterprise. In the Soviet period this took the form of 'projects of the century' such as the Baikal–Amur railway. In post-communist Russia there has been an equivalent increase in the concentration of financial and industrial groupings.

A stronger business class and financial institutions can mean more investment, better-paid jobs, the introduction of new technology, and an improvement in the level of service. But it can also mean short-term enrichment and the formation of close and sometimes corrupt relations between business and the state itself, particularly when there are few effective mechanisms to express the views of citizens and to hold government to account. The old system in which the *nomenklatura* originated was based upon a single party that could not legitimately be challenged; but it was a party that by the same token had no need to justify its actions and seek a continuing mandate from citizens, and one that found it could not count on their support when its performance began to disappoint them. The members of Russia's post-communist elite face a comparable challenge in attempting to combine their own enrichment with the consent of the mass electorate on whom their position ultimately depends.

Notes

This study draws in part upon the Soviet Elites Project based at the University of Glasgow, which is supported by the UK Economic and Social Research Council and directed by Evan Mawdsley and Stephen White. In a related paper, 'From Soviet *nomenklatura* to Russian elite', *Europe–Asia Studies,* 1996, no.5, we deal more directly with the composition of the contemporary political elite and its origins in the Soviet *nomenklatura*.

1. See Vilfredo Pareto, *Treatise on General Sociology* (New York: Harcourt, Brace and Jovanovich, 1935).
2. *Argumenty i fakty,*1994, no.35 (popularity of USSR); and ibid., 1994, no.23 (communists still in power). In an April 1995 survey 67 per cent of Russians gave a positive evaluation to the old Soviet system of government, compared with 26 per cent who evaluated the present regime in the same way: see Richard Rose, *New Russia Barometer IV: Survey Results* (Glasgow, Centre for the Study of Public Policy, 1995), pp. 42–3.
3. See Zdenka Mansfeldova, 'The Emerging New Czech Political Elites', paper prepared

for the ECPR Joint sessions at Madrid, April 1994.

4. See for instance Adam Pogorecki, 'The Communist and post-communist *Nomenklatura*', *Polish Sociological Review* **106**, no.2 (1994), pp.111–23. See also Jacek Wasilewski (ed.), *Konsolidacja elit politycznych 1991–1993* (Warsaw: Instytut Studiów Politicznych, 1994); Jacek Wasilewski, 'The Crystallization of the Post-communist and Post-Solidarity Political Elite', in Edmund Wnuk-Lipiński (ed.), *After Communism* (Warsaw: Institute of Political Studies, 1995), pp.117–33; Edmund Wnuk-Lipiński and Jacek Wasilewski, 'How Much Communism Is Left With Us?', *Politicus*, August 1995, pp.39–44; and Ivan Szelenyi *et al.* (eds), *Elity w Polsce, w Rosji i na Węgrzech* (Warsaw: Instytut Studiów Politicznych, 1995).

5. David Lane and Cameron Ross, 'The Changing Composition and Structure of the Political Elites', in David Lane (ed.), *Russia in Transition* (London: Longman, 1995), p.68.

6. Up to 80 per cent of local functionaries were the same as they had been in the Soviet period, according to *Rossiiskaya gazeta*, 4 March 1992. Yeltsin himself claimed there was less continuity at national level: *Izvestiya*, 27 March 1992. A comparison between the 'old' and 'new' elites is presented in B.V. Golovachev *et al.*, 'Formirovanie pravyashchei elity v Rossii', *Ekonomicheskie i sotsial'nye peremeny: monitoring obshchestvennogo mneniya*, 1995, no.6, pp.18–24, and 1996, no.1, pp.32–8. This finds that 'three-quarters of the former *nomenklatura* either remained in high state and management positions, or occupied positions close to them' (ibid., p. 37). The same investigation is drawn upon in N.S. Yershova, 'Transformatsiya pravyashchei elity Rossii v usloviyakh sotsial'nogo pereloma', in T.I. Zaslavskaya and L.A. Arutyunyan (eds), *Kuda idet Rossiya?* (Moscow: Interpraks, 1994), pp.151–5; it reports that 'over 60 per cent' of the former *nomenklatura* still occupied elite positions (p.154).

7. See Thomas A. Baylis, 'Plus ça change? Transformation and Continuity Amongst East European Elites', *Communist and Post-Communist Studies* **27**, no.3 (September 1994), pp.315–28.

8. *Nezavisimaya gazeta*, 3 December 1992.

9. For a more general treatment that emphasises elite cohesion see John Higley and Jan Pakulski, 'Revolution and Elite Transformation in Eastern Europe', *Australian Journal of Political Science* **27**, no.1 (March 1992), pp.104–19; and John Higley and Jan Pakulski, 'Elite Transformation in Central and Eastern Europe', *Australian Journal of Political Science* **30**, no.3 (November 1995), pp.415–35. See also Hellmut Wollmann, 'Change and Continuity of Political and Administrative Elites from Communist to Post-communist Russia', *Governance* **6**, no.3 (July 1993), pp.325–40.

10. An alternative reputational approach is available in David Lane, 'Gorbachev's Political Elite in the Terminal Stage of the USSR: A Reputational Analysis', *Journal of Communist Studies and Transition Politics* **10**, no.1 (March 1994), pp.104–16, and David Lane, 'Political Elites Under Gorbachev and Yeltsin in the Early Period of Transition: A Reputational and Analytic Study', in Timothy Colton and Robert C. Tucker (eds), *Patterns in Post-Soviet Political Leadership* (Boulder, CO: Westview, 1995).

11. These investigations are as follows: (i) 'Kto pravit Rossiei? (Issledovanie elity Rossiiskoi provintsii)', 1994; (ii) 'Lidery Rossiiskogo biznesa', 1992–94; (iii) 'Rossiiskaya politicheskaya elita', 1993; (iv) 'Sobstvennost' v Rossii', 1993; (v) 'Material'nyi uroven' zhizni v Moskve i Rossii', 1993; (vi) 'Politicheskie partii i tsentry vliyaniya Rossii', 1992–93; (vii) 'Politicheskaya elita Brezhnevskoi formatsii', 1991–93; (viii) 'Vliyatel'nye lyudi pri Gorbacheve i Yel'tsine', 1992; (ix) 'Obshchestvennoe mnenie

o bogatykh i bogatstve', 1992; (x) 'Biznes i reformy', 1992; (xi) 'Byvshie sotrudniki KGB v novoi roli predprinimatelei', 1992; (xii) 'Biznes i politika', 1992; (xiii) 'Stsenarii politicheskikh izmenenii v Rossii', 1992; (xiv) 'Rossiiskie menedzhery', 1991; (xv) 'Komanda Yel'tsina', 1991; (xvi) 'Sovetskie millionery', 1991; (xvii) 'Novaya sovetskaya elita', 1990; and (xviii) 'Administrativnaya sistema i ee sub"ekty', 1989–92. Sponsorship for these studies was obtained from a variety of agencies including the Administration of the President of Russia, the French Defence Ministry, the UK Economic and Social Research Council, Columbia University, and the newspapers *Delovoi mir* and *Moskovskie novosti*.

12. Our principal biographical sources included the following: *Izvestiya TsK KPSS* 1990, nos. 8, pp.8–61, 10, pp.28–61, and 11, pp.32–62; *Deputaty Verkhovnogo Soveta SSSR: Odinnadtsatyi sozyv* (Moscow: Izvestiya, 1984); *Sostav tsentral'nykh organov KPSS izbrannykh XXVI s"ezdom partii. Spravochnik* (Moscow: Politizdat, 1982; a corresponding volume for the 27th Congress is available in the Centre for the Preservation of Contemporary Documentation, Moscow); A.S. Barsenkov *et al.*, *Politicheskaya Rossiya segodnya*, 2 vols (Moscow: Moskovskii rabochii, 1993); Vladimir Pribylovskii, *Kto est' kto v rossiiskoi politike*, 3 vols (Moscow: Panorama, 1993); *Kto est' kto v Rossii i v blizhnem zarubezh'e: Spravochnik* (Moscow: Novoe vremya, 1993); V.N. Berezovskii and V.V. Chervyakov (eds), *Sto partiinykh liderov: kratkii biograficheskii spravochnik* (Moscow: RAU Press, 1993); *Elita rossiiskogo biznesa* (Moscow: Darin, 1993; rev. edn, 1994); I. Bunin *et al.*, *Biznesmeny Rossii: 40 istorii uspekha* (Moscow: Oko, 1994); P. Gazukin and V. Pribylovskii (eds), *Pravitel'stvo Rossiiskoi Federatsii: biograficheskii spravochnik* (Moscow: Panorama, 1995); *Vlast'. Deputaty Gosudarstvennoi Dumy. Kratkii biograficheskii spravochnik*, 4 parts (Moscow: Institut sovremennoi politiki, 1994); Jeanne Vronskaya and Vladimir Chuguev, *Kto est' kto v Rossii i byvshem SSSR* (Moscow: Tetra, 1994); A.S. Barsenkov *et al.*, *Federal'noe sobranie Rossii. Sovet Federatsii. Gosudarstvennaya Duma* (Moscow: Fond Foros, 1995); and V.S. Bondarev (ed.), *Kto est' kto i pochemu. Politicheskaya elita Rossii v portretakh* (Moscow: Skriptorii, 1995).

13. See for instance Michael Voslensky, *Nomenklatura: Anatomy of the Soviet Ruling Class* (London: Bodley Head, 1984).

14. For a discussion of the changing composition of the Central Committee and of what Robert Daniels described as the 'job slot' system, see Evan Mawdsley, 'Portrait of a Changing Elite: CPSU Central Committee Full Members 1939–1990', in Stephen White (ed.), *New Directions in Soviet History* (Cambridge: Cambridge University Press, 1991), pp.191–206.

15. See T. H. Rigby, *Political Elites in the USSR* (Aldershot: Edward Elgar, 1990), Chapter 4; V.G. Sirotkin, 'Nomenklatura (zametki istorika)', *Vestnik Akademii Nauk SSSR*, 1990, no.6, pp.12–26; T.P. Kozhikhina and Yu.Yu. Figatner, 'Sovetskaya nomenklatura: stanovlenie, mekhanizmy deistviya', *Voprosy istorii*, 1993, no.7, pp.25–38; and O.T. Dzhavlanov and V.A. Mikheev, *Nomenklatura: evolyutsiya otbora* (Moscow: Luch, 1993).

16. A full listing of the positions that were included in the national party *nomenklatura* is now available in the party archives: see Tsentr po khraneniyu sovremennoi dokumentatsii, Moscow, *fond* 89, *perechen'* 20, document 77, 7 August 1991.

17. Voslensky, *Nomenklatura*, pp.213ff.

18. See for instance Mervyn Matthews, *Privilege in the Soviet Union* (London: Allen & Unwin, 1978); and Il'ya Zemtsov, *Chastnaya zhizn' sovetskoi elity* (London: Overseas Publications Interchange, 1986). The party's own investigation into privilege was

reported to the Central Committee in December 1990: *Materialy Plenuma Tsentral'nogo Komiteta KPSS 10–11 dekabrya 1990 goda* (Moscow: Politizdat, 1991), pp.86–95.

19. *Moskovskie novosti*, 24 April 1988.
20. Trotsky's views on this subject were most fully set out in his *The Revolution Betrayed* (New York: Doubleday, Doran and Co., 1937).
21. Ligachev was reported to have used this term by the director of the Centre for the Scientific and Technical Creativity of Youth attached to the Bauman district committee of the CPSU, Anatolii Churgel'. For his assistance with this part of our discussion, we are indebted to A. Pavlyukov; we have also drawn upon interviews for the Soviet Elites Project with former Komsomol first secretaries Viktor Mishin and Viktor Mironenko.
22. Bunin *et al.*, *Biznesmeny Rossii*, pp.35–6, 141, 199–200 (Zatulin was also chairman of 'Rossiiskii broker') and 170. A recent investigation found that 7 per cent of young entrepreneurs had emerged from the Komsomol apparatus: *Moskovskaya pravda*, 5 November 1995.
23. For the Central Committee's resolution see V.N. Sungorkin and I.A. Savvateeva, (compilers), *Firma pri gorkome* (Moscow: Molodaya gvardiya, 1990), p.222. For their purposes, see *XX s"ezd Vsesoyuznogo Leninskogo Kommunisticheskogo Soyuza Molodezhi. 15–18 aprelya 1987 goda: stenograficheskii otchet*, 2 vols (Moscow: Molodaya gvardiya, 1987), vol.1, p.65.
24. *Dokumenty TsK VLKSM 1987* (Moscow: Molodaya gvardiya, 1988), pp.64–7; for the establishment of the All-Union Co-ordinating Council see *Sobranie postanovlenii pravitel'stva SSSR (otdel pervyi),* 1987, no.20, art.76.
25. *Dokumenty i materialy II plenuma TsK VLKSM* (Moscow: Molodaya gvardiya, 1987), pp.38–41.
26. *Dokumenty TsK VLKSM, 1988* (Moscow: Molodaya gvardiya, 1989), p.187.
27. *Sobranie postanovlenii pravitel'stva SSSR (otdel pervyi)*, 1988, no.29, art.81.
28. For the text of the law as adopted see *Vedomosti Verkhovnogo Soveta SSSR,* 1988, no.22, art.355 (at p.383).
29. *Dokumenty TsK VLKSM 1989* (Moscow: Molodaya gvardiya, 1990), p.205.
30. *Dokumenty i materialy XXI s"ezda Vsesoyuznogo Leninskogo Kommunisticheskogo Soyuza Molodezhi 11–18 aprelya 1990g.* (Moscow: Molodaya gvardiya, 1990), p.28.
31. Ibid, pp.40–1.
32. Churgel' interview.
33. This account is based upon the testimony of Vladimir Shcherbakov, whose father took particular responsibility for 'grain business' with the USA within the USSR Ministry of Foreign Trade.
34. Here and elsewhere we have drawn upon the studies conducted for 'Lidery Rossiiskogo biznesa'.
35. Zatulin discussed his own career in *Biznesmeny Rossii*, pp.199–206; he was 'very grateful' for the experience he had acquired working in the Komsomol headquarters (p.200).
36. On Bukato, see *Kommercheskie banki Rossii. Spravochnik,* 2 vols. (Moscow and New York: Intelbridge, 1995), vol.1, p.411; on Dubenetskii, *Kto est' kto v Rossii i v blizhnem zarubezh'e*, p.222. This section also draws upon the 'Lidery Rossiiskogo biznesa' investigation.
37. Bunin *et al.*, *Biznesmeny Rossii*, pp.69–70; *Kommercheskie banki*, vol.1, pp.388–91.
38. For a discussion of these changes see Juliet Ellen Johnson, 'The Russian Banking

System: Institutional Responses to the Market Transition', *Europe–Asia Studies* **46**, no.6 (1994), pp.971–96, and *Delovye lyudi,* no.55 (April 1995), pp.6–94.

39. For an overview of the contemporary Russian elite see Vladimir Berezovskii's articles in *Svobodnaya mysl'*, 1993, no.1, pp.56–65, and no.2, pp.93–105; 1994, no.19, pp.67–86. Eberhard Schneider, 'The Downfall of the *Nomenklatura* and the New Russian Elite', paper presented to the 16th Congress of the International Political Science Association, Berlin, August 1994, concentrates upon the parliamentary elite.

40. This account is based upon 'Kto pravit Rossiei', part 1: Krasnodar *krai.*

41. Kvantrishvili was assassinated on 5 April 1994: see *Izvestiya,* 7 April 1994.

42. For most of what follows we have drawn upon Olga Kryshtanovskaya, 'Finansovaya oligarkhiya', *Izvestiya,* 10 January 1996.

43. See for instance *Izvestiya,* 8 February 1995.

6 Elites, Institutions and Democratisation in Russia and Eastern Europe

Judith Kullberg, John Higley and Jan Pakulski

The collapse of communist regimes in Russia and Eastern Europe between 1989 and 1991 inaugurated a period of momentous political change, the ultimate outcomes of which are still unknown. With few exceptions, post-communist political leaders have committed themselves to transforming their countries' political and economic institutions in accord with the Western liberal model. The politics of the region have thus been dominated since the late 1980s by efforts to replace the institutions of state socialism with those of the market economy and representative democracy.

Despite the formal commitment of elites to system transformation, significant problems have appeared *en route* to democracy, problems that were either absent or muted in successful Southern European and Latin American democratic transitions. In the past five years, most of the new democracies of the former Soviet Union and its East European satellites have experienced serious political conflicts and a general decline in popular support for democratic values and institutions. Routine manipulation of the press, censorship and state intimidation of opposition groups have returned in several countries. These and related developments have prompted observers to question the authenticity of some post-communist democracies,[1] or even to argue that the liberal experiment in the east is failing.[2]

While many scholars and analysts believe that something is going wrong, it is not clear what. Although most agree that the social and political malaise is a 'legacy' of Leninism, there is considerable disagreement about how this legacy is being transmitted. Some depict it as primarily structural, others as cultural, and still others as centred upon traditional state–society relations in Eastern Europe. Without a clear identification of the causes of the problems plaguing post-communist polities, it will be difficult to arrive at viable solutions.

This chapter proposes a theoretically parsimonious alternative to the imprecise concept of legacy. We take the position that the dynamics and trajectories of political change in post-communist countries can be explained almost entirely as a function of the structure and behaviour of elites. As in transitions from non-communist authoritarian regimes, elites have been the crucial variable in the demise of the old Leninist order and construction of new democracies. Paradoxically, although elites initiated the fundamental reforms that destroyed communism, post-communist elites are hindering democratic development, except in those few countries where fundamental alteration in the composition, interaction patterns and behavioural norms of post-communist elites have already occurred. The persistence of communist structural and behavioural patterns among elites, albeit in fragmented forms, has undercut the performance of new democratic institutions, particularly parliaments, and it has contributed to the emergence of semi-democratic, still noticeably authoritarian regimes. While all post-communist regimes suffer from these residues of Leninism, it is abundantly clear that the trajectories of political change across the region nevertheless vary considerably. We trace this variation to the divergent evolutionary paths of elites both before and after the collapse of communism. The number of cases and the extent of variation among them provide an opportunity to improve our understanding of the connections between elites and institutions, the evolution of political orders, and the directions of history.

The chapter begins with a brief overview of elite theory and a discussion of the connections between elites and institutions. It then presents a model of Leninist elite structure prior to the onset of fundamental reform under Gorbachev, contrasting the Leninist model with a model of elite structure in liberal democracies. From this contrast, the qualitative changes necessary for a change from the Leninist model to the liberal model are identified. We then compare our expectations with actual patterns of change in Russia and Eastern Europe. Since Leninism was endogenous to the Soviet and Russian political experience, we begin our analysis of actual cases with the Soviet Union and post-Soviet Russia. The Soviet and Russian path is then compared with the paths taken in Hungary, Poland, the Czech Republic, Bulgaria, Romania, Slovakia and

Ukraine. In conclusion, we shall return to questions about the relationship between elite structure, institutional choice and democratic development, discussing their implications for theories of democratisation and for research on democratic transitions.

Elites and Institutions

Elites are individuals and small groups holding top positions in a society's largest or otherwise most resource-rich organisations, and who are able to deploy the power of those organisations to affect political outcomes in a significant and systematic way. Elite structure refers to the social composition, patterns of interaction, norms and codes of behaviour of a given elite. The founders of elite theory held that elite structure powerfully shapes the character of states and regimes (that is, how government decision-making power is organised and exercised), and they urged that a science of politics be built upon the study of elites.[3]

Classical elite theory explored at great length the effect of socio-economic and historical context on the structure of elites. At the same time, it emphasised the relative autonomy of elites: that is, the independent effect, controlling for other variables, of elites on short- and long-term political outcomes.[4] From its start, elite theory has been centrally concerned with the relationship between social structure, conceived as the enduring patterns of interaction in society, and agency, conceived as the reasoned, purposive choices and actions of individuals.[5]

Although elite theory has been attentive to social structure, it has not devoted sufficient attention to institutions, which contemporary social theorists view as important parts of social structure. Following Hall, we define institutions as the 'formal rules, compliance procedures, and standard operating practices that configure the relationships between individuals in various units of the polity and the economy'.[6] Institutions are typically depicted in elite theory and research as creations of the elite – the instruments through which ruling elites exercise control and influence over society. This notion of institutions as tools of elites is challenged by organisational theory and the new institutionalism, which see the state, institutions and organisations as imposing powerful constraints on actors, and as moulding elite behaviour.[7] Some institutionalists assume not only the primacy of institutions over individual actors, but that institutions possess their own goals and internal rationality[8].

Elite theory and the new institutionalism thus hold opposing views of the causal connections between elites and institutions. But these views are not as incompatible as many theorists claim. Indeed, if they are merged, the theoretical one-sidedness of each can be redressed by the strengths of the other. This involves conceptualising the ways in which elites and institutions are linked. We propose a model of regime emergence and change which synthesises the two approaches. We shall then use this model to analyse and account for the varying trajectories of post-communist regimes.

In step with elite theory, our model assumes that elites are responsible for the creation of political institutions and thus the character of political regimes. Elites establish the rules which allow for (1) a political decision-making process that is binding for the entire society or collectivity; (2) the selection of individuals who make political decisions; and (3) the enforcement of political decisions. We further assume that the institutional preferences of elite persons and groups are influenced by their behavioural norms and patterns of interaction, the key components of elite structure. In the absence of other motivating factors such as dire crises and external threats, elites are likely to prefer and contrive institutions that conform to their existing norms of behaviour and patterns of interaction.

Although existing norms of behaviour and patterns of interaction thus constrain the range of institutions that are acceptable to elites, elite disagreements and conflicts over proposed institutions are nonetheless frequent. Few elites are homogeneous; almost always they contain identifiable groups that have differing interests and therefore differing institutional preferences. The configuration of institutions which emerges in any polity is therefore a result of the relative resources various elite groups are able to expend in negotiations and conflicts, as well as the political skills that such groups possess. The importance of elite political skills must not be overlooked, for as Riker[9] has shown, the adoption of rules by a collectivity is often a consequence of the way in which questions about rules are framed and presented politically. In short, elites with greater strategic resources, political skills or both exert disproportionate influence on institutional selection.

Once institutions are established, they may change in several ways: (1) as a consequence of alteration in elite structure, that is, change in the composition, behavioural norms or interaction patterns (or a combination of these) of elites; (2) as a consequence of conscious elite action, often in response to external or internal threats to society or elite interests or both; (3) through elite articulation of the interests and preferences of wider social groups and interests. These 'paths' of institutional change are not mutually exclusive. As we shall see in examining transitions from communism, they often occur simultaneously.

In step with institutionalism, our model assumes that institutions also have effects of their own. Their primary effect is to reinforce, elaborate and stabilise elite norms and interaction patterns. Through this effect on elite behaviour, institutions influence long-term political change, usually by inhibiting or limiting its scope. But even in conditions of systemic collapse, in which an old institutional configuration is formally eliminated or fundamentally re-configured, if the elites who operated the old order persist (as they usually do), there will be an important degree of continuity in the norms and interaction patterns that were previously reinforced, elaborated and stabilised by the old institutions. These continuing norms and interaction patterns among elites are likely to influence the choice of new institutions and the general character of an emerging regime. In this indirect way, and despite systemic collapse, old institutions influence the selection of new ones.

The Transition from Communism to Democracy

This elite or institutional model of political change can be used to elucidate the transition from communism to representative democracy. The success of these transitions depends not only on replacing one set of formal institutions with another, but also on transforming elite structure. The sequencing of these two aspects of change is thus a crucial factor in democratic transformation and consolidation: the most successful transition has occurred in those countries where initial elite negotiations formed the institutional frameworks for (partial) elite replacement and change, and where the emergent elite structure facilitates further institutional consolidation. To provide a clear understanding of how elite structures in communist societies must be transformed if they are to support robust democracies, we contrast Leninist and liberal-democratic models of elite structures, both presented here in the form of an ideal type.

The Leninist Model

The dominant feature of the Leninist elite was its uniformity. Drawn exclusively from members of the Communist Party, the Leninist elite did not permit competition by other parties or organisations; indeed, the only other parties that were allowed to exist were completely under the Communist Party's control. Furthermore, under the party's anti-factionalism rule, no formal or even hidden internal differentiation of the party, other than that corresponding to administrative–territorial divisions, was tolerated. Thus, in principle, the Leninist elite was undivided, committed to one ideology, and had but a single interest – to maintain its power. Consistent with its mono-organisational base, the elite was arranged in a seamless, strict hierarchy that ran from the top leadership of the party directly down to regional and local actors. Decision-making was highly centralised, and the autonomy of elite groups below the highest party–state leadership was always narrow. The control of higher officials and the top leader was secured in no small part by the system of elite recruitment and appointments – the *nomenklatura* system – which made officials at each organisational level directly dependent on those above them. Hierarchy and centralisation were also sustained by the party's behavioural norms, which were inculcated through intense ideological indoctrination and socialisation. Commitment to the party's values and behavioural code was exhibited through unquestioning obedience and self-sacrifice. The authority of higher-level officials over those below was reinforced by coercion and fear.

Although to outside observers the unity of Leninist elites seemed virtually complete, it was a façade that masked deep mistrust of actors towards one another. Elite interactions and norms amounted to a zero–sum game in which competition was non-iterative: winners won everything, losers lost all and were destroyed or permanently expelled from politics. Consequently, elite insecurity was deep and pervasive. The reliance by the top party elite on hierarchy and fear to exercise its control over lower-level elites and cadres produced unintended behavioural consequences. The latter created informal circles of camaraderie and patronage to shield themselves from terror and the oversight of high party authorities, to carve out personal domains relatively immune from central control, and to compete with other mid-level actors for higher positions. In many respects, these relations, particularly those involving patrons and clients, were pre-modern in character.[10] A 'formalised informalism' – in which social proximity to key leaders was the route to power – prevailed. The prevalence of these behaviours and norms fostered corruption, and it undermined the performance of Soviet-style socialism.

This elite structure was connected with a specific social-structural and institutional configuration, the latter often analysed in terms of partocracy.[11] The extreme hierarchy and centralisation of the Leninist elite – the party dictatorship – was achieved and maintained through the suppression of all social and economic interests and organisations outside the party–state, a suppression made possible by state ownership of the entire economy. Centralisation of decision-making authority was also sustained through subordination of the state and its elaborate bureaucratic structure to the party. Law and legal institutions were also subordinate in that no laws applied to the party and its officials, particularly its highest officials; instead, their words and decisions were the laws that applied to all others.

The Liberal Model

In contrast to the single organisational origins and ties of a Leninist elite, the elite in a representative democracy is typically drawn from a wide range of organisations and sectors, each of which possesses significant political and economic resources.[12] Rather than the mono-archic structure typical of Leninist elites and partocratic apparatus, the Liberal elites have a polyarchic structure,[13] and they operate within the predominantly bureaucratic and technocratic administrations. Interactions among elites are largely horizontal, and they appear as a constantly shifting kaleidoscope of alliances and coalitions. Consistent with Pareto's[14] thesis that all democracies are governed through 'pluto-democratic' elite cartels, some researchers have found that elites in democracies such as the United States, Australia and the former West Germany are distinguished by exceedingly complex formal and informal networks of friendship, acquaintanceship and influence. These networks overlap and interlock so greatly as to constitute 'webworks' that encompass and tie together all important elite groups.[15]

Instead of a struggle for power conducted among highly insecure but powerful actors, democratic politics is a game conducted by relatively autonomous elite groups played according to widely-accepted rules and norms. Also unlike the game played in a Leninist elite, the democratic game within a Liberal elite has no ultimate goals, no telos; it is inherently open-ended. Played in committees and other collegial *loci*, it revolves around 'deferred reciprocal compensations' according to the code of *do ut des* – 'give in order to get'.[16] The absence of coercion and strict hierarchy, as well as the relatively even distribution of power and economic resources among the actors in a Liberal elite, dispose them to see politics as a non-zero–sum game. Each elite group is able to defend and advance its interests sufficiently to motivate its continued participation. Thus, the Liberal elite game is also an iterative one in which today's losers are able to become tomorrow's winners.[17] Winning and losing are relative and partial, rather than absolute, outcomes.

The horizontal interactions and dispersions of a Liberal elite reflect and to a great extent emerge from diverse market-generated 'interest blocs' consisting of relatively identifiable and stable segments of the society and economy. No single interest predominates. The holding of most political positions is determined by open, limited electoral contests. Individuals hold positions for limited periods, at the end of which they must again compete in electoral contests whose outcomes are always basically uncertain. In principle, all competing interests and persons have equal standing, enforced by an independent legal system. No political official is above the law and all must adhere to it. Thus, the exercise of power is tightly constrained and basic civil liberties are strongly protected. The economic and political institutions of liberal democracies are essential for the maintenance of mutual elite security, which, some elite theorists contend, is the *sine qua non* of consolidated democracies.[18]

Leninist Elites and Their Evolution

Taking the Leninist elite structure as the starting-point and the Liberal elite structure as the end-point, we can specify the changes in a Leninist elite which would be necessary for a successful transition from a communist to a democratic regime. First, there should be significant change in elite composition, as well as substantial pluralisation and diversification of the elite. Second, hierarchical patterns of elite interaction should be replaced by a dense web of horizontal, negotiated relations. Third, the neo-traditional clientelistic 'family circles' and 'mutual protection societies' that existed behind the monolithic façade of Leninism should fade and be replaced with shorter-term, consensual alliances among actors who pursue specific, limited ends. Finally and most crucially, elite norms and behaviours should be transformed so that politics are no longer played as a non-iterative, zero–sum game, but rather as a repeated game with benefits for most, if not all, competitors.

The power and independent effects of organisations and institutions must be given a place in the change from a Leninist to a Liberal elite. Two of the classical elite theorists, Mosca and Michels,[19] appreciated the need for this. Mosca discussed the growing autonomy of the modern state, particularly the liberal state. He argued that elites – his 'ruling class' – had responded to the increased complexity of industrialised society by expanding the size of the state and developing bureaucracies to manage or monitor key economic sectors and to address diverse and conflicting social interests. Consequently, the state had become more than the tool of a single ruling elite. In his famous analysis of the evolution and internal operation of socialist and working-class parties, Michels likewise strongly emphasised the influence of organisations and institutions, reversing the causal arrows leading from elites to organisation by arguing that organisation inevitably creates elites or 'oligarchies' and that it also strongly shapes their interests.

As noted above, elite theory has been assailed by institutionalists for over-estimating the autonomy of actors and for not attending to the structural factors which constrain day-to-day elite behaviour and choices. But this institutionalist critique of elite theory has in return been attacked for its strong determinist thrust and for allowing too little place for what individual actors do.[20] In institutionalist analyses, behaviour is mapped by organisational rules and norms. If actors appear at all, it is as mere executors of institutionalised preferences, lacking interests and preferences of their own. The tension between the emphases of elite theory and institutionalism finds clear expression in T.H. Rigby's observation about the Soviet elite during the 1980s: 'On the one hand they enjoy an extraordinary independence of the rest of society, but on the other they are subject to an extraordinary dependence on the state, in the person of its top officials, its inquisitorial and coercive agencies and their own hierarchical supervisors.'[21]

Let us encapsulate the interdependencies of elites and institutions in the original communist seizures of power and in the subsequent evolution of communist elites and regimes.

The revolutionary victory of the small, doctrinaire and secretive Bolshevik elite in Russia's war-induced apocalypse between 1917 and 1922, the similar victory of Tito's partisans in war-torn Yugoslavia between 1943 and 1945, and the Soviet imposition of communist elites on the satellite countries of East–Central Europe immediately following the Second World War destroyed pre-existing elites, institutions and regimes.[22] To defend and perpetuate their sudden ascendancy, the communist elites chose to centralise power sharply. In making this choice, they transferred the interaction patterns and norms of behaviour from the organisation most relevant to them, namely the party, to the state. Thus, the original structure of communist elites shaped the character of the emergent Soviet and Soviet-imposed institutional orders and regimes.

Thereafter, control over all institutional sectors was exerted through a strict elite hierarchy that ran through the party and was based eventually in the *nomenklatura* system which licensed individuals for elite positions according to their political–ideological credentials. The principles of 'democratic centralism' and the party's 'leading and guiding role' reinforced and justified the single, monolithic hierarchy. Party structure, elite structure, and state structure largely coincided. Although institutional sectors and the elite groups heading them became more articulated with industrialisation and greater social complexity,[23] the autonomy of elite groups other than the highest party–state leadership was always narrow. Elite interactions and norms during the earliest (Leninist–Stalinist) phase of communist rule amounted to a zero–sum game in which competition was non-iterative, and elite insecurity was great. Down to Stalin's death in 1953, the Soviet elite was a study in fear and fratricide. Soviet imposition of this configuration on Central–East European countries after the Second World War likewise produced deeply insecure, socially isolated elites recruited largely from outside the traditional political class or intelligentsia. The imposed elites engaged in vicious factional struggles (often fanned by their Soviet sponsors) and in massive purges in which losers (as well as their families and clients) were socially degraded, imprisoned and often executed.

Although there was some national variation (for example, Yugoslavia), this elite configuration was quite uniform throughout the region until the late1950s. However, upon Stalin's death in 1953, a consensus quickly developed within the CPSU Politburo that the secret police should be placed under firm party control and the practice of dictatorship replaced by the principle of collective leadership.[24] Motivated by a desire for security and stability, this elite agreement amounted to an important alteration in the Soviet institutional arrangement and led to significant, albeit incremental, elite changes across East–Central Europe. In this regard, Khrushchev's 'secret speech' at the party's XX Congress in 1956 was a critical watershed, for it directly challenged the Leninist–Stalinist patterns of elite interaction and norms of behaviour. The unchecked power of coercive apparatuses such as the Soviet Ministry of State Security was curbed, and elites in the satellite countries were allowed more autonomy. The outcomes of factional struggles were made less absolute, with losers no longer facing mortal sanctions. Marxist-Leninist ruling formulas were loosened, and the *nomenklatura* system was institutionalised so that the importance of propinquity and leadership discretion in elite recruitment was reduced. Elite persons drawn from the intelligentsia once again became numerous. Most important, elites in the USSR and its key satellites achieved a rough *modus vivendi* ('*nomenklatura* communism') characterised by more civilised norms of interaction and what amounted to life tenure in elite positions.[25] This was not, to be sure, the configuration of mutual elite accommodation and security that is characteristic of democratic regimes; rather, the public fidelity of elites to Marxist-Leninist tenets, to the party's dominant role and to Soviet leadership was blended with pragmatic notions about building socialism by winning consent instead of liquidating opponents.

In Hungary and Poland, the incipient post-Stalin alterations among elites triggered explosions in the form of bloody revolts during 1956. The elite members who led the Hungarian uprising were subsequently executed by the Soviet-backed Kádár government. This was, however, the last instance of systematic violence among communist elites, and it signified the end of the pristine Leninist elite configuration, institutional pattern and monolithic regime in most of the region. The Polish uprising led to elite-level changes that were embodied in the rise of Gomułka's 'nationalist' faction to power. In Czechoslovakia, post-Stalin elite alterations occurred in two steps: a somewhat less repressive regime after Novotný's elevation to the presidency in 1957, followed by the Dubček faction's failed effort in 1968 to establish peaceful political competition and greater elite autonomy without eliminating the party's 'leading and guiding role'. In Romania, the death of Gheorghiu-Dej in 1964 enabled the independence-minded Ceauşescu to take over. In Bulgaria, on the other hand, Zhivkov's continuing hold on power made significant change at the elite level hard to discern.

Another phase of elite change became apparent in a few countries under 'late communism' – the dozen or so years before the 1989–91 democratic transitions. This involved a partial decentralisation of power and relative pluralisation and autonomisation of elites, their widespread professionalisation through intakes of highly educated and specialised personnel, and a further loosening of interaction patterns and norms. In Hungary, 'political stability' and 'reform' became the watchwords of elites who knew and feared the alternative of bloody revolt and repression. They signified a don't-rock-the-boat understanding to avoid discussing where economic reforms undertaken by the Kádár government might be leading.[26] This process of opening up and professionalising Hungarian elites was diagnosed even by dissidents who spoke of a merger between the communist partocracy and the intelligentsia.[27]

In Poland, the Gierek government's largely unsuccessful economic reforms during the mid-1970s spawned bloody clashes in 1976 and a stand-off between increasingly demoralised communist elites on the one side and Church, intellectual and (after 1980) Solidarity leaders on the other. This was interrupted by the martial law crackdown on Solidarity, undertaken in response to Soviet demands, during 1981-83. But when martial law was lifted, there was no reversion to the earlier post-Stalin elite configuration. Party and military elites continued a reformist line, punctuated by finely targeted repressions. Opposition elite groups were excluded from power but tolerated, and both elite camps respected minimal 'rules of engagement' that, following a wave of strikes and economic difficulties in the summer of 1988, led directly to the Round Table negotiations which began in earnest in February 1989. These further modifications of elites were not mirrored in the countries neighbouring Hungary and Poland, however. Ceauşescu's dictatorship continued in Romania, Czechoslovak elites remained 'frozen' in the wake of the Prague Spring débâcle, and in Bulgaria Zhivkov was content to mimic Gorbachev's reforms while overseeing a draconian repression of the country's restive Turkish minority.

In the Soviet Union, the late communist period involved a further evolution of the elite structure. The relative autonomy and dispersion of top-ranking leaders increased, and the practice of building support and even coalitions on particular issues, rather than simply imposing them from above on unwilling subordinates, became more common.[28] This shift towards more stable patterns of elite interaction was accompanied by the very important, but less frequently noticed, emphasis upon 'raising the qualifications' of cadres so that the party could better direct the economy in the face of new industrial and information technologies. Resulting in a rapid and impressive increase in educational attainments among party officials, the decision to staff organisations with the best-educated cadres possible had the largely unintended effect of producing better informed, less ideological and more pragmatic elites.

Not only did the increased educational attainments of elites lessen their attachment to Soviet orthodoxy, but they made the boundary between the party and the intelligentsia more porous. Relative to the fear with which the intelligentsia lived more or less continuously from 1918 until 1953, the increased reliance on and expanded trust in the intelligentsia by the post-Stalin regime was remarkable. Particularly during the Brezhnev era of infatuation with the potential of the 'scientific–technological revolution', the Soviet leadership strove to increase the rationality of decision-making by incorporating the expertise of knowledge-based sub-elites.[29] As a consequence of this increased interaction and exchange of ideas between the political elite and the sub-elite intelligentsia – particularly scientists, policy analysts, sociologists and writers – the general orientations and world-views of the intelligentsia infiltrated the party, especially its second echelon of younger and better-educated leaders.[30] Like the intelligentsia, this generation of aspiring elite members came to perceive by the mid-to-late 1970s that a social and moral malaise plagued the Soviet Union. Many shared the opinion that the nagging problems, particularly in the economy and in production, with which they struggled daily, were embedded in the organisation and institutions of the Soviet system.[31]

Upon Gorbachev's accession to the post of General Secretary in 1985, these critical evaluations of 'the system' were translated into the broad-based reform programme of *perestroika* and *glasnost*. In its rearrangement of basic authority relations and its attempt to transform the partocracy into a law-governed state, the reform programme fatally undermined the legitimacy and internal coherence of the party, although not intentionally, as Russian extremists have subsequently alleged. Assaulted from without by radical reformers and broad-based popular movements in virtually every republic, the party fragmented long before the attempted August 1991 coup.[32] The way in which the CPSU weakened, through intense intra-elite conflict and fragmentation, has significantly affected elite interaction patterns and behavioural norms, as well as the character of emerging institutions and regimes, in all the former Soviet republics.

It is evident from this encapsulation that no single pattern of elite change was followed by all East European countries during the post-Stalin and 'late' phases of communist rule. Particular legacies of pre-communist and early communist politics, plus the contingencies that bulk large in elite choice and action, produced different elite and regime trajectories across the region. These greatly affected the possibilities for further elite changes in the post-communist period. We have elsewhere tried to assess these recent developments.[33] We now want to take stock of current elite configurations in the region, paying particular attention to continuities and changes in elite structures. Let us consider the continuities first.

Elite Continuities since 1989–91

To the surprise of most observers, the collapse of communist rule, which occurred most clearly between 1989–91, involved no comprehensive change in the composition of elites. Although continuity in elite composition has been marked in all countries of the region, there have nevertheless been important variations. Comparing the holders of roughly 900 top political, economic and cultural elite positions in Russia, Hungary and Poland, respectively, in 1988 with the holders of the same or equivalent 900 positions in each country in 1993, Wasilewski[34] found that about one-third of the position-holders in 1988 remained in elite positions in 1993 (35.3 per cent in Russia, 32.6 per cent in Hungary, 40.8

per cent in Poland). In specific sectors this continuity was more pronounced: 48.2 per cent of Russia's political elite, 40.8 per cent of its cultural elite, 50.7 per cent of Poland's economic elite. Wasilewski found, moreover, that substantial proportions of the 'new' holders of elite positions in 1993 had in fact been sub-elites or 'deputies' located just below the top *nomenklatura* ranks in 1988: 49.0 per cent in Russia, 37.4 per cent in Hungary, 26.0 per cent in Poland. When he tallied the total numbers of 1988 *nomenklatura* members who retained or moved up to elite positions between 1988 and 1993 with those who lost such positions during the five-year period, Wasilewski found the ratios to be 86:10 in Russia, 23:10 in Poland, and 22:10 in Hungary.[35]

These figures probably overstate the continuity of Russian elites because they do not cover the considerable turnover that Gorbachev effected among political and state-administrative elites during 1985-88.[36] By the same token, the figures probably understate the continuity of Hungarian and Polish elites because they do not take into account the electoral victories of ex-Communists in Poland in September 1993 and in Hungary in May 1994. Those victories returned a number of old faces to top elite positions. In any event, the observed patterns of elite continuity in all three countries clearly support Wasilewski's conclusion that 'East European revolutions were not particularly painful to former rulers. The process of social demotion affected [a] minority of them. In Poland and Hungary this minority is fairly numerous, whereas in Russia – nearly negligible.'[37]

Limited data and anecdotal evidence about other countries point to similar continuities in elite composition. Examining political elites in the former Czechoslovakia, Thomas Baylis observed that no 'oppositional "counter-elite" really took the place of the former Communist rulers, although opposition figures played a more prominent role in the first phase of the transition.'[38] In the Czech Republic since its 1992 divorce from Slovakia, Baylis found that political elite turnover had been unusually low, while turnover in Slovakia had been higher but only because of the brief replacement of Vladimír Mečiar's HZDS government by a diverse coalition between March and November 1994. In Bulgaria, Romania, Ukraine and Serbia – not to mention Belarus, Georgia, Kazakhstan, Turkmenistan and Uzbekistan – the persistence and dominance of 'ex-communist' elites has been pronounced, and it supports Baylis's conclusion that, except in the former East Germany, 'the transition from communist to democratic rule is being managed by leaders who were, with few exceptions, not notably uncomfortable under the old order, and who frequently were part of its support system.'[39]

This continuity in elite composition has occurred principally because the collapse of communist regimes did not entail destruction of the state apparatus. Instead, the most exposed and discredited party-political leaders were removed and the key governmental institutions were freed from communist party oversight and patronage, while incremental changes in constitutional rules increased the importance of those institutions. Sets of elite positions in the private sector emerged through a blending of previously covert economic 'lobbies' and newly-formed private enterprises. Turnover of persons in top political positions was offset by continuity among elite and sub-elite administrative personnel.[40] In countries where the turnover of political leaders was most pronounced it involved incorporating leaders of formerly excluded groups: Solidarity in Poland; Democratic Forum and Christian Democrats in Hungary; Charter 77, Civic Forum and Public Against Violence in Czechoslovakia. This inflow of new and often movement-propelled leaders, however, was soon arrested. In Czechoslovakia, the 'moral' elites were largely replaced by more professional elites in the 1992 elections.[41] In Poland and Hungary, popular backlashes against painful economic measures propelled rapid comebacks by ex-communist political leaders.

Except for some top political figures, then, elites generally survived the transitions to post-communist regimes. The nature of elite changes that occurred before the communist collapse help to explain this survival. The younger and better-educated persons who attained elite positions during 'late communism' possessed transferable skills and cultural capital that were not much threatened by the transitions. Especially if they were politically untainted, these 'expert' elites suspected that they would do well under a new regime and economic system, and they therefore either supported or did not actively oppose regime change. Also during late communism, many elites developed wide patron–client networks which cushioned them during the 1989–91 upsets. Credits accumulated in those networks were cashed in to avoid displacement or demotion. Still other elites apparently anticipated communism's collapse, if not its precise form or timing, and they made the necessary political and commercial preparations. Thus, financial malpractices and other nest-feathering measures were rife among elites before the democratic transitions.[42]

During the transitions, established elites scrambled to protect their power bases or convert them into new bases.[43] Their manoeuvres were varied. Some donned the nationalist mantle, repudiated ties to the USSR, and proclaimed themselves fighters for national independence.[44] Others negotiated places for themselves in post-communist regimes at the Round Tables.[45] Many metamorphosed into capitalists by appropriating large parts of state industrial enterprises ('*nomenklatura* privatisation'), while others colluded in 'mafia' activities to profit from weakened state oversight and regulation. Most communist party elites repackaged themselves as socialists and social democrats, and in this guise they prevailed or at least held their own in parliamentary and electoral arenas against inexperienced, poorly organised and badly divided opposition elites and movements. If one asks, in short, why the elites associated with communist rule did not go down fighting against the inroads of democratic and capitalist forces, a large part of the answer is that they had little need to do so: their survival as elites was more likely if they did not fight.

The continuity in elite composition accounts in considerable measure for the generally peaceful nature of the transitions from communist to post-communist regimes. By and large, established elite groups and persons did not confront mortal challenges; some fancy footwork was usually enough to retain power and privilege, and guns were not much needed. The most discredited and politically visible members of the communist establishments were removed quickly and publicly – moves that forestalled more profound changes. The first round of freely contested elections and plebiscites produced some further turnover in political positions, but they proved less catastrophic for established elites than expected. Given the decentralisation of power and widened range of influential positions, the main consequence of the elections was elite supplementation rather than replacement. And as noted, subsequent elections have tended to produce comebacks by elites who were marginalised in the first electoral round. Generally, there have been few losers and many winners within elite ranks.

This situation at the elite level in turn helps to explain why mass publics in the region stayed mostly on the sidelines. For one thing, the nationalist postures which many communist elites quickly adopted resonated with those publics. For another, because elites were concerned to shore up existing power bases or jump to different ones, dismantling collective farms, state bureaucracies and state industrial enterprises, large militaries and other bases of power (except for the party itself in a few countries), or abolishing the pervasive governmental subsidies that sustained them, were not much on the elite agenda. Dependent on these entities and subsidies for jobs and modest perquisites, most categories of the public were therefore not immediately – or at least not devastatingly – affected by the elite game of musical chairs, and they made no serious effort to interrupt it. In Poland where such dismantling did occur in earnest during the 'shock therapy' engineered by Leszek Balcerowicz, elite positions were secured by the very strong and broad electoral mandate given to the first Solidarity-based government.[46]

Another consequence of continuity in elite composition, however, has been conflicts and doubts about the authenticity of post-communist regimes. They suffer from a chronic moral deficit. Among liberal-democratic forces there has been a widespread tendency to view the new regimes as façades behind which the *nomenklatura* continues to rule. Liberal democrats have accordingly been riven over the extent to which they should oppose or collaborate with government and state officials who survived the transitions. Partly as a consequence of this infighting, liberal-democratic forces have been organisationally divided and in poor condition to compete in elections. This has been especially evident in Russia where suspicions of the Yeltsin government and wider regime among liberal democrats increased to the point where they nearly withdrew their support during 1994 and early 1995, leaving the government and regime in parlous condition. Similar situations have been evident in all other ex-Soviet republics (the Baltic states excepted), and in Bulgaria, Romania, Slovakia and Serbia.

An important question about the continuity in elite composition is the extent to which it has also meant continuities in elite interaction patterns and behavioural norms. Although there have been important changes in both respects since 1989–91, some were already under way, as we have discussed, before those pivotal years. This was especially true of Hungarian and Polish elites among whom covert nationalism during the 1980s promoted widening access to party–state decision-making processes, coupled with more tolerance of elite dissent.[47] Before the 1989 Round Table negotiations between Polish elites, for example, rules of the political game proscribing inter-elite violence and behaviour inconsistent with 'patriotic responsibility' were evident. By the start of the regime transitions, most important elite groups in the region agreed that open electoral contests were desirable, or at least inevitable, and although they were primarily symbolic gestures in countries like Bulgaria and Romania, the Round Tables manifested the readiness of elites to negotiate the conditions and timing of such contests. Even where they first involved restrictions, as in Poland's June 1989 elections, or where they closely resembled plebiscites or were greatly delayed, as in Romania in 1990 or in Belarus and Ukraine in 1994, open, freely contested elections were a rule of the game that the vast majority of contenders for power accepted.

The East European transitions were in many ways unique and paradoxical: the revolutionary (in their scope and speed) changes were instituted by a rather 'non-revolutionary' mixture of old and new elites.

Romania apart, the old regime had few defenders; it was deserted by most of its leaders and beneficiaries, thus opening the way for swift 'velvet' and 'walk-over' transitions. With the disappearance of Soviet sponsorship, the broad array of nationalist and reformist groups – often spawned within the partocratic apparatus – faced no opposition. These were revolutions not only without the Leninist-type revolutionaries, but also without revolutionary ideological blueprints. The ascendant elites were determined to emulate the Western liberal models of market economy and liberal-democratic polity, and they did it within the largely preserved state structures. Continuity in elite composition has thus gone hand-in-hand with the continuity of the state but also with significant changes in elite interactions and norms. Let us examine these changes more closely, paying particular attention to how they have affected the relative security or insecurity of elites.

Elite Changes since 1989–91

In broad outline, the Soviet and Russian transition and subsequent political developments have proceeded essentially through coups and elite power struggles, rather than elite negotiations and accommodations. Elite fragmentation, high levels of tension and fundamental disagreements over the character of reform began in the late Soviet period and have continued into the post-communist present.[48] The interactions and behaviour of Russian elites show amazing continuities with the old Soviet (and even tsarist) elite structures and norms. These continuities have strongly shaped the character of the new Russian regime.

In the past five years, the struggle for control of Russia has involved three dramatic showdowns between elite actors, two of which were violent and featured the military in decisive roles. The failed August 1991 coup can be accurately depicted as the last gasp of the old-guard Soviet elite against the rising power of republican elites, most especially the Russian President and parliament and their respective apparatus. The second coup, this one peaceful and successful, was led by Boris Yeltsin, in collusion with Ukraine's party boss Leonid Kravchuk and with Stanislav Shushkevich, chairman of the Belarus parliament. While committed publicly to hammering out a new Union treaty with Gorbachev that would specify the relative powers of the Soviet central state and the republics, the three met secretly near Minsk in December 1991 and signed an agreement that dissolved the Soviet Union and established in its place the Commonwealth of Independent States. This agreement constituted a seizure of the power, resources and facilities of the Soviet state by Boris Yeltsin and the Russian government. In one fell swoop, Yeltsin eliminated his nemesis Gorbachev from power and took over the Kremlin. After dismembering the elite of the CPSU and the Soviet state, however, Yeltsin and the newly-ascendant Russian elite groups began the internecine quarrel which turned allies into bitter, irreconcilable enemies and which culminated in the third coup – Yeltsin's dissolution of parliament and his ordering of army units to shell and capture the Russian White House in October 1993.

In retrospect, it is clear that the 'democratic' institutions, laws and norms promoted by Gorbachev, which were meant, first and foremost, to alter Soviet elite structure and behaviour, were poorly grasped and only sporadically practised, and have therefore had relatively little effect on Russian elites since 1991. The main reason why their effects have been so limited is that, rather than being forged on the basis of a new elite consensus concerning the desirability of open and restrained political contests, they were imposed from above by the highest party elite as a means of enhancing its control over the system. Gorbachev's new institutions, laws and norms signified not the party's abandonment of its claim to power, but an attempted *obnovlenie* or renewal of political life through the grafting of democratic procedures, such as popular nomination and election, on to Soviet institutions such as the soviets and the CPSU.

Factionalism and polarisation have thus plagued elite relations since the last years of the Soviet empire and they have threatened the political stability not only of Russia, but also of most other states on the former territory of the USSR. To achieve democracy, elites, most of which comprise former communists, must not only devise and implement new institutions, but they must alter fundamental patterns of behaviour, authority and power relations of which they themselves are the bearers. Self-evidently, this has proved difficult. Instead of fashioning interaction patterns and norms of behaviour that facilitate the operation of democratic institutions, Russian and other former Soviet elites appear to be following the old scripts. For most of the actors, politics is still perceived as a zero–sum game.

Thus, top figures in Russia continue to accumulate power through personal networks, and they maintain it by extending the administrative hierarchies over which they preside. For example, the Russian Federation has been claimed to have 1.7 times more bureaucrats than the Soviet Union had in 1989, despite there being 130 million fewer people to administer.[49] Sub-elites and aspiring elites continue to be rewarded for support and loyalty, and they are swiftly punished for disobedience or even for inclinations towards independent action. Formal rules of the game are routinely ignored and often wilfully violated. Thus, the degree to which Russian elites (as well as elites in Ukraine, Belarus and most other post-Soviet republics) accept the rules and norms of open, freely contested electoral competition is unclear. Registration procedures in the 1993 Russian elections were designed to favour the government and its allies. The election commissions have been little modified since the collapse of the Soviet system and are widely perceived as instruments of those in power. As was evident during the run-up to the 1995 State Duma elections and even more during the turbulent months before the mid-1996 presidential election, the necessity for elections continues to be questioned, and there is nothing like a 'level playing field' for contesting elections.

Boris Yeltsin's mercurial leadership has been a crucial factor in moulding the Russian regime. Immediately after the August 1991 coup, the President, not bound in a firm coalition with any group and standing above party politics, sought to implement reforms through decrees without consulting his former allies or creating a firm base of elite support. Demanding the support of all democratic forces, he made few efforts to develop reciprocal ties or even open communications with those forces. There can be little doubt that Yeltsin's strategy and imperious behaviour, which he later blamed on his adviser Gennadii Burbulis, contributed to the presidential–parliamentary stand off that was broken only by force two years later.

The type of institutional arrangement which has thus emerged in the Russian fray can accurately be characterised as presidentialist, or even 'super-presidentialist'.[50] Linz and Stepan[51] have consistently warned against adopting such an arrangement during or after democratic transitions, arguing persuasively that because of the constraints it places upon legislative authority, presidentialism fails to provide adequate incentives for elites to create autonomous bases of power, particularly political party organisations. Without the emergence of autonomous elite power bases, the pluralistic and accommodative elite configuration associated historically with the development of representative democracy is unlikely. It is clear that Russian presidentialism has impeded the formation of viable non-state elite organs, and it has contributed to the continuation of court and Kremlin politics, the pattern of elite interaction and behaviour that was deeply embedded in tsarist Russian and then Soviet politics. Cliques, shadowy power brokers and lobbies connected with new entrepreneurial 'structures' and the 'mafia' compete with fragile governmental institutions for control of Russia. Russian political analysts and commentators have frequently noted the essential elite and institutional continuities between the old and new regimes. The President, dependent upon the military and the other 'power ministries', especially the Ministry of the Interior and the Federal Counter-Intelligence Service (formerly the KGB) has augmented the role of the Security Council in which the ministries exercise direct control over the policy formulation, as the Chechnya débâcle has shown. Observers compare the Council to the Politburo and the continually expanding presidential administration to the apparatus of the Central Committee Secretariat. Following the 1996 electoral alliance, the Council fell into the hands of General Aleksandr Lebed, whose meteoric rise in popularity threatened Yeltsin's supporters. Dismissal of Lebed in October 1996, amidst rumours of *coup d'état* and declining health of the President, opened a new phase of the intra-elite conflicts.

In marked contrast to the Soviet and Russia case, Czech, Hungarian and Polish elites appear to have completed the changes in interaction patterns and norms necessary to move from a Leninist to a liberal elite structure. Elites in all three countries are operating largely free of fear and deep ideological division. This condition has emerged most rapidly and perhaps surprisingly among Czech elites, whereas among Hungarian and Polish elites it is much more the outgrowth of trends that were evident during the 1980s. At the start of 1989, the Czechoslovak elite configuration remained frozen in the hardline Husák regime. By the end of the year, however, it was substantially (we are tempted to say 'gracefully') transformed. Secret contacts between top regime officials and their most visible opponents (especially Václav Havel) led almost immediately to negotiations and a brief sharing of power with leaders of the hastily-organised Civic Forum and Public Against Violence movements. However, a massive eleventh-hour switch of loyalties among political and state-administrative elites away from the regime and towards a putative democratic order made the power-sharing arrangement largely superfluous. In spite of public pressure, no vindictive measures were taken against the communist leaders who quickly departed from the scene, while some of those who led the Prague Spring experiment twenty years earlier were welcomed back into elite positions and circles. Much of the credit for this dramatic, potentially violent, but eminently peaceful and smooth transition properly went to Václav Havel, whose influence and example did much to secure elite management of it. Subsequently, the split with Slovakia removed ethno-nationalist tensions and bolstered the accommodation and broad policy consensus among Czech elites, with the strong leadership provided by Václav Klaus being particularly important.

Because Hungarian elites achieved substantial pluralism and practised restrained interactions during 'late communism', elaborate negotiations were unnecessary for their further change.[52] The Round Table negotiations between June and September 1989 thus served to reinforce and put the seal on an already changed elite structure, and they led directly to open and peaceful electoral contests between political forces in which 'hold-over' elite members were conspicuous. When economic discontentment enabled the ex-communist Socialists to win a sweeping electoral victory in May 1994, power sharing with the Free Democrats was nevertheless quickly agreed in order to continue economic reforms with minimal political friction.

Finally, although there were mutually understood 'rules of engagement' between them, Polish elites were divided into opposing camps on the eve of the 1989 democratic transition. This was due most immediately to the 1981 suppression and subsequent remobilisation of Solidarity. After a Round Table agreement to share power during the transition, the election in 1990 of Solidarity's leader, Lech Wałęsa, as President further propitiated part of the Solidarity elite camp, although a more radical wing adopted a posture of extra–parliamentary opposition, together with leaders of the Peasant Party. Accommodation of these somewhat disaffected elites proved difficult, and there were divisive institutional questions about parliamentary-executive relations. But while Polish elites have appeared to be more fragmented than their Czech and Hungarian counterparts, no important elite group, including the comparatively radical Labour Union party on the left and the Christian National Union on the right, has questioned the democratic order.

A different pattern of post-communist elite change unfolded in Bulgaria and Slovakia, however. In both countries, strong coalitions of ex-communist and nationalist elites resisted accommodation and power-sharing with opposition elites. The emergence of horizontal, negotiated interaction patterns that would provide all significant elites with access to power has been halting. Elite divisions and conflicts have remained large, and they have been papered over by emergency measures and *ad hoc* positional reshuffles. Winning and losing have thus been more marked in Sofia and Bratislava than in Prague, Budapest and Warsaw, with a more definite exclusion of losers from political influence. In Bulgaria, the Communists, re-packaged as Socialists, dominated the regime transition and the politics which followed. Only the threat of a national strike pushed Socialist leaders into desultory Round Table talks during 1989, and opposition elites were excluded from the interim governments which ensued during 1990. Elites under the Union of Democratic Forces banner have since remained fragmented and politically ineffectual, and the Socialists again showed that they had the upper hand by winning a majority of parliamentary seats in the September 1994 elections. Ideological and ethnic divisions remain substantial among Bulgarian elites, and during 1996 Bulgarian financial institutions effectively collapsed. Serious elite divisions are also apparent in Slovakia where a coalition of ex-communist and nationalist elite groups led by Vladímir Mečiar has regularly and plausibly been accused of purging its opponents from elite positions, operating a 'new *nomenklatura*' and stifling political discourse through heavy-handed control of state-owned media.

To the extent that one can speak of elite change in Romania and Ukraine – yet another pattern – it began with pre-emptive coups within the Communist Party aimed at fully controlling the regime transitions. In both countries, the removal of discredited top party leaders occurred under the pressure of momentary popular mobilisations, but it was followed by internal party reshuffles rather than negotiated power-sharing arrangements with opposing elites. The *loci* of power have continued to be concentrated in the states of both countries and in the repackaged ex-communist parties that dominate them, turnover of elite personnel has been limited to a few executive positions, elite interactions appear not to cross the boundary between pro- and anti-government elites, and norms of elite behaviour have a distrustful and defensive colour. The two-session Romanian 'Round Table' (a label never used by participants) at the end of January 1990 was a smokescreen for reorganising relations among the anti-Ceauşescu party and military leaders of the Christmas 1989 coup. Fragmented opposition elites were effectively excluded from power through a plebiscitary presidential election in May 1990. Nor did the long-lasting government coalition (from April 1991 to September 1996) led by the ex-communist Social Democrats (PSDR) reach out to opposition elites. The PSDR elite has instead consolidated its grip on power, placing its supporters throughout the state administration and in key institutions such as state television and the judiciary while consistently favouring business interests closest to it.

Likewise in Ukraine, a pre-emptive 'independence coup' against Soviet dominance carried out by local party boss Leonid Kravchuk was not followed by significant negotiations with elites leading the Rukh movement and other nationalist forces, which themselves became increasingly disorganised and fragmented. Continued political domination by the ex-communist ruling coalition (the 'party of power') was achieved through a closed elite network running through the executive branch, the state security organisations and other state institutions.[53] Contested elections were delayed until 1994, and the presidential election of July that year revealed a deep ethnic–territorial split among voters. Instead of convening a Round Table, the new government led by Leonid Kuchma entered into a temporary post-election pact with two major parliamentary opponents, one of whom (Vitaliy Masol) was subsequently defeated politically and accused of corruption. In short, elites in Romania and Ukraine have not managed political change in a collaborative fashion but have instead sought to exclude and confront each other in conflicts that perpetuate their divisions and insecurities. In both countries, falls from elite positions remain steep and costly, and the distinction between winners and losers is sharp.

Conclusions

Russia and Eastern Europe have constituted *par excellence* an arena for applying and refining elite theory during the twentieth century. Their experience of power seizures by revolutionary elites that then created previously unknown elite structures, institutions and regimes during the century's first half, the subsequent, tortured evolution of these elites, institutions and regimes between the mid-1950s and the late 1980s, the regime transitions between 1989 and 1991, and the varying trajectories that elites, institutions and regimes have since followed are without parallel in the twentieth-century world.

This chapter has drawn on elite theory's institutional stream to explore a model that might capture the contours and dynamics of this extraordinary political record. The model holds that elite structures and political institutions are interdependent. The basic character of political regimes is the outgrowth of this interdependence. In everyday political life, institutions constrain the choices which elites make, channel their interactions, and provide the practical contexts in which informal, mostly tacit norms of elite behaviour are to be observed. Thus they are not only the constrainers, but also, and perhaps more significantly, the resources and 'capacitors' for elites. But institutions are themselves the product of choices that elites made and of interaction structures and norms that they constructed or significantly modified at key historical junctures. Thus the interdependence of elites and institutions is not as circular as it sounds. On occasions such as the Russian Revolution and war-induced Soviet control of Eastern Europe, Stalin's death, the decision to professionalise elites and sub-elites, and Gorbachev's attempt to rejuvenate elite effectiveness, the withdrawal of Soviet power from Eastern Europe towards the end of the 1980s, and finally the collapse of the USSR in 1991, elite choices changed elite structures, altered institutions and eventually brought about an array of regime transitions. This transition appears to be most successful where the initial elite pacts and agreements among the old and new elites formed informal institutional frameworks for further political transformations, involving elite changes and the consolidation of new institutional orders.

Theorists and students of elites need to pay more attention to the complex relationship between elites, institutions and regimes. While extremely welcome, the new generation of elite studies in Russia and Eastern Europe risks concentrating too much on the displacement and circulation of elites. Working mainly from the stratification rather than the institutional stream of elite theory, these studies are tending to replace the earlier juxtaposition of 'red' versus 'expert' elites with a juxtaposition of 'old' ex-communist versus 'new' non-communist elites. The 'new' elites are assumed to be carriers of democratising and marketising changes, while the 'old' ex-*nomenklatura* are assumed to be opponents of change. This chapter has tried to show that such dichotomies oversimplify complex mixtures of continuity and change in elite structures and give too little attention to the constraints of institutions on elite change, despite such radical political disjunctures as those that have recently occurred in Russia and Eastern Europe.

Notes

1. Boris Kagarlitsky, *How Russian Democracy Got Derailed* (New York: Monthly Review Press, 1995); Carol Skalnik Leff, 'Dysfunctional Democratization? Institutional Conflict in Post-Communist Slovakia', *Problems of Post-Communism* 43, no.5 (1996), pp.36–50.
2. Charles Gati, 'If Not Democracy, What? Leaders, Laggards, and Losers in the Postcommunist World', in Michael Mandelbaum (ed.), *PostCommunism: Four Perspectives* (New York: Council on Foreign Relations, 1996), pp.163–98.
3. Vilfredo Pareto, *The Mind and Society* (New York: Dover, 1916; 1935); Gaetano Mosca, *The Ruling Class* (New York: McGraw-Hill, 1896; 1923; 1939); G. Lowell Field and John Higley, *Elitism* (London: Routledge & Kegan Paul, 1980); and Eva Etzioni-Halevy, *The Elite Connection: Problems and Potential of Western Democracy* (Oxford: Basil Blackwell, 1993).
4. Moshe Cnudkowski, *Political Elites and Social Change: Studies of Elite Roles and Attitudes* (DeKalb: Northern Illinois University Press, 1983).
5. Jürgen Habermas, *On the Logic of the Social Sciences* (Cambridge, MA: MIT Press,

1988); Anthony Giddens, *The Constitution of Society: Outline of the Theory of Structuration* (Cambridge: Polity, 1984); Anthony Giddens, *Social Theory and Modern Sociology* (Stanford, CA: Stanford University Press, 1987); Nicos P. Mouzelis, *Back to Sociological Theory: The Construction of Social Orders* (New York: St Martin's Press, 1991)

6. John Hall, *Governing the Economy* (New York: Oxford University Press, 1986), p.19.

7. Douglass North, *Institutions, Institutional Change and Economic Performance* (Cambridge: Cambridge University Press, 1990).

8. James G. March and Johan P. Olsen, *Rediscovering Institutions: The Organizational Basis of Politics* (Englewood Cliffs, NJ: Prentice Hall, 1989), pp.17–18.

9. William Riker, *The Art of Political Manipulation* (New Haven, CT: Yale University Press, 1986).

10. Kenneth Jowitt, *The Leninist Response to National Dependency* (Berkeley, CA: Institute of International Studies, 1978); Kenneth Jowitt, 'Soviet NeoTraditionalism: Political Corruption of a Leninist Regime', *Soviet Studies* 35, no.3 (July 1983), pp.275–97.

11. Abdurakhman Avtorkhanov, *The Communist Party Apparatus* (Chicago: Henry Regnery, 1966); Jan Pakulski, 'Bureaucracy and the Soviet System', *Studies in Comparative Communism* 19, no.1 (1986), pp.3–21.

12. Etzioni-Halevy, *The Elite Connection*.

13. Robert A. Dahl, *Polyarchy: Participation and Opposition* (New Haven, CT: Yale University Press, 1971).

14. Vilfredo Pareto, *The Transformation of Democracy*, edited by Charles J. Powers (New Brunswick, NJ: Transaction, 1984; first published in 1921).

15. S.E. Finer, 'Pareto and Pluro-Democracy: The Retreat to the Galapagos', *American Political Science Review* 62, no.2 (June 1969), pp.440–50; John Higley, Ursula Hoffman-Lange, Charles Kadushin and Gwen Moore, 'Elite Integration in Stable Democracies: A Reconsideration', *European Sociological Review* 7 no.1 (1991), pp.35–53.

16. Giovanni Sartori, *The Theory of Democracy Revisited: The Contemporary Debate* (Chatham, NJ: Chatham House, 1987), p.224.

17. Adam Przeworski, 'The Games of Transition', in Scott Mainwaring, Guillermo O'Donnell and J. Samuel Valenzuela (eds), *Issues in Democratic Consolidation: The New South American Democracies in Comparative Perspective* (South Bend, IN: University of Notre Dame Press, 1992).

18. John Higley and Richard Gunther (eds), *Elites and Democratic Consolidation in Latin America and Southern Europe* (Cambridge: Cambridge University Press, 1992).

19. Mosca, *op.cit.*; Robert Michels, *Political Parties: A Sociological Study of the Oligarchical Tendencies of Modern Democracy* (New York: The Free Press, 1962).

20. Kathleen Thalen and Sven Steinmo, 'Historical Institutionalism in Comparative Politics', in Sven Steinmo, Kathleen Thelen and Frank Longstreth (eds), *Structuring Politics: Historical Institutionalism in Comparative Analysis* (Cambridge: Cambridge University Press, 1992), pp.1–32.

21. T.H. Rigby, *Political Elites in the USSR: Central Leaders and Local Cadres From Lenin to Gorbachev* (Aldershot: Edward Elgar, 1990), p.2.

22. Richard Pipes, *The Russian Revolution 1899–1919* (New York: Knopf, 1990); Richard Pipes, *Russia Under the Bolshevik Regime* (New York: Knopf, 1994); Gale Stokes, *The Walls Came Tumbling Down: The Collapse of Communism in Eastern Europe* (New York: Oxford University Press, 1993); Martin Malia, *The Soviet Tragedy* (New York: The Free Press, 1994).

23. Judith Kullberg, *The Origins of the Gorbachev Revolution* (unpublished PhD disserta-

tion, University of Michigan, 1992).

24. Carl A. Linden, *Khrushchev and the Soviet Leadership* (Baltimore, MD: Johns Hopkins University Press, 1966); George Breslauer, *Khrushchev and Brezhnev as Leaders: Building Authority in Soviet Politics* (London: Allen & Unwin, 1982).

25. Malia, *The Soviet Tragedy*, pp.348ff.

26. Rudolf Andorka, 'Regime Transitions in Hungary in the 20th Century: The Role of National Counter-Elites', in Hans-Ulrich Derlien and George J. Szablowski (eds), *Regime Transitions, Elites and Bureaucracies in Eastern Europe*, special issue of *Governance* **6**, no.3 (1993); Malia, *The Soviet Tragedy*.

27. George Konrad and Ivan Szelenyi, *Intellectuals on the Road to Class Power* (New York: Harcourt Brace Jovanovich, 1979).

28. Jerry F. Hough, *The Soviet Union and Social Science Theory* (Cambridge, MA: Harvard University Press, 1977); Valerie Bunce, *Do New Leaders Make a Difference? Executive Succession and Public Policy under Capitalism and Socialism* (Princeton, NJ: Princeton University Press, 1981).

29. Thane Gustafson, *Reform in Soviet Politics: Lessons of Recent Policies on Land and Water* (Cambridge: Cambridge University Press, 1989); Georgii Arbatov, *Zatyanuvsheesya vyzdorovlenie (1953–1985gg.)* (Moscow: Mezhdunarodnye otnosheniya, 1991).

30. Roy Medvedev, *On Socialist Democracy* (New York: Norton, 1975).

31. Eduard Shevardnadze, *The Future Belongs to Freedom* (New York: The Free Press, 1992).

32. Graeme Gill, *The Collapse of a Single-Party System: The Disintegration of the Communist Party of the Soviet Union* (Cambridge: Cambridge University Press, 1994); David Lane, 'The Gorbachev Revolution: The Role of the Political Elite in Regime Disintegration', *Political Studies* **44**, no.1 (April 1996), pp.4–23.

33. John Higley and Jan Pakulski, 'Elite Transformation in Central-Eastern Europe', *Australian Journal of Political Science* **30**, no.3 (1995), pp.415–35; Judith Kullberg, 'The Ideological Roots of Elite Political Conflict in Post-Soviet Russia', *Europe–Asia Studies* **46**, no.6 (September 1994), pp.929–53.

34. Jacek Wasilewski, 'Elite Circulation and Consolidation of Democracy', paper presented the conference on Elites in the Systemic Transformation, Warsaw, August 1995.

35. Ibid., p.10.

36. Kullberg, *The Origins of the Gorbachev Revolution*.

37. Wasilewski, 'Elite Circulation', p.10.

38. Thomas A. Baylis, 'Political Leadership After Communism: Eastern Germany and Czechoslovakia', paper presented to German Studies Association, Dallas, Texas, 1994, p.8.

39. Ibid.

40. Klaus von Beyme , 'Regime Transition and Recruitment of Elites in Eastern Europe', in Derlien and Szablowski, *Regime Transitions*, pp.409–25; Thomas A. Baylis, 'Plus ça Change? Transformation and Continuity Among East European Elites', *Communist and Post-Communist Studies* **27**, no.3 (1994), pp.315–28.

41. Lubomir Brokl and Zdenka Mansfeldova, 'Czech Political Elites and Elites of the Legislative Power', paper presented to the conference on Elites in the Systemic Transformation, Warsaw, August 1995.

42. Jadwiga Staniszkis, *The Dynamics of Breakthrough in Eastern Europe* (Berkeley: University of California Press, 1991); David Pryce-Jones, *The War That Never Was:*

The Fall of the Soviet Empire 1985–1991 (London: Weidenfeld & Nicolson, 1995).

43. Elemér Hankiss, *East European Alternatives* (Oxford: Clarendon Press, 1990); Andorka, 'Regime Transitions in Hungary'; Staniszkis, *The Dynamics of Breakthrough*.

44. For example, John B. Dunlop, *The Rise of Russia and the Fall of the Soviet Empire* (Princeton, NJ: Princeton University Press, 1993); Alexander J. Motyl, *Dilemmas of Independence: Ukraine After Totalitarianism* (New York: Council for Foreign Relations, 1993).

45. Helge Welsh, 'Political Transition Processes in Central and Eastern Europe', *Comparative Politics* **26**, no.4 (1994), pp.379–94.

46. Włodzimierz Wesołowski, 'Parlamentarzyści jako część elity politycznej' [Parliamentarians as part of the political elite], in Jacek Wasilewski and Włodzimierz Wesołowski (eds), *Początki Elity Parlamentarnej* [The Beginnings of Parliamentary Elites] (Warsaw, IFiS PAN and the Research Group on Eastern Europe, 1992), pp.9–72; Ireneusz Bialecki and Bogdan Mach, 'Orientacje społeczno-ekonomiczne posłów na tle poglądów społeczeństwa' [Socio-economic orientations of MPs compared with public views], in ibid., pp.119–56; Mirosława Grabowska and Tadeusz Szawieł, 'Anatomia Elit Politycznych: Partie Polityczne w Postkomunistycznej Polsce 1991–93' [Political elites: political parties in post-communist Poland, 1991–93] (Warsaw: Institute for Sociology, University of Warsaw. 1993).

47. Andorka 'Regime Transitions in Hungary'; Rudolf L. Tőkés, *Hungary's Negotiated Revolution* (Cambridge: Cambridge University Press, 1996); Janina Frentzel-Zagorska (ed.), *From a One-Party State to Democracy* (Amsterdam: Rodopi, 1993); George J. Szablowski, 'Governing and Competing Elites in Poland', in Derlien and Szablowski, *Regime Transitions*, pp.341–57; Jacek Wasilewski, 'Kontraktowy Sejm jako miejsce formowania się elity politycznej' [Contract Sejm as a place of political elite formation], in Wasilewski and Wesołowski, *Początki Elity Parlamentarnej*, pp.275–304.

48. Lane, 'The Gorbachev Revolution'.

49. *The Financial Times*, 27 June 1995.

50. Juan J. Linz and Alfred Stepan, *Problems of Democratic Transition and Consolidation* (Baltimore, MD: Johns Hopkins University Press, 1996).

51. Juan J. Linz and Alfred Stepan, *The Breakdown of Democratic Regimes* (Baltimore, MD: Johns Hopkins University Press, 1978); Linz and Stepan, *Problems of Democratic Transition*.

52. Tőkés, *Hungary's Negotiated Revolution*.

53. Marko Bocjun, 'The Ukrainian Parliamentary Elections in March–April 1994', *Europe–Asia Studies* **47**, no.2 (March 1995), pp.229–49.

7 Elites and the Russian Transition

Graeme Gill

The collapse of the Soviet Union and consequent emergence of an independent Russia was accompanied by high hopes that the new state would proceed rapidly and peacefully towards the construction of a democratic political structure and a market-based economic system. Such hopes were fuelled both by the stated aims of the Russian leadership and by the recent experience in Latin America and Southern Europe where the successful replacement of authoritarian regimes by those of a democratic stripe had occurred. Indeed, this experience was seen as being so significant that one observer referred to it as the 'third wave' of democratisation.[1] However, such hopes were not always accompanied by a sober recognition either of the immense problems Russia would face in traversing these twin paths, or the differences between the Russian situation and that of these other parts of the globe.[2] Clearly the physical size of Russia, its ethnic diversity, the particular effect on its development of seventy years of communist rule and the problems of transforming a centrally-directed economy into a market-based system all set it apart from those Latin American and Southern European states which had made the transition to democracy in the 1970s and 1980s. But despite these differences, there are some commonalities. One of the most important is the central role that will be played in shaping the contours of the transition[3] by the political elite; the course of development in Russia will be shaped, as it was in these other countries, in large (but not exclusive) part by the nature of elite politics.

Analysis of transitions in Latin America, in particular[4], suggests that crucial to a successful and peaceful process of democratisation is the question of elite unity and how it is achieved. If the elites at the head of the major sectors of national life (in particular the political and military elites, but also those in the economic sphere) remain agreed and broadly united around the aim of democratisation and the policies designed to achieve that aim and about how the course of politics is to be structured, the better able they will be to manage this process and the less likely the disruption of the process by elite conflict will be. However, if there is conflict within the elites – and as argued below this will be inevitable at some stage of the process – and this cannot be resolved quickly, the effect is likely to be serious for the process of transition. Violent elite conflict can result in both leadership and policy instability, with an inability to pursue the sort of stable and consistent line essential to the achievement of an ordered course of development. Furthermore, such conflict can lead to attempts by segments of the elites to mobilise sections of the populace into politics, thereby introducing an element of spontaneity and arbitrariness which can also upset the emergence of an ordered process of transition. Successful transition therefore involves the resolution of elite conflict before it derails the course of change.

Such a focus upon the importance of resolving elite conflict is consistent with the view which dominates much of the literature on the transition to democracy that the key to the successful move from an authoritarian regime to a democratic one is the structuring of elite relations. This assumes that what is important for democratic development is the construction of appropriate political institutions and the embedding of appropriate principles of political activity within the new system. The principal actors in producing such an outcome are the elites. These are the people who build the institutions and whose actions lay down the patterns of activity which become entrenched as the 'normal' way of doing things. This view contrasts sharply with that of many earlier scholars who argued that essential for the consolidation of democracy was the development of a democratic political culture.[5] Unless widespread commitment to democratic values existed in the population, in this view, a democratic structure could not be consolidated. The focus upon elites sees such popular democratic values as less important than the existence among elites of a basic consensus about the rules of the game. While accepting that there may be limits to the substantive consensus that can be achieved on policy issues, such theorists emphasise the way in which a procedural consensus can be built up through a process of 'crafting'[6] of political institutions and practices. Elite interaction and the way it develops, including the way conflict is resolved, fundamentally shapes the contours and nature of the emergent political system.

The process of transition is bound to create tensions within elites. Unless there is an immediate wholesale turnover of elites, with those in power under the old regime totally replaced by people who had neither commitment to nor standing in that regime, ambiguity towards the transition is bound to remain present within elite circles. Not everyone will agree on the need for transformation, and even among those who do, there will be differences of opinion about how far and how fast it should be pursued. These latter differences are likely to be present even if there is an immediate and complete turnover of the elite. Substantive policy differences will be inevitable. It is also likely that differences over process, over how politics is to be conducted and power distributed, will emerge regardless of the nature of the elites. Such tensions may be complicated by institutional differences and the way that elites seek to act to protect the interests of those institutions which they head. The clearest instances of this concern the bureaucratic struggles between individual government ministries, but perhaps the most important in terms of the successful course of transition in Latin America and Southern Europe was the military. Thus it is clear that tension and conflict are likely characteristics of elite politics during a transition: tension between old and new, between proponents of different policy positions and between different institutional constituencies will be stimulated by the uncertainties intrinsic to the whole process of transition. The issue is how the elites handle this tension.

A couple of strategies have been evident in the way elites in states undergoing the shift from authoritarian to democratic rule have sought to deal with such tension. One way of seeking to gain the peaceful removal of the old elite, or the section of it opposing change, has been through the granting of 'exit guarantees'.[7] These are promises made to members of old elites to grant them certain favours or advantages providing they leave their positions and refrain from becoming involved in public life. Such promises often take the form of provision of immunity from prosecution for deeds committed under the old regime. Historically these have been very successful in obtaining the removal of old elites and clearing the way for a new elite to consolidate itself in power; for example, such guarantees were instrumental in the withdrawal of the army and the consolidation of the Menem regime in Argentina.[8] Another strategy designed to bring about elite unity has been called 'elite settlement'.[9] This occurs where conflicting elites seek to reorganise their relations by negotiating compromises over their basic disagreements. Such compromises may be embodied in pacts which will, even if loosely, codify agreed principles of action and political conduct.[10] They are more likely to be directed at bringing about a procedural consensus, defining the rules of the political game, than a substantive consensus related to policy concerns, although the latter is not impossible. Such settlements can be crucial to the stable functioning of elite politics, particularly when the former system has been totally discredited and new elites vigorously reject its legacy. It has also been an important means of coming to grips with the problems of institutionally-based conflict noted above. Of course, the other way of eliminating tension and conflict has been for one segment of the elite to use force to eliminate its challengers. Such a mechanism by its very use ensures that the process of transition will not be peaceful, but if it is quick and its effects are limited, it could in the long term be beneficial to the cause of elite unity and system stability. But it is usually a high-risk strategy.

Another aspect of the nature of the elite which is important in shaping the course of the transition is the degree of the political elite's autonomy. This is crucial for the way in which elite relations are structured, and therefore for the means whereby elite conflict is resolved. Three aspects of this are relevant: autonomy from other elites, autonomy from the mass, and autonomy from international forces. The first aspect refers to the relationship between the political elite and such groups as military and economic elites. The greater the degree to which the political elite is autonomous from, and even in control of, these other elites, the greater its capacity to implement its will in society. By contrast, if the political elite is dependent upon or controlled by either of these elites, its freedom of action is thereby moderated and, if these other elites can act on their own account, the greater the likelihood of the need for compromise if stability is to be achieved. Similarly, the greater the autonomy of leading elites from the mass of the population, the greater their capacity to implement the policies they prefer. If an elite must always be concerned about the likely impact of what it does on the mass of the population, the more likely it is to seek to moderate its policies in order to maintain mass support. This is, of course, a crucial factor in any process of democratisation which is combined with economic transformation, because the latter is bound to lead to some economic hardship, with potentially disastrous electoral consequences for political decision-makers.[11] Finally, the relationship between national elites and international forces may be crucial. In much of the literature on Latin America, the subordinate place of the economies of those states in the world economy has been a point of emphasis.[12] That location has shaped the economic problems and possibilities that have faced the new elites and thereby done much to shape the transition process. Similar considerations apply in all cases of transition; the relationship with major economies and with international financial organisations is important in all cases of transition, particularly those involving major economic change. Similarly the relationship with foreign political forces may be important. American support for right-wing domestic forces in Latin America is well known and has been important in shaping the course of political development there. Such factors have also been present in other cases of transition. To the degree that national elites are autonomous from such forces, then the course of transition is likely to be shaped more by national than by international factors.

The question is, how have these issues been played out in the Russian transition? Has the elite conflict that emerged in Russia been resolved in ways which would facilitate the emergence and consolidation of a democratic political structure?

Elite Contours in Russia

The emergence of the Russian political elite as the key political actor in an independent Russia came about in part as an unavoidable result of the larger political process. The dissolution of the Soviet Union immediately eliminated the Soviet political elite from the political stage. As an entity, the Soviet Party and government leadership disappeared, while most of its individual members also left political life; some went into retirement, others into commerce, with only a few harbouring aspirations to continue to play a role in the political life of the new state. The displacement of the Soviet elite does not appear to have been accompanied by explicit exit guarantees on the part of their Russian successors. Although there were rumours of a deal between Yeltsin and Gorbachev, no details of this have been forthcoming, and even if a deal had been made, in the aftermath of the August coup attempt it is unlikely that such a deal would have embraced the entire former Soviet leadership, or even large sections of it. Indeed, if anything, there is some evidence of a threat to the former elite on the part of the new rulers of Russia: the opening of hearings in mid-1992 by the Constitutional Court into the constitutionality of the Communist Party's activity during the Soviet period potentially threatened to open the way to the laying of charges against former political leaders. The Court's decision that there was no need to rule on this matter because the party had already ceased to exist was a strange decision in law, but was consistent with a political imperative of reassuring former members of the elite about their security. The parliamentary granting of an amnesty to the leaders of the August coup (and Yeltsin's parliamentary opposition from autumn 1993) in February 1994 sent a similar message. While there may have been no explicit pact or guarantee, such action involving a forthright rejection of the formal calling to account of members of the former elite served the same purpose. It allowed the Soviet elite to accept its withdrawal from the scene by guaranteeing its future security from legal action. This removal of the Soviet elite left in power in the republics of the former Soviet Union those people who had gained leadership positions in the republics in the final years of Soviet power.

The Russian elite differed from those in many of the other republics in one important institutional way. In Russia a separate Russian Communist Party had been established only in 1990, with the result that it had no basis independent of the Soviet party. Thus even if the Russian elite had not been led by a man determined to break the power of the party, Boris Yeltsin, once the Soviet party had been eliminated, the Russian party leadership would have lacked the institutional capacity to maintain its position in republican elite councils. Thus unlike the governing elites in many of the other republics, initially the post-independent Russian political elite did not have a clear and identifiable party faction (even if elsewhere that party faction went under a different party name), although it did contain significant numbers of people who had recently been members of the CPSU.

It is important to recognise that the rise to prominence of the Russian political elite did not constitute a case of insiders being replaced by outsiders, but of the top rank of the elite (the Soviet leadership) being displaced in Russia by those on the second rung.[13] The President and Vice-President, heads of the presidential administration, members of the Supreme Soviet and Congress of People's Deputies, members of the government and heads of state ministries were mostly people who had worked their way up the Soviet power structures and had spent much of their political lives in the ranks of the Communist Party. Many were imbued with the norms and principles of Soviet politics and possessed the sorts of informal networks of contacts that had been so central to the functioning of the Soviet system. In this sense they were not a revolutionary elite coming in from the outside to overturn that which they inherited, but were actually part of the structure that was the legacy of the Soviet Union.

One of the characteristics of the Soviet elite is that it was highly integrated, in the sense that the different segments of it (political, economic, military) constituted integral parts of the whole; they were not autonomous from each other but were interlinked through institutional and informal personal channels and networks. Initially this was less a feature of the contours of Russian elite life; the links between the political elite on the one hand and the military and economic elites on the other were more attenuated and the elites themselves did not form a single coherent entity. As the legally recognised successor state to the USSR, Russia inherited the vast bulk of the former Soviet military forces. However, during the Soviet period, the leadership of those forces had been part of the broader Soviet, not Russian, elite. This meant that, in the new post-Soviet conditions, the Russian political and military elites were neither highly integrated nor, in most cases, personally close. Certainly some members of the political elite such as Vice-President Rutskoi had close contacts with the military, but for the elite as a whole the military remained a group apart. Possessed of its own institutional ethos and interests, which were for much of this period seen as being under attack, the military initially lacked the sorts of established and secure channels of access into the political elite which they had .enjoyed in Soviet times.

Similarly the inclusion of the leaders of the economic sector in the Soviet elite was not a situation fully translated into the post-Soviet period. While those people in charge of the central economic institutions of the state, for example the Ministry of Finance and the Central Bank, remained part of the political elite, economic reform and the form it took generated new forces in the economic sphere that looked to the political elite for support. One has been that group of senior managers and people in authoritative positions from the Soviet period who were able to take advantage of the opportunities that occurred during the last years of Soviet power and of the privatisation provisions of the Yeltsin government to establish their personal control over major economic enterprises.[14] Many of these people who had been playing managerial or supervisory roles in the Soviet production process retained established links with senior personnel in the government ministries taken over by the Russian government from its Soviet predecessor. It is probable that their lines of communication, and potentially of influence, remained relatively unchanged while the personnel from the Soviet period continued to occupy leading positions in the relevant ministries. In addition, this group sought to consolidate its influence through leading members of the government thought to be sympathetic to their views, including such people as Chernomyrdin, Soskovets and Shumeiko. But in addition to this group, whose basis is to be found in economic institutional structures inherited from the Soviet regime, another grouping has emerged based principally in the new and expanding spheres of banking and retail trade. While some of these have begun to build commercial success upon Soviet institutional legacies, including most importantly some of the Soviet banking structures, the new freedom created by economic reform has enabled some of these people to accumulate significant wealth and economic power. In structural terms this was a new group with no established channels into the political elite. This will be discussed further below.

Crucial to the institutionalisation of a new political system is the stabilisation of the patterns of interaction between elites. However, the generation of such stable patterns was substantially hindered by the lack of unity within the political elite. One of the crucial differences between the course of the displacement of the Soviet regime in Russia and the similar events throughout much of Eastern Europe is that in the former there was no equivalent of the Round Table discussions which effectively mapped out some of the contours of the transition in some of the countries of the latter. In part this was because of the nature of the post-Soviet elite, with political forces within it inadequately defined to provide the basis for such negotiations. Also important was the nature of the displacement of the Soviet regime. The period from June 1990 was one in which the Russian political elite was concerned first of all both to assert and effectively to consolidate its independence from the Soviet centre, with the result that it had little time or inclination to engage in the sorts of negotiations about how the post-Soviet future might be restructured. The coup attempt in August 1991, which accelerated the drive for independence, followed by the agreement to disband the USSR stimulated further discussion about the circumstances under which the old regime could be replaced, but did not push major discussions about future political forms into the foreground of the Russian elite's attention. As a result, when Russia emerged as an independent entity at the end of 1991, there was no agreement among Russian elites about how the new politics should be structured.

Despite the lack of a negotiated set of rules of the game, the Russian political process was not completely devoid of regulating mechanisms. In formal terms, the Constitution of the Russian Soviet Federated Socialist Republic introduced in 1978 was still in operation despite the collapse of the USSR. However, apart from the symbolic aspect of retaining a Soviet-era constitution, this document was not really suitable for an independent Russia. It had been written for a Russia that had been a constituent part of the Soviet federation, and despite numerous amendments both in the Soviet and the post-Soviet eras, it remained unsuitable as a guide to political practice. Indeed, many of the amendments had made the document more complex and internally contradictory, with the result that on many issues it was unable to act as the final arbiter in the way that constitutions should. Nevertheless, its existence meant that even if it was unsuitable, there was a set of rules which formally was meant to structure political life.

In addition, the members of the Russian elite carried with them into the post-Soviet era a baggage of norms, principles and practices that had helped to define politics in the Soviet period. The rules of the Soviet political game, while not codified in any document, were nevertheless widely understood by Soviet political actors.[15] These rules had been what enabled the formal highly structured system to function effectively, and they could not be wiped from the consciousness of Russian political actors simply because the institutional structure within which they were embedded had disappeared. But once that system had disappeared, the utility of the rules which had been associated with it was greatly reduced; the principles associated with the rhetoric of democracy sat uneasily with the secrecy, patronage and lack of popular involvement that were essential parts of the informal rules of Soviet politics.

Thus while for the Russian elite sets of both formal and informal rules of the game did exist, there was limited agreement within that elite about the normative authority possessed by those rules. For many, the rejection of the Soviet model of politics also meant the rejection of the rules that were associated with it, and therefore of the Soviet-era Constitution and the informal rules of the game. But with the rejection of the Soviet-era rules and the absence of any Round Table procedure of negotiation, there was no agreement about what was to replace them. There was therefore no procedural consensus in the elite, no clearly established rules of the game to structure political life which all accepted.

The Fracturing of the Political Elite

This absence of procedural consensus was not initially important. The early unity of the Russian elite had rested upon the struggle against the Soviet centre. Since the 12 June 1990 Declaration of Sovereignty of Russia closely following Yeltsin's election as Chairman of the Presidium of the Supreme Soviet (effective President) on 29 May 1990, the Russian government had waged a continuing campaign to loosen its ties with the Soviet centre. This campaign had accelerated following the popular election of Yeltsin as President on 12 June 1991 and the August 1991 coup attempt against Gorbachev. This struggle had been a unifying force for large sections of the Russian elite. The initial election of Yeltsin as Chairman by the legislature in May 1990 had been by only a narrow majority.[16] The opposition to Yeltsin both personally and on a policy basis was reinforced by concerns in the legislature about the development of an expansive presidential role,[17] a concern which was subsequently to become increasingly important. However, these concerns were moderated by the desire not to disrupt the struggle with the Soviet centre by excessive disunity, with the result that Yeltsin's opponents did not press their concerns. Nevertheless, the unity that characterised the Russian elite was only weakly based, and towards the end of 1991 actions were taken which would sunder that unity completely.

If there was no procedural consensus among the Russian elite, nor was there widespread substantive consensus.[18] From the time the Russian government sought to weaken its ties with the Soviet centre, that government was characterised by a range of views about the nature of the relationship which should exist between Russia and the Soviet Union and about the shape of economic reform. Formally all accepted the need for a revision of the arrangements which underpinned the Soviet federation and for the shift to a market economy, but there was no clarity about the way those arrangements should be revised or about exactly what was meant by a 'market economy' and how it was to be achieved. The first of these issues, the relationship with the Soviet centre, was resolved with the dissolution of the USSR at the end of 1991, and although sections of the elite continued to place their hopes in the new Commonwealth of Independent States as a mechanism for rebuilding some sort of union, this did not become a major issue of contention within the elite. However, this was not the case with the question of economic reform, a question which almost immediately became complicated by the intrusion of procedural issues.

On 28 October 1991, before the Soviet Union had been formally dissolved, Yeltsin announced a plan of radical economic shock therapy designed to speed the transformation of the economy into one based on the free market. Involving economic stabilisation through a tight monetary and credit policy, price liberalisation, privatisation and reorganisation of the financial system,[19] this programme was to be implemented progressively, with the main impact coming with price liberalisation beginning on 2 January 1992. On 1 November 1991 the Congress of People's Deputies granted Yeltsin extraordinary powers valid until 1 December 1992 to appoint ministers and introduce decrees designed to facilitate economic reform.[20] Five days later Yeltsin also took over the position of Prime Minister, ostensibly to expedite the process of economic reform. These moves created significant unease within sections of the political elite. The adoption of shock therapy and the rhetoric which accompanied it was a clear signal that its proponents favoured the shift to a market economy in which the state played very little role; rather than the so-called 'regulated market' which many had seen as a means of moderating the excesses of market forces through state involvement, shock therapy seemed to be associated with a system in which market forces were untrammelled by virtually any form of state regulation. The expansion of Yeltsin's role, although in part agreed to by the legislature, revived the fears about an expansive presidential role that had been evident earlier. These concerns erupted into open elite conflict in April 1992 at the Sixth Congress of People's Deputies, and lasted until September–October 1993.

The fracturing of the Russian political elite occurred broadly along institutional lines, with the bulk of the presidential apparatus (although from late-1992 Vice-President Aleksandr Rutskoi crossed to the anti-Yeltsin side) and the government supporting Yeltsin, shock therapy and an expansive view of the presidency, and the legislature (both Congress of People's Deputies and Supreme Soviet) headed by Supreme Soviet speaker Ruslan Khasbulatov opposing these. The institutional division is logical: an expansive presidency would have meant a reduced role for the legislature, and given that the increased power accorded to Yeltsin was specifically related to the implementation of economic reform, opposition to that reform was one way of opposing the drift towards a presidential system of government. But this institutional division was also a function of the way the leading actors chose to play out their roles. Within the legislature there was a core of support for Yeltsin, as shown by the course of the voting for the chairmanship of the Presidium of the Supreme Soviet in 1990. In theory, this section of the legislature could have been mobilised by Yeltsin in a continuing fashion to counter those opposed to him within that institution. While those who could be counted as firm supporters of Yeltsin were not a majority within the chamber, there would probably have been sufficient waverers who, if joined to this core, could have offset the group more firmly opposed to the President. However, Yeltsin made no continuing attempt to mobilise his potential support. By not reaching out to potential supporters but instead taking a firm stance against the legislature, he crystallised the institutional divisions and exacerbated the conflict.

The dynamics of the intra-elite conflict are important for an understanding of the role of elites in the Russian transition, but we do not need to retell the story of that conflict here.[21] The bases upon which each side sought to rest its case were very different. Khasbulatov and his supporters from within the legislature based their claims about excessive presidential power and the need for the legislature to be the primary arm of the state upon a reading of the Soviet-era Constitution. They thus made a claim for legal–rational authority, and for the view that the President was in breach of the Constitution. It was this which formally provided grounds upon which there was talk of impeaching Yeltsin. On economic matters they argued that the short-term costs of shock therapy were excessive and the long-term prospects for success dim. In contrast Yeltsin's position rested much more upon a view of himself as the representative of the people, giving voice to their hopes and aspirations. He argued that he was directly and personally responsible to the people, using his June 1991 election as proof, and that their will overruled and was more important than any formal constitutional provisions.[22] On economic reform, he accepted the argument that short-term pain was necessary for longer-term economic success. Thus, as well as the differing views on the economy, the two sides counterposed different bases of authority: legal–rational authority was opposed by what amounted almost to a claim for charismatic authority, or at least a special personal relationship with the people.[23]

It may be thought that Yeltsin's claim to a personalised authority independent of constitutional provisions would have encouraged him to conduct his part of the struggle without regard to the provisions of the Constitution. However, in practice both sides substantially adhered to the Constitution and demonstrated significant moderation in their actions thoughout most of this period. The main tactics used by the legislative side included criticism of Yeltsin and his policies and practices both within the chamber and publicly, the adoption of legislation designed to counter measures taken by Yeltsin, the building up of pseudo-governmental structures to shadow and block Yeltsin's own presidential administration, moves to impeach the President, and appeals to the Constitutional Court. For his part Yeltsin conducted the struggle through public appeals for support, threats to go to the people or in March 1993 to establish 'special rule', the adoption of decrees, the generation of a range of new bodies in the presidential apparatus designed to concentrate power there, and appeals to the Constitutional Court. On a number of occasions, Yeltsin also offered compromises to his opponents, particularly over the composition of the government, and in these Khasbulatov was often a willing partner. During the conflict, the Constitutional Court often acted as a sort of umpire, especially during the early stages of the conflict; if it ruled that one of the parties had acted illegally, that judgement generally was accepted, even if not always in good grace. Thus, while the conflict was pursued on a continuous basis, it was always characterised by a sense of moderation; neither side seemed willing to go beyond the brink in order to be successful, and when the possibility of this happening threatened, both sides would pull back.

The series of compromises which were reached between the two sides, despite their ultimate lack of success, may be seen as attempts to resolve procedural differences, but they should not be seen as attempted pacts; they were more limited in scope and were therefore not by themselves means of achieving the sort of stability of operating environment that is characteristic of pact-making. Yeltsin's agreement to give up the position of Prime Minister in April 1992, the December 1992 agreements giving the legislature the right to confirm in office the Prime Minister and the power ministers and over the holding of a referendum, and the mid-1993 attempt to design a new Constitution are the clearest instances of attempted compromise. Ultimately all these attempts at compromise failed. This was because, while both sides were willing to compromise temporarily at the tactical level, neither was willing to compromise on its fundamental position. But while neither side was willing to moderate its basic stance, and as long as support for both sides within the political elite remained solid, there was no way that the conflict could be resolved within the bounds of that elite. Some sort of circuit-breaker had to be introduced from outside if the debilitating conflict were to be ended.

For most of its duration, the course of conflict within the political elite was confined substantially to the bounds of that elite, with the mass of the population excluded from meaningful political involvement. Certainly elite actors appealed to the populace for their support during the conflict, and although at times public opinion as reflected in opinion polls seemed to give a fillip to one side or the other, this had little practical effect on the course of the conflict. Seemingly more important was the referendum held on 11 April 1993, in which the overall results seemed to boost Yeltsin considerably;[24] levels of popular support for the President and his policies were higher than had been expected and the view that the legislature should face early election was much stronger than the view that Yeltsin himself should go to the polls. But while the referendum was followed by a comparative lull in attacks on Yeltsin, it had no lasting impact.[25] Thus, in the period up until late 1993, the mass of the populace was largely excluded from the course of elite conflict and played no active part in its unrolling.

The emerging economic elite may have played some part in the course of the conflict within the political elite, but this was not a clear and vigorous intervention into that conflict. Many of the economic elite, and particularly those who had gained control of privatised enterprises, were concerned about the effects of shock therapy and the rapid shift to the market. The continued viability of their enterprises often depended upon the continuation of substantial state subsidies, a practice which clearly ran counter to the strict monetary and credit policies intrinsic to shock therapy. This group should therefore have been firm supporters of the legislative criticism of Yeltsin's economic policies and of the continuing loose monetary policy followed by the Central Bank under the chairmanship of Viktor Gerashchenko. The Central Bank was responsible to the legislature rather than to the President, and under Gerashchenko followed a policy favouring the continued minting of currency and the extension of loans and subsidies to economic enterprises, elements clearly in conflict with the main thrust of Yeltsin's reform. This policy was supported by many industrialists, who would therefore have been expected to support Khasbulatov and the legislature. However, the effect of this may have been offset by the fact that many industrialists and entrepreneurs hoped to make and to consolidate the personal gains made through the Yeltsin administration's policy of privatisation, and were therefore wary of acting in ways which might cause that administration to act contrary to their interests. In any event, the economic elite did not throw its support decisively behind either side in the elite political conflict, and there is no evidence that that elite played a part in structuring the course of the conflict, except in so far as it was instrumental in bringing about changes in the composition of Yeltsin's government (see below).

Initially the main force behind shock therapy was Yegor Gaidar, first Acting Prime Minister and then Prime Minister in his own right. Gaidar's background was as an academic economist.[26] He did not come out of the Soviet productive sector and did not have close contacts with it. Nor, in the view of his critics, did he have much appreciation about the real conditions in that sector. As the conflict continued, Gaidar became a major focus of attack. Under pressure in April 1992, Yeltsin introduced three new members into his government, Viktor Chernomyrdin, Georgii Khizha and Vladimir Shumeiko, all of whom were seen as representatives of the so-called industrial lobby and therefore as supporters of a moderation of the more radical aspects of shock therapy. All had spent significant time working in the Soviet industrial or energy sectors, and all were seen as in some sense the bearers of the interests of industrialists. In December 1992, Gaidar was replaced as Prime Minister by Chernomyrdin. Although Chernomyrdin's influence in the economy was never supreme and was always balanced against that of both the presidential administration and the state ministries, his presence at the head of the government was seen as both a compromise by Yeltsin and a symbol of the potential importance of the new economic elite. But even if these individuals did represent the industrial wing of the emerging economic elite, they did not support the legislature in its conflict with the President: when the showdown came in autumn 1993, they remained supportive of the President.

The other elite group, the military, was to have a central role in the main attempt by Yeltsin to resolve the conflict within the political elite. In September 1993, following attempts by Khasbulatov actively to expand the conflict beyond the bounds of the political elite by courting support within the security and armed forces sectors and the local soviets, Yeltsin announced the dissolution of the Congress of People's Deputies and Supreme Soviet, the holding of elections to a new bicameral assembly on 11–12 December, and declared that in the interim the country would be ruled by decree.[27] In response to this unconstitutional action, Khasbulatov, Rutskoi and some supporters barricaded themselves in the parliament building. A stand-off ensued, but following Rutskoi's incitement of his supporters to violence, Yeltsin called upon the military forcibly to end this situation. With some reluctance,[28] the military elite ordered its forces into action and the deputies inside the building were removed. Rutskoi and Khasbulatov were arrested. The conflict within the political elite was thus semingly resolved through the intervention of the military elite and the removal of one side to the conflict. The victorious fragment of the elite headed by Yeltsin now sought to consolidate its victory by seeking the imprimatur of the masses through both the election of a new legislature and the adoption of a new Constitution drafted in Yeltsin's office. Yeltsin made some efforts to structure this process in such a way as to ensure the outcome he wanted. He forbade some parties and groups from participating in the election (officially those who had been involved in the so-called parliamentary rising, but who were also uncompromising critics of the President), temporarily closed some newspapers, and threatened action against party leaders who used the election campaign to criticise the President or his actions. During the campaign a new draft Constitution was unveiled which shifted power substantially towards the President and away from the legislature.[29] Debate on this was one-sided: those who supported the draft dominated the media, with opponents having very little opportunity to air their views. Clearly the election and plebiscite on the Constitution were conducted under conditions that seemed tailor-made to validate the results of the conflict within the political elite.

Thus in the two years following the fall of the Soviet system, conflict erupted in the political elite over both procedural and substantive issues. Despite attempts at compromise, there was little real likelihood of a resolution through pact-making or through elite settlements. With neither side willing to compromise on its basic position, there was no common ground upon which a stable settlement or pact could rest. The resort to force broke this deadlock and severely weakened one side of the conflict, enabling the other effectively to impose a solution. The issue is whether this created the conditions for a stable and continuing settlement of elite differences.

Post-Election Elite Consolidation?

At a superficial level, this mobilisation of the mass into politics to ratify the victory of the Yeltsin fragment of the elite was successful, with an apparent stabilisation of the political system and acceptance by all sides of the contours of the newly-instituted political process. What is the evidence for this view? While relations were not smooth, with the President suffering adverse votes (including the granting of a parliamentary amnesty to his opponents in February 1994) and the holding of votes of no confidence in his government, the tensions were contained. Furthermore, legislative and presidential elections were held respectively in December 1995 and June–July 1996, broadly on schedule, without disruption, and with the losers accepting the verdict. Most of the leading political actors (except for the Communist Party of the Russian Federation, the Agrarian Party and the reformist bloc, Yabloko) publicly committed themselves to a course of moderation through the signature of the Yeltsin-sponsored Pact on Social Accord in April 1994. This was designed to set out some ground rules for political activity. But perhaps the best argument for broad acceptance of the state of affairs created by the autumn 1993 showdown concerns the Constitution. Although it was announced at the time that the Constitution had been approved by 58.4 per cent of voters,[30] later reports suggested that in fact less than half of the electorate had participated in the vote, thereby rendering it invalid.[31] If true, this would also have rendered the new Constitution invalid and thereby re-injected considerable ambiguity into the question of the shape of the formal rules of the game. But no major group took up this issue and thereby challenged the validity of the new constitutional arrangements, a fact consistent with a form of *de facto* elite settlement: all sides accept the new arrangements, despite concerns among many about the precise distribution of power embodied in them, because they realise the damage continuing political instability could cause to the emergent political system and the country. But does this represent the embedding of new, commonly-agreed rules of the game in the political system?

The emergence and consolidation of a new set of rules is usually an extended process, requiring a substantial period of humdrum politics in which patterns and practices can take hold without the disruption caused by crisis or exceptional events. With the results of the December 1993 election seen by many as only an interim and unsatisfactory situation (because of Yeltsin's intervention into the electoral process noted above), and with a new legislative election due in December 1995, it is unlikely that the conditions would have been sufficient to embed new rules of political practice firmly into the political structure. Rather there are strong reasons for thinking that the moderation of elite activity reflected shorter-term practical considerations rather than a longer-term commitment to new norms of behaviour. In the procedural sphere, the new Constitution and the shift in power that it involved eliminated the uncertainty that had given rise to the argument over whether executive or legislative should be the more powerful institution. In the policy sphere, economic reform was pursued less vigorously after December 1993 than it had been in 1992, thereby removing a major source of antagonism. Moreover, the events of autumn 1993 had made clear to everyone the potential consequences of continuing conflict, and for those opposed to the President, the lengths to which he would go to vanquish them. In any case, they could reconcile themselves with the view that the elections due at the end of 1995 gave the possibility of recasting the contours of the elite and thereby delivering into their hands the power to achieve their ends. All these considerations reflect a pragmatic evaluation of the post-December 1993 political situation, not a commitment to a new mode of political functioning.

But even if the apparent stabilisation of the system in 1994–95 stemmed from these sorts of pragmatic concerns rather than an embedding of democratic principles of the political game, it is possible that such a period of regularity could lead to the generation of the sort of commitment to the system widely seen as necessary for the consolidation of democracy. It may be that the lack of any disruption to the political process as a result of the defeat of the pro-Yeltsin forces and the success of the Communists in December 1995, of Yeltsin's victory in July 1996 and of the prolonged absence and relative inactivity of Yeltsin after the presidential election means that commitment to such principles has become consolidated in Russia. But, as for the earlier period, this is by no means unproblematic. The post-December 1995 moderation may have been more a result of political circumstances than of adherence to embedded norms: in the first half of 1996 all sides were awaiting the outcome of the presidential election in the knowledge that this was the main contest for power in Russia, while what we have seen since the middle of 1996 has been less a sense of moderation resulting from acceptance of certain principles of operation than a process of drift as all sides awaited the outcome of the President's illness. The response of political forces to the longer-term outcome of Yeltsin's illness, and to the way in which he re-asserts presidential authority, will be crucial in showing the degree to which modes of operation within the political sphere have been accepted by political elites, and therefore the extent to which a stable elite settlement has been reached. But if such a settlement has been arrived at, it must be recognised that it has been less the result of negotiated compromise than of the acceptance of rules laid down by one side.

What of relations between the political elite and other forces?

Elite Autonomy?

The relationship with the mass of the population remains one in which elite autonomy has not been substantially reduced through the development of effective mechanisms of responsibility or accountability. While the holding of the election and constitutional plebiscite in December 1993 and the legislative and presidential elections in December 1995 and June–July 1996 seem to represent an expression of elite accountability to the populace, this appearance is significantly weakened by the claims of electoral fraud surrounding the 1993 poll and the refusal of the authorities to do anything about this. By refusing to act to rectify the results of electoral malpractice, the elite has allowed the will of the people to be subverted by manipulation from within that elite. The result of the presidential election has also been demeaned by the way in which the electorate was kept in ignorance of Yeltsin's severe health problems, thereby permitting the confirmation in office of someone who was physically incapable of carrying out the duties of that office. The meaning of popular mandate, and thereby of accountability, is cast into doubt if a mandate is given to someone who cannot carry it out, and if power is thereby wielded by unelected officials. Furthermore, the under-developed nature of the political parties means that they are not able to act as effective mechanisms of popular control even over the legislators, let alone over the government which, as a result of the 1993 Constitution, is not responsible to the legislature. Nor have labour organisations been able to play a significant role in projecting popular opinion, let alone control into the political arena.[32] Moreover, the high levels of popular apathy and lack of interest in politics registered in opinion polls[33] suggests that there is little pressure for the strengthening of popular control over political leaders. The autonomy of the political elite from the mass of the populace has barely been reduced.

The involvement of the military in the resolution of the autumn 1993 crisis raised questions about the role the military elite would play in Russian politics. The military carried with them into the post-Soviet period a tradition of non-involvement in politics and obedience to civilian command. Clearly this tradition has been placed under some strain. The running down of military spending, the reduced military role and responsibilities with the decline from superpower status, and the treatment of army personnel (especially the absence of facilities for returning soldiers), their mobilisation to resolve the conflict within the political elite, and the circumstances surrounding the involvement in Chechnya all placed strains on this relationship. But there is no sign of any fundamental change in the position of the military elite. Despite suggestions of Yeltsin's need to make concessions to the military in the wake of October 1993 (the chief evidence for this is seen to be the new military doctrine introduced shortly afterwards),[34] the President's prolonged unwillingness to take action against Defence Minister Pavel Grachev in the wake of the Chechnya affair, and loose talk about a so-called 'party of war' in Moscow, there is no hard evidence to suggest that the military elite has gained a position of significant influence within decision-making councils in Russia. Indeed, the lack of military response to the sacking of Grachev in mid-1996 and then of Security Council secretary Aleksandr Lebed in October 1996, both of whom were seen as representing military interests, suggests a continuing ethos of military non-involvement in civilian affairs. Clearly the military will always be a powerful interest group and it will always have relatively open access to political elite circles, but such access is likely to remain best conceptualised in terms of interest group or bureaucratic politics activity rather than of the displacement of a civilian political by a military elite, or the dependence of the former on the latter.

A common complaint emanating from the opposition side of politics in Russia has been that the government has been subservient to Western economic interests. This is a large topic that involves the politico-economic relationship between the Russian and the international economy and cannot be explored fully here. However, it is clear that the post-Soviet Russian government has been influenced in the economic policies it has pursued by the views of Western advisers and in particular by such international bodies as the IMF and World Bank. While there is no evidence that these bodies have played a direct, independent policy-making part, they have clearly influenced important economic decision-makers in the policies they have implemented. Initial shock therapy, continuing attempts at fiscal restraint and the push for privatisation are all clear examples of such policies. The hold such international organisations have over Russian decision-makers is access to the loan funds and credits which are seen as crucial to Russia's long-term economic success. But despite the importance of such considerations and despite the arguments that policy in many areas has been shaped according to Western dictates,[35] there is no hard evidence that the Russian elite is acting at the behest of foreign forces. While it must certainly take these into account, it is not responsible or accountable to them; indeed, on a number of occasions (including the Chechen war, the proposed expansion of NATO, extravagant election promises, and events in the former Yugoslavia) the Russian government has acted in ways divergent from the wishes of many of its Western supporters.

But the most important aspect of the question of autonomy relates to the economic elite. The process of economic change has had as one of its major elements the construction of a private sector. This has involved, in principle, two paths of the development of private interests: through the privatisation of state assets, and through the generation of new, independent economic activity. The productive, industrial and financial sectors have mainly been concentrated in the former, the retail sector in the latter. But despite their different origins, elites in all sectors of the economy have been concerned about the uncertainties surrounding the emergence of the new private sector. The inadequacy of the Russian legal regime, the under-developed nature of market institutions, and the prevalence of criminal activity combined to increase levels of uncertainty among economic elites. One response to this has been to look to the government for support and to create the environment of certainty and predictability which a market system requires. However, the weakness of the Russian state, reflected in its inability to deal satisfactorily with criminal activity and to collect its own tax revenues, has encouraged those seeking support to rely less upon the formal channels and public operations of the state than upon the sorts of unofficial contacts and processes that might be classed by some as bordering on the corrupt.

Olga Kryshtanovskaya and Stephen White have shown in an earlier chapter how significant elements of the Soviet *nomenklatura* were able to transform their administrative power in Soviet times into economic power in post-Soviet times.[36] The privatisation programme of the Russian government was effectively a means of guaranteeing the privileges of much of the old Soviet elite. It was also a means of transforming many former managers and employees of Soviet productive enterprises into the employees of private concerns. These people retained their connections with those sections of the former state apparatus which were not privatised, with the result that the newly-emergent private sector has remained linked into and networked with the state bureaucratic structures responsible for economic activity. This connection has been most obvious at the levels of elite politics where, for example, Prime Minister Chernomyrdin, former Deputy Prime Minister Soskovets and presidential chief of staff Chubais have had very close connections with respectively the energy sector, the defence industry sector and the financial sector. The closeness of the personal and institutional links between leading political figures and specific economic sectors, resting principally upon *nomenklatura*-generated personal networks,[37] provides the potential for the growth of much greater unity between the political and this section of the economic elite than would be desirable in a genuinely democratic political system. It involves, potentially, an interlocking of power where established personal networks reinforced by the prospect of personal gains underpin the merging of political and economic power. It also means that the autonomy of the political elite from the economic could become substantially compromised.

But this process would not necessarily help that section of the economic elite which is making its money from the expanding retail sector. This group, which seems to form a considerable part of the new rich in Russia, does not seem to have the sort of personal entrée enjoyed by the productive and financial sectors of the economy. Nevertheless, the wealth that they are accumulating, added to the primitive nature of the rules regulating propriety in public office and the reputation many Russian politicians have of being open to inducements, suggests that this section of the emergent economic elite is well able to look after its interests in the political sphere. Despite the relatively small number of businessmen in public politics and the absence of an obvious representative in upper political ranks, it is likely that this sector is well placed to strengthen its ties with the political decision-makers.

Conclusion

Like all transitions from authoritarian rule, that in Russia has been moulded significantly by elite activity. The elite that has played the biggest part has been the political elite, largely inherited from the Soviet period but from among the second and now also lower rungs of that structure. Economic elites may have exercised some influence in a more indirect way, while the military elite has played an important part on one occasion, but then at the behest of a fragment of the political elite. In this sense, the transition has been overwhelmingly managed by the political elite. The mass of the population has been essentially a passive actor in this process, and given the high levels of apathy that were recorded throughout 1994–95 and the lack of reaction to subsequent political events, this may remain the case in the short term. But although the political elite has dominated the process, there is not yet a consolidated political elite culture at the apex of the Russian structure. Once the contours of the elite have been re-formed through the elections in 1995 and 1996 and the effects of Yeltsin's illness have been played out, the conditions may exist to allow such a consolidation to occur. But for this to come about there will need to be a wide-ranging consensus on both procedural and substantive issues within the political elite. Given the challenges still facing Russia, it is not clear that conditions favourable for that to occur will exist.

Notes

1. Samuel P. Huntington, *The Third Wave: Democratization in the Late Twentieth Century* (Norman: University of Oklahoma Press, 1991).
2. See the discussion of the relevance of other literature in Sarah Meiklejohn Terry, 'Thinking About Post-Communist Transitions: How Different Are They?', *Slavic Review* **52**, no.2 (Summer 1993); Philippe C. Schmitter and Terry Lynn Karl, 'The Conceptual Travels of Transitologists and Consolidologists: How Far to the East Should They Attempt to Go?', *Slavic Review* **53**, no.1 (Spring 1994); Valerie Bunce, 'Should Transitologists be Grounded?', *Slavic Review* **54**, no.1 (Spring 1995) and discussion in *Slavic Review* **54**, no.4 (Winter 1995).
3. Use of this term does not assume that the process of transition will inevitably end in democracy and a market economy. But regardless of the end-point, the process of change will be fundamentally shaped by the nature of elite politics. In this chapter, the term 'elite' refers only to those at the head of the political, military and economic sectors of national life in the Russian Federation.
4. For example, Guillermo O'Donnell, Philippe C. Schmitter and Laurence Whitehead

(eds), *Transitions from Authoritarian Rule: Latin America* (Baltimore, MD: Johns Hopkins University Press, 1986).

5. The most famous example of this is Gabriel A. Almond and Sidney Verba, *The Civic Culture. Political Attitudes and Democracy in Five Nations* (Boston, MA: Little, Brown, 1965).

6. To use the term of Giuseppe Di Palma, *To Craft Democracies: An Essay on Democratic Transitions* (Berkeley: University of California Press, 1990).

7. Guillermo O'Donnell and Philippe C. Schmitter, *Transitions from Authoritarian Rule: Tentative Conclusions about Uncertain Democracies* (Baltimore, MD: Johns Hopkins University Press, 1986), pp.29–30. Also the discussion in Robert H. Dix, 'The Breakdown of Authoritarian Regimes', *Western Political Quarterly* 35, no.4 (1982).

8. Marcelo Cavarozzi, 'Patterns of Elite Negotiation and Confrontation in Argentina and Chile', in John Higley and Richard Gunther (eds), *Elites and Democratic Consolidation in Latin America and Southern Europe* (Cambridge: Cambridge University Press, 1992), p.232.

9. Higley and Gunther, *Elites and Democratic Consolidation*, p.xi.

10. On pacts see O'Donnell and Schmitter, *Transitions from Authoritarian Rule*, Chapter 4.

11. For one discussion see Adam Przeworski, *Democracy and the Market: Political and Economic Reform in Eastern Europe and Latin America* (Cambridge: Cambridge University Press, 1991), Chapter 4.

12. In particular, see the literature on bureaucratic authoritarianism: for example, David Collier (ed.), *The New Authoritarianism in Latin America* (Princeton, NJ: Princeton University Press, 1979), Part 3.

13. One observer, citing the view of the co-founder of the East German New Forum, Jens Reich, has labelled the group from which the post-communist political elite in Eastern Europe has come the 'lower nobility' of the communist era: Thomas A. Baylis, 'Plus ça Change? Transformation and Continuity Among Eastern European Elites', *Communist and Post-Communist Studies* 27, no.3 (1994), p.323.

14. On this see Michael McFaul, 'State Power, Institutional Change, and the Politics of Privatization in Russia', *World Politics* 42, no.2 (January 1995); see also below.

15. For one discussion of this see T.H. Rigby, 'Khrushchev and the Rules of the Game', in R.F. Miller and F. Fehér (eds), *Khrushchev and the Communist World* (London: Croom Helm, 1984).

16. In the fourth round of voting, Yeltsin gained only four votes more than was needed: Jonathan Steele, *Eternal Russia: Yeltsin, Gorbachev and the Mirage of Democracy* (London: Faber & Faber, 1995), pp.244–5.

17. For one discussion of this see Richard Sakwa, *Russian Politics and Society* (London: Routledge, 1993), pp.46–7.

18. For an argument that the basis of policy dissensus lay in the diverse views present in the elite in the last days of Soviet power, see Judith S. Kullberg, 'The Ideological Roots of Elite Political Conflict in Post-Soviet Russia', *Europe–Asia Studies* 46, no.6 (1994), pp.929–54.

19. *Rossiiskaya gazeta*, 29 October 1991.

20. Ibid., 2 November 1991.

21. This has been outlined in many places: see, for exmple, Steele, *Eternal Russia*; Sakwa, *Russian Politics and Society*, Chapter 2. For the views of the major players, see Boris Yeltsin, *The View from the Kremlin*, translated by Catherine A. Fitzpatrick (New York: Harper Collins, 1994), and Ruslan Khasbulatov, *The Struggle for Russia:*

Power and Change in the Democratic Revolution, edited by Richard Sakwa (London: Routledge, 1993).

22. For example, *Izvestiya*, 22 September 1993.
23. For the argument that this should be seen as a form of 'delegative democracy', see Paul Kubicek, 'Delegative Democracy in Russia and Ukraine', *Communist and Post-Communist Studies* **27**, no.4 (1994), pp.423–41.
24. *Izvestiya*, 6 May 1993.
25. It is possible, however that the favourable outcome for Yeltsin in April strengthened his determination to act against his opponents in September–October.
26. For personal details of leaders, see *Politicheskaya Rossiya segodnya*, 2 vols. (Moscow: Moskovskii rabochii), 1993).
27. *Rossiiskaya gazeta*, 23 September 1993.
28. For Yeltsin's account, see Yeltsin, *The View from the Kremlin*, Chapter 9.
29. For the Constitution, see *Rossiiskaya gazeta*, 25 December 1993.
30. This comprised only 30.7 per cent of the electorate: see Richard Sakwa, 'The Russian Elections of December 1993', *Europe–Asia Studies* **47**, no.2 (March 1995), p.211.
31. *Izvestiya*, 4 May 1994.
32. For an excellent discussion of labour unions, see Linda J. Cook, 'Workers in the Russian Federation: Responses to the Post-Communist Transition, 1989–1993', *Communist and Post-Communist Studies* **28**, no.1 (1995).
33. For example, *Segodnya*, 8 and 15 April 1995.
34. Archie Brown, 'Political Leadership in Post-Communist Russia', in Amin Saikal and William Maley (eds), *Russia in Search of its Future* (Cambridge: Cambridge University Press, 1995), p.42. On the military doctrine, see *Izvestiya*, 4 November 1993.
35. For an argument that the dissolution of the legislature was linked to the role of international capital, see Jonathan W. Moses. 'The *Eighteenth Brumaire* of Boris Yeltsin', *Security Dialogue* **25**, no.3 (1994), pp.335–47.
36. Also see Olga Kryshtanovskaya and Stephen White, 'From Soviet *Nomenklatura* to Russian Elite', *Europe–Asia Studies* **48**, no.5 (July 1996), pp.711–33.
37. According to one survey, 42.3 per cent of members of the government had come from the Soviet *nomenklatura*: see *Izvestiya*, 10 January 1996; see also the chapters by John P. Willerton and by Olga Kryshtanovskaya and Stephen White in this volume.

8 Russia as a Post-Communist Country

Leslie Holmes

In a recent comparative book on post-communism,[1] I proposed a descriptive model of this new phenomenon, as one way of attempting to define and delimit it. The model comprises fourteen salient features of post-communism, the particular configuration of which distinguishes post-communist countries from other systems, including other transition societies. The first seven characteristics relate to political cultural implications of the legacy of communism, while the remainder are concerned with the comprehensiveness and salient features of their attempts at transitions, and the overall context in which such attempts are being made. In this chapter, recent developments in Russia will be tested against that model, as one way of attempting to conceptualise them. The basic argument is that Russia is in many ways *less* different from other post-communist states than is often claimed, even though it is from some important perspectives *sui generis;* of these, its own identity problems constitute perhaps the most significant. While maintaining that the qualitative differences between Russia and many other post-communist societies are fewer than is often appreciated, it is acknowledged that some of the problems are deeper, and reactions to them more extreme, than in some other countries. Given Russia's size and strategic significance, these differences matter.

A Descriptive Model of Post-Communism

Many comparative analysts argue that the recent transitions in Eastern Europe and the former Soviet Union (FSU) are not unique, but rather can be understood in terms of existing paradigms of transition that have been derived primarily from experiences in Latin America and Southern Europe.[2] There can be no doubt that there *are* similarities between what has been happening in the former communist world and what has occurred in these other regions since the 1970s. On the other hand, there are also sufficient differences to warrant the use of the term post-communism, and to argue that this is a unique phenomenon.[3] The following model seeks to highlight the salient features of post-communism. There is no question that several of the factors can be found in similar form in other parts of the world. Nevertheless, the particular blend identified here is unique to Eastern Europe, the FSU, and, to a lesser extent, a small number of Asian states that rejected the Soviet–communist model at about the same time as their European and Eurasian counterparts. The individual characteristics are not analysed in general terms here, since that has been done in the source mentioned above. Rather, they are used simply as a starting-point for examining recent developments in Russia from an analytical perspective.

One final introductory point is that the following is not a model of transition; this would be a different exercise, and well beyond the parameters of the present one. Hence, there is no consideration of the *processes* of transition, such as the role and nature of founding and subsequent elections or privatisation methods.

1. Assertion of Independence and the Rise of Nationalism

Russia is in a special position in terms of the assertion of independence. For the vast majority of post-communist states, the double-rejective revolutions that began in Poland and Hungary in 1988–89 and soon spread represented a rejection of both the existing system of communist power and external domination. For most of the East European states, the rejection was of Soviet domination. For most of the Yugoslav republics, it was of Serbian domination. And for many of the Soviet republics, it was of Russian domination. But Russia itself was in a very different situation as the anti-communist revolutions spread. It had been the centre of a huge empire since at least 1721 (when the Russian Empire was proclaimed by Peter the Great). It was the dominant actor in a major economic bloc (the Council for Mutual Economic Assistance – CMEA) and a major military bloc (the Warsaw Treaty Organisation – WTO). And it was one of only two true superpowers. Far from rejoicing about overthrowing a foreign yoke, many Russians felt lost and humiliated. Instead of bonding and enjoying their new-found sense of independence, Russians began to blame each other for the loss of empire and the fact that their country was no longer treated by the world with the awe it had so recently inspired. In this sense, Russia's position was unique.[4]

But precisely this loss – or at least confusion – of identity and subsequent need to find a 'new' one has contributed to a growth of Russian nationalism that makes Russia more typical of post-communist states.[5] This nationalism is by no means confined to the followers of Zhirinovskii and the ironically-named Liberal Democratic Party of Russia. It is also a salient component of the policy programme of the largest party in the Russian legislature, the Communist Party of the Russian Federation (CPRF), and in many ways played a more significant role in the 1996 presidential manifesto of communist leader Gennadii Zyuganov than did his social and economic promises. Yeltsin himself, while not as blatant a nationalist as Zyuganov or Zhirinovskii, has played on Russia's success in partly reconstituting the former USSR,[6] and became more hawkish about NATO expansion in 1993 on one level in order to play the nationalist card.[7] Finally, the ill-fated incursion into Chechnya in December 1994 was in part designed to demonstrate to all that the Russians were not prepared to allow ethnic minorities to humiliate them even more by seceding from the Russian Federation and thereby further reducing Russia's boundaries.

2. *Near Absence of a Culture of Compromise*

Russia is typical of post-communist states in having little tradition of compromise. After all, this was the home of Tsarist autocracy and Leninist democratic centralism. From 1921 until its collapse in 1991, factionalism had formally been banned even within the Communist Party itself. The legislature had been a rubber-stamping agency until well into the Gorbachev era, and then became an arena for open political conflict.

This absence of a tradition of compromise helps to explain the unstable, often dysfunctional, and sometimes even farcical nature of Russian politics in the 1990s. At its most extreme, this inability to compromise has resulted in violence. In terms of elite politics in Moscow, clearly the best example of this was President Yeltsin's closure of parliament in September 1993, followed by the physical attack on the White House in October. But it can also be seen in the fighting in Chechnya.

This is not to deny that there have also been important signs that most Russian politicians can and will compromise with each other when this appears to be necessary. The *relatively* peaceful relationship between the President and the parliament for most of 1994 is a good example. While there were significant political differences between Yeltsin and the new parliament elected in December 1993, both sides had been sobered by the success of the Liberal Democrats in that election, and proved willing to compromise because of the common threat of the so-called Zhirinovskii factor. However, this relatively harmonious period was short-lived; the president's decision to use coercion in Chechnya led to widespread condemnation in parliament. With Zhirinovskii's poor showing in the first round of the presidential election of 1996, moreover, the centripetal force of the Zhirinovskii factor in Russian politics was essentially spent. Since this factor had led to such a relatively short period of compromise, and since it took what was perceived to be an extreme threat to bring the two sides closer together, the significance of this exception should not be exaggerated.

3. High Expectations of Leaders

Both opinion surveys and electoral behaviour reveal that many Russians have high expectations of their leaders, and become very cynical and even angry when leaders fail to live up to the unrealistic standards expected of them.[8] The near-total rejection of Mikhail Gorbachev from about 1990 is a prime example.[9] At one time hailed as a liberator, Gorbachev was perceived to have brought chaos to the Soviet people, and to have played a major role in the break-up of the Soviet empire. Although Yeltsin succeeded in winning the 1996 presidential election, this was to no small extent because the mass media had painted a dismal picture of life under alternative candidates; most Russian voters *were* disillusioned with Yeltsin, but many of those who voted for him did so because of apprehension about the alternatives.[10] This said, many voters appear to have believed that life would substantially improve under a 'strong' leader,[11] which is a major reason for the relatively impressive performances of Zyuganov, Lebed and, to a much lesser extent, Zhirinovskii. By September 1996, Yeltsin's coronary illness and related incapacity to work his normal hours had led many Russians to turn to Yeltsin's strong-man national security advisor, Aleksandr Lebed. But Lebed's popularity was at least a short-term hindrance to him; it was unquestionably a major reason for his dismissal in mid-October 1996, since Yeltsin, Prime Minister Chernomyrdin and others saw him as a threat to their own weakening positions.[12]

It could be objected that the Russian attitudes just described are in essence no different from attitudes frequently encountered among Western voters. Three points need to be borne in mind, however. First, the argument in this chapter is that the particular aggregation of characteristics is unique to post-communism, not that individual phenomena cannot be found in other systems. Second, the real power of the General Secretary during the communist era or of the President now is far greater in Russia than the power of any other agency, notably the legislature. In this sense, ordinary citizens are more dependent on the Russian President than they would be in a system with a more genuine division of powers. Although the President's powers are often exaggerated – he *is* more dependent on the legislature than is generally appreciated – it is public perception that matters most. This focus on one individual often results in both unrealistically high expectations early in a new leader's 'reign', and a more extreme sense of disappointment when that person fails to meet these expectations. Finally, it is vital to bear in mind the Russian context when comparing the situation with other countries. The identity crisis mentioned above, plus the high levels of political instability and economic insecurity in Russia during the 1990s, mean that the position of 'the' leader is both more critical and more fragile than it would be in most Western states.

4. Cynicism Towards and Mistrust of Political Institutions

A number of attitude and opinion surveys suggest that many Russians are cynical about their political institutions.[13] One reason is the communist legacy; there was so often a glaring gap between claims of 'socialist democracy' and the actualities of elitist communist power so that many Russian citizens became deeply cynical about claims of democracy. While the earliest stages of post-communism in Russia were accompanied by a raising of hopes about more democratic politics and less elitism, many now believe that politics have again become personalised and conspiratorial.

The events of September–October 1993 were a major impetus in the development of widespread cynicism.[14] But the situation has been exacerbated since the June 1996 elections, largely because of President Yeltsin's very poor state of health. Not only were there concerted efforts before the elections to keep the Russian electorate ignorant of just how unwell their President was (as part of the campaign to increase his electoral chances), but the presidential staff strove for several weeks even *after* the election to down play the seriousness of Yeltsin's health problems. At the same time, and for reasons that were inadequately explained, the President initially refused to see Lebed to discuss the peace proposal which the latter had agreed with Chechen leaders, even though Chechnya had by then become the single most pressing issue on the political agenda. All this led to a widespread popular perception that politics had become conspiratorial again, while Western observers were beginning to wonder if they would have to resurrect the Kremlinological skills that so many of them had honed during the communist period.

A final reason for widespread cynicism has been the perceived increase in corruption among the political elite. Corruption is an unusual crime, in that there is often no obvious victim who would complain to the authorities; this is just one of many reasons why it is impossible to measure the scale of venality. Whether or not corruption has actually increased, it is clear that many citizens *believe* that it has, which is exerting a negative influence on the Russian transition. One reason for this perception is that, precisely because of the uncertainty and low legitimacy levels of the Russian post-communist political arrangements, many politicians have sought to increase their own standing in the public's eyes by attempting to undermine their opponents with allegations of corruption.

Perhaps the best-known case occurred in 1993. At the beginning of that year, President Yeltsin charged his then Vice-President, Aleksandr Rutskoi, with investigating alleged corruption among senior politicians. By mid-year, and in addition to a series of allegations against lower-ranking officials, Rutskoi had claimed that one former Acting Prime Minister (Yegor Gaidar), Yeltsin's aide Gennadii Burbulis, and two Deputy Prime Ministers (Aleksandr Shokhin and Vladimir Shumeiko) had all corruptly benefited from the privatisation process. But these allegations had been made just days after Yeltsin had humiliated Rutskoi, and could be construed as sour grapes on the part of the Vice-President. In an ironic twist, Rutskoi was himself charged with corruption in August 1993: it was alleged that the Vice-President, via a foundation which he chaired, had been syphoning millions of dollars into a Swiss bank account.[15]

Another major example of allegations of corruption among senior officials occurred in mid-1996. At the beginning of July, the Chairman of the Duma's Defence Committee, Lev Rokhlin, accused the recently-dismissed Defence Minister Pavel Grachev of permitting wide-scale embezzlement in the military, and directly charged five generals (including Grachev's own brother-in-law) with corruption. The Duma then demanded a full legal investigation, which was still continuing at the time of writing.[16]

The most important point about the kinds of allegations just described is that some of them appear to be motivated primarily by personal vendettas among leading political figures rather than the objective pursuit of justice. While it is too early to know whether or not this is true of the mid-1996 allegations, the 1993 episode was almost certainly a function of Rutskoi's clashes with Yeltsin, rather than being based on substantial concrete evidence. The charges against Rutskoi were finally dropped in December 1995. The whole episode was almost certainly another example of the kind of problem identified by V. Marsov and A. Poleshchuk in a front-page article in one of Russia's leading newspapers in 1993, when they argued that 'Today, the struggle against corruption is above all a struggle against a political opponent.'[17] But such incidents, added to the many genuine cases of official corruption that have been widely reported in the media, serve to undermine the legitimacy of the post-communist arrangements, and to increase the public's mistrust of Russia's new institutions.[18]

5. Rejection of Teleologism and Grand Theories

In most post-communist countries, the open abandonment and rejection of Marxism-Leninism was accompanied by a cynicism towards grand theories and teleological ideologies altogether. Even if it is assumed that Russia is still on its bumpy way to democracy and capitalism, this does not reflect the adoption of a new *telos* or grand theory. Ralf Dahrendorf is probably going too far when he argues that democracy and capitalism are neither teleological nor even systems as such;[19] their whole point, he suggests, is that they represent the sum total of lots of individual actions and beliefs, and are not based on any one all-encompassing premise. Nevertheless, the advocacy and pursuit of 'democracy' is at most a vague and – almost by definition – contested concept, quite different from the putative omniscience of 'scientific socialism'. At all events, it appears that many citizens and even politicians in the post-communist world, including Russia, have been very wary of theories that claim to embrace and explain all or most aspects of human existence.

Two final points need to be made about this fifth characteristic. First, the post-communist rejection of grand theories has little to do with the post-modern rejection of meta-narratives; rather, it is primarily a function of the disappointment with the loftier and more abstract aspects of the communist project.[20] Second, there are signs that attitudes towards teleologism *may* now be changing; but this is more appropriately considered in the conclusions.

6. Ideological Vacuum

Intimately connected with the last point is the wariness by now of all ideologies, not merely overtly teleological and all-encompassing ones. Even the initial faith that many appear to have had in vague notions of 'democracy' and 'the market' in the earliest days of post-communist Russia has by now either faded or completely disappeared. As the Director of the All-Russian Centre for Public Opinion Research in Moscow, Yuri Levada, has argued:

> ... the populace shunned ideology and gave the sacramental formula, 'What is to be done', a pragmatic reading, doing what it could to muddle through everyday life ... Public consciousness became thoroughly deideologised, and the absence of credible political programs or leaders did not seem to alarm Russian citizens.[21]

This disillusionment is quite understandable, given the political and economic problems Russia has experienced in recent years. Conversely, the absence of an agreed general framework for the future is likely to frustrate attempts to pull Russia out of its current quagmire.

7. Moral Vacuum

Another closely related point is that the collapse of Marxism-Leninism also meant the end of an ethical system for many citizens. There was at least a relatively clear ethical code during the Soviet era; even though many Russians used to claim they rejected the mores of Marxism-Leninism, they were subject to the pervasive effects of the ideology's language, symbols and values. Dominant attitudes towards inequality, for instance, appear to have been very different in Russia from those in most Western societies.[22] Citizens were discouraged from developing personal (individualistic) moral value systems, partly because this was at odds with the collectivist orientation of Marxism-Leninism, and partly because it was perceived by the authorities as threatening to communist rule.

In post-communist Russia, many Russians have been able to fill the moral void by turning to – or espousing more openly than in the past – religion. Indeed, there has been a marked revival of religion, especially of Russian Orthodoxy, since the late 1980s. According to Igor Troyanovskii, the number of operating Orthodox churches almost doubled between 1985 and 1991, from 6,806 to some 12,000.[23] Although overall levels of church-going and affiliation may now have peaked and even be waning (reliable data are not available), one important *symbol* of support is the vast sums of money impoverished Russians have shown themselves willing to contribute to the reconstruction of the Christ the Saviour Cathedral in Moscow, which had been destroyed on Stalin's orders in 1931.

But religion has not been an attractive proposition for many. Several factors, many of them related, help to explain this. One is the effects of decades of anti-religious propaganda by the communists. Another is the widespread secularising impact of modernisation. A third is the severe resource problems, both human and financial, currently being experienced by the Orthodox church. Finally, there is the fact that many Russians are so depressed and cynical at present that, as argued earlier, they are disinclined to turn to any teleology or macro value system. Whatever the reasons, and despite some increase in religious affiliation in recent years, the churches in Russia are not succeeding in providing many citizens with the moral framework they seek and need.

Opinion surveys certainly suggest that large numbers of Russians believe there has been a decline of morality, and perceive this as a serious problem. The start of the rot is often associated by Russians with the later communist period, though many believe it has accelerated in the 1990s. According to one unpublished survey conducted by what was at the time the All-Union Centre for Public Opinion Research, almost a third of those polled in a February 1991 survey believed there had been a sharp decline in public morality in recent years; a little over one-third believed there had been little change, but that *glasnost'* had made it appear there had been a decline; only 21 per cent believed that public morality had improved (13 per cent of respondents were unable to judge).[24] More recent surveys suggest that there is now a widespread sense that the new Russia is in a moral crisis.[25]

One of the difficulties of creating a new morality in post-communist Russia relates to the point touched upon earlier about communist attitudes towards *individual* morality. Clearly, some citizens were prepared to challenge the Soviet authorities and the latter's notion that there could and should be only a collective communist code; among the best-known examples of such critics are Aleksandr Solzhenitsyn and the late Andrei Sakharov. But many citizens appear to have internalised the notion that they did not have to develop their own individual morality to any great extent, even if they were privately critical of much of what the communists espoused and did. With the all-pervasive state claiming the right to make most moral decisions on behalf of ordinary citizens, the latter were not encouraged to develop their ability to exercise individual (free) *choices* on major ethical issues. Although the situation began to improve by the 1960s, insufficient progress had been made by the time of the collapse of communist power for a widespread individual-based ethical code to take root. This must be seen as one of the principal reasons for the moral deficit in post-communist Russia. After all, Igor Kon is surely correct when he argues that, '... freedom of choice is the very essence of morality'.[26] Russians have not, in general, been used to the level of freedom of choice that is required to fill the current moral void in their country.

8. Comprehensive Revolution

Like virtually all other post-communist countries, Russia has faced a multiple transition with the collapse of the communist system. Claus Offe has referred to the 'triple transition' being undertaken by the post-communist countries, by which he means major change in the political system, the economic system, and the boundary (territorial and citizenship) restructuring of the post-communist world.[27] The changes in both the political system and the economic system have been extensively analysed elsewhere, and need not detain us; suffice it to say that Russia had a Communist Party monopoly system until the late 1980s that has now been replaced by a genuine multi-party system, and a centrally-planned and largely state-owned economy that has now been replaced by a far more marketised system in which there is a genuine mixture of ownership forms.

Post-communist Russia's own boundaries have not yet changed to any meaningful extent.[28] Of course, since many Russians used to see themselves as part of a large empire that has now collapsed, *perceptions* that the boundaries of the country have dramatically shrunk are easy enough to find. Many Russians considered themselves Soviet as much as specifically Russian, and in this sense their boundaries have been considerably redrawn. But it is precisely because Yeltsin and other leaders have resisted moves to alter boundaries to what they perceive as the disadvantage of the world's largest country (in terms of territory) that the war in Chechnya erupted in 1994. Moscow's reaction cannot be understood solely in terms of wanting to keep the relatively small Chechnya part of Russia; indeed, many Russians have negative (racist) attitudes towards the Chechens,[29] and would prefer to have as little contact with them as possible. Rather, the Russian leadership appears to have believed that ordinary Russians had already suffered enough humiliation with the collapse of the Soviet empire, and that to start permitting the break-up of Russia itself would be the straw to break the camel's back. Since it was clear that it was not only many Chechens who would prefer to leave Russia and form their own sovereign state but also many citizens of Bashkortostan, Tatarstan, Tuva and elsewhere, many Russian leaders were concerned that if they granted independence to one group, they would be opening a Pandora's Box – or, more appropriately here, a *matrioshka* doll. Add to this the political point that many communists have since 1991 been blaming Yeltsin for the collapse of the Soviet empire, and that they have accused him of being prepared to permit the break-up of Russia itself,[30] and it becomes even more obvious how sensitive the issue of boundaries is in contemporary Russia. This helps to explain why Moscow has been unwilling to cede the four most southerly Kurile Islands (which the Japanese call the Northern Territories) to Japan, even though it would almost certainly be to Russia's longer-term economic benefit to do so.

As part of their endeavours to resurrect something along the lines of a more egalitarian version of the Russian and Soviet Empire, the Russians have keenly advocated and developed the CIS. Although this was in its early years a very fragile organisation, the CIS had by the mid-1990s become more stable, though still far from consolidated.[31] Certainly, the Russians have enjoyed some success in reintegrating the military commands of the Soviet successor states. For example, the defence ministers of ten of the twelve member-states agreed in November 1995 to create a joint air defence system that would ultimately be under Russian control (and largely funded by Russia).[32] This followed an agreement made in April 1994 between the Central Asian and Transcaucasian states (excluding Azerbaijan) and Russia that the latter would be co-responsible for defending the former's southern borders. And in April 1996, Belarus signed a union treaty with Russia, thus moving much closer to its centuries-old partner, in a way many Russian leaders almost certainly hope will be emulated by other former Soviet republics. Meanwhile, the Duma voted in March 1996 to deepen the integration of the peoples previously united within the USSR, at the same time as it condemned the December 1991 agreement (the Belovezhskaya Pushcha Accords) that had dissolved the USSR and established the CIS. Although Yeltsin condemned the Duma's resolution, the lower house's act revealed just how shaky the CIS was, and that there was an important force in Russian politics committed to attempting to reconstruct something akin to the former USSR. Hence, the boundaries of Russia are still very much in flux, and, unlikely though this appears at present, there could yet be attempts to create a third Russian empire (that is, after the Tsarist and Soviet).

The political, economic and territorial revolutions are not the only ones Russia has been experiencing in the 1990s. A fourth is a social revolution. Like other post-communist states, Russia had very little by way of a bourgeoisie at the time of the collapse of communist power. The emergence and development of such a class was seen by many analysts as necessary if Russia's economic and political revolutions were to succeed, since it is widely accepted that privatisation and marketisation will be successful only if there is a substantial group in society with a vested interest in their success. Even if it is the case that many members of the new bourgeoisie are members of the old communist *nomenklatura,* their class position and ideological perspective is often very different from what it was during the communist era.[33]

It was mentioned above that Russia has been re-forging military links with many of its former Soviet neighbours. But there are other ways in which Russia has been restructuring its military allegiances, in what can only be described as a revolutionary way. Until the late 1980s, the Soviet Union had *basically* treated the West as the enemy (and *vice versa*). Although the relationship had been warmer at some periods (for example, the early 1970s) than at others, the fact was that the USSR was the most powerful member of the WTO that treated NATO as its primary antagonist. The WTO collapsed in 1991. While the Central and Southeast Europeans were far more enthusiastic about its end than were the Soviet peoples, especially the Russians, it is indisputable that Gorbachev played a very significant role in reducing the tensions between East and West that resulted in the ending of the Cold War; whether or not the Soviet Union intended it, this set the stage for the WTO's collapse. Within a very short period of time following this collapse, there was a dramatic improvement in relations between NATO and Russia. Given tensions between these two since late 1993, it is easy to forget that the Russian leadership had until September 1993 declared itself comfortable with the improved relations between NATO and the East European states, and even appeared to accept that many of its former WTO neighbours would one day join the Western military alliance.[34] For reasons that were initially related more to domestic politics than to major changes in foreign policy perspectives, Yeltsin adopted a very different policy towards the West and NATO following the September–October 1993 political crisis; suddenly, Russia was claiming to feel threatened by Western expansionism on or close to its borders. Even since that time, however, Russia has not reverted to an essentially similar position towards NATO to that of the USSR. Despite the alleged fears, Russia has co-operated with NATO by joining the Partnership for Peace Program, and has been granted special status by NATO; while the latter has emphasised that Moscow will not have the right of veto over East European states' applications to join the Western alliance, it has on various occasions promised to consult Russia over future expansion plans.[35] All this can only be described as a revolutionary change from the Soviet era.

9. Temporality

By definition, post-communism is a transitional phenomenon, in that it is still dominated by the past rather than being a consolidated entity of the present and future. Once a given post-communist state is widely perceived to have arrived *and settled* at a given destination, such as Western-style democracy or populist democracy or military dictatorship, and once that arrangement is seen as far more salient than the fact that a given country is still coping with the legacy of the past and finding its way, then a country can no longer justifiably be described as post-communist.

Russia is still very much in a phase of uncertainty. The June 1996 elections revealed that a substantial minority of Russian voters were attracted to politicians whose conception of and commitment to democracy in the Western senses would be questioned, even though the most popular of these (Zyuganov) had consciously distanced himself from the more traditional elements in the Communist Party in the months preceding the election. With Yeltsin's incapacity following the elections, the fact that one of the leading contenders for power (Lebed) had recently indicated his reservations about too much democracy for a country in Russia's precarious situation was just one sign that Russia's moves towards stable democracy in the 1990s *might* prove to be no more than a passing flirtation.

10. Dynamism

Some of the post-communist states are still well on course to become typical Western- style systems by early in the next millennium. The most obvious examples are the Czech Republic, Hungary, Poland and Slovenia, while some of the Baltic states and even some Balkan countries might also fit into this category.[36] Although many have experienced a 'return' of 'communists', the significance of this should not be exaggerated; the 'communists' are in most cases better de-scribed as radical social democrats, and their electoral victories as exam-ples of understandable protest politics. How does Russia fit into this pattern?

Russia's dynamism is much less clear than that of several of the Visegrad states. Although Yeltsin's July 1996 victory might from some perspectives imply continuation along an essentially unidirectional path, the reality is more complex. Following close shaves, Yeltsin has often changed direction on significant issues. One example – relating to NATO – has already been cited. Another was the personnel changes, and related shifts of emphasis in economic policy, following the December 1993 parliamentary elections. Then, following the first round of the 1996 presidential elections, Yeltsin felt obliged to make concessions to Lebed. For instance, he *eventually* appeared to agree to Lebed's radical ap-proach to the Chechen issue, even though this represented a virtual volte face on his part. In short, Russia's direction is less obvious than the continuity of leader might suggest.

One major reason for Russia's meanderings is that it is subject to deeper political cleavages than are many of its neighbours to the West. As intimated above, the notion of rejecting a common oppressor had acted as a cohering element for many in the post-communist world in the earliest days of the new arrangements. This is not to deny the existence of significant political differences in most early post-communist states; clearly there were many. But it *is* to argue that the level of self-question-ing and scapegoating in most East European countries was less than in Russia, which had been the great loser in this process. This is almost certainly a major reason why the level of hostility in Russia between many of the leading exponents of the major political platforms appears to be greater than that between the main political leaders in many other communist states.

While other post-communist presidents have shut down parliaments (for example, Lech Wałęsa in Poland in May 1993, Nursultan Nazarbaev in Kazakhstan in March 1995[37]), there has been nothing to compare with the unconstitutionality and violence involved in the Russian closure of parliament in 1993. Nor has there been anything in most other commu-nist states to compare with the attempted coup of August 1991. The argument here is that these extreme events testify to the deeper divisions within Russia than in most other post-communist states, troubled though these are and have been.

11. Instability

It is obvious that Russia has been in a very unstable position since 1991. There are a number of concrete indicators of this; while the existence of just one or two of them would not necessarily suggest basic instability, their aggregate effect does.

One sign is the frequency of elections. Between 1991 and 1996, Russia has experienced two parliamentary and two presidential elections. The latter took place some five years apart, and in this sense their frequency was perfectly normal for a stable society. But it is unusual for a presidential election to be postponed several times, as the second one was, and for there to be serious doubts that they would take place at all, as there were in Russia right up until June 1996. It is also unusual to have two parliamentary elections only two years apart, and for one of them to have been brought about because of the violent closure of the parliament.

There has also been a relatively high number of government changes, reflective of Yeltsin's strained relations with both parliament (and his perceived need to make concessions on occasion) and his own lieutenants. The most significant examples of the former relate to a man in whom Yeltsin once showed great confidence, Yegor Gaidar. In November 1991, at the peak of his own standing, Yeltsin announced that he would assume the post of Prime Minister, in addition to the presidency. Gaidar was Yeltsin's First Deputy Prime Minister, and as such played a crucial role in the introduction of radical economic reform in January 1992. But parliament (at that time and in this context meaning the Congress of People's Deputies) became increasingly uneasy about the concentration of power in Yeltsin's hands, and in April 1992 succeeded in pressuring Yeltsin to transfer many of his powers to Gaidar, who became Acting Premier. But tensions between Yeltsin and the communist-dominated legislature continued to build, and by December 1992 Yeltsin felt obliged to make major concessions. The principal victim of the President's moves was Gaidar, whose radical economic policies were increasingly criticised by parliament; Gaidar lost his position as Acting Prime Minister, to be replaced by the more centrist Viktor Chernomyrdin.

Probably the best example of Yeltsin's conflicts with his own lieutenants is the struggle between the President and his deputy, Vice-President Aleksandr Rutskoi, during 1992 and 1993. Rutskoi and Yeltsin had been very close in the aftermath of the August 1991 attempted coup. But by 1992, Rutskoi was becoming increasingly critical of the President. This peaked in 1993, by which time Rutskoi, together with the parliamentary speaker (Chairman of the Supreme Soviet), Ruslan Khasbulatov, had become the most outspoken critic of the President. Without elaborating every stage of the breakdown of relations between Yeltsin and Rutskoi, suffice it to note that Rutskoi was eventually arrested in October 1993 for his role in the parliamentary stand against the President (he was released in late February 1994). In terms of its long-term implications, more significant than the fate of Rutskoi himself was the fate of his post. Between Yeltsin's removal of Rutskoi (at the time of the latter's arrest), and the publication in the following month of a draft Constitution that was confirmed by referendum in December, the post of Vice-President had disappeared. This fact had become extremely important by mid-1996, as Yeltsin's poor state of health raised the major question of who would actually run Russia were the President to be seriously incapacitated. Although Article 92 of the 1993 constitution conferred this responsibility on the Prime Minister, this would be only a temporary solution; while the Constitution requires a new presidential election within three months in the case of permanent incapacity of the incumbent, it is not clear how such permanent incapacity is to be determined if the existing President is unwell but considers himself able to carry on with his duties. Nor is it clear how long the Prime Minister may deputise for the President on a 'temporary' basis. Conversely, if there had been agreement on new presidential elections in late 1996 or in 1997, it is not entirely obvious that this would be a desirable development. Given how recently such elections had taken place, and given that many citizens apparently believed they had been misled by the Yeltsin team at the time of these elections, the holding of further elections could prove to be a destabilising factor. Had there been a Vice-President who could have taken over (as in the US arrangements) and ruled until the next scheduled elections (namely until the year 2000), many of the fears of potential serious instability relating to Yeltsin's illness could have been allayed. Inasmuch as the constitutional arrangements in Russia since the end of 1993 had been very much the product of one man, it could be argued that the continuing personalisation of Russian politics was one of the reasons for its continuing instability.

A third sign of instability is the frequency and scale of changes within political parties. Having been a one-party state for so long, it is understandable that, once legalised in the late 1980s, new political parties sprang up like mushrooms. Once again, Russia was similar in this respect to many other post-communist countries.[38] However, two factors have made the consolidation process more problematic than elsewhere. The first is the point made earlier about identity problems and the deeper divisions within Russian society. While it is possible to conceptualise some of these differences in terms of traditional debates between the Slavophiles and the Westernisers that have surfaced in Russian intellectual life on numerous occasions since the 1840s, the important point is that these two approaches are fundamentally at odds and represent deeper differences than are to be found in most East European countries. This has rendered it that much more difficult to consolidate parties than in some other countries. The second is the sheer size of Russia. Despite having lost both an external and an internal empire, Russia is still considerably larger than any other country on earth. One ramification of this, plus the fact that Russia was not as developed as 'First World' states, was the relatively poor state of communications. This factor is not insurmountable, however, and communications have been slowly improving during the 1990s. A more significant ramification is that Russia is a highly regionalised country; this is reflected in its federal structure, which is untypical of post-communist states. The sense of regional over national loyalty appears to be strong in many parts of the country, and renders the consolidation of parties with essentially similar outlooks much more difficult.[39]

12. A Widespread Sense of Insecurity

A considerable body of survey data exists by now to indicate a widespread sense of insecurity in contemporary Russia.[40] There are a number of very obvious reasons for this feeling. The communist state in Russia and elsewhere has been described as having had a 'cradle to grave' or 'womb to tomb' approach to citizen welfare. While this approach has been criticised by many Western observers, who believe it discourages autonomous citizen behaviour (for example, the development of civil society) and represents a paternalistic or even patronising attitude on the part of the state, it did mean that few had to worry about being unemployed or homeless, or without adequate medical cover. There can be no question that there were prices to be paid for this, in addition to the tacit agreement not to challenge the state. Thus the right to work was accompanied by the duty to work; housing was often very cramped and poorly equipped; and health-care facilities were typically crowded and lacking the latest technology.[41] Yet there was a comparatively high level of security; the very limited freedom of choice that many Westerners might find unacceptable was partly compensated for by the comfort of a bartered security.

Hence unemployment is a relatively new phenomenon for Russians.

Although the rates in Russia have been much lower than in most other post-communist states with the exception of the Czech Republic,[42] they have been climbing as the impact of economic reforms has taken hold, and look set to increase in the future.[43] But the novelty of unemployment was not the only reason for a sense of insecurity. Another has been the very poor condition of the Russian welfare state. Although an unemployment scheme became operational in July 1991, when the first Soviet unemployment exchanges were opened, this has experienced a number of teething problems. Moreover, Russians can see *employed* people not being paid by the state,[44] let alone the unemployed, and know that people entitled to receive state benefits may not in fact be paid even the very modest sums due to them.[45] In addition, Russia currently has no social security scheme for the long-term unemployed; once a recipient has been unemployed for twelve months, the unemployment benefits dry up.[46] Particularly if unemployed individuals do not have family to support them through such difficult times, it is far from clear how they are supposed to survive.

Hyper-inflation is also a new phenomenon that is disturbing for most Russians. According to the Economist Intelligence Unit, the annual inflation rate of consumer prices in Russia was a relatively modest 5 per cent in 1990; this rose to nearly 93 per cent in 1991, 1354 per cent in 1992, 883 per cent in 1993, and 320 per cent in 1994.[47] Although it has slowed down in the mid-1990s, such rates have clearly been a major source of concern to Russians, particularly in the light of the above-mentioned uncertainties of being paid (if employed) or receiving benefits (if unemployed or on some kind of pension).

Moves towards further privatisation of housing have added to the feelings of insecurity. Tenants are often unsure that their apartment will still be available to them in the future; even if it is in principle, rent increases in some parts of Russia have been so high that they cannot be certain they will be able to afford to stay where they are.[48]

Yet another reason why many Russians feel insecure in the 1990s in a way they did not in the communist era is that the break-up of the USSR has seen many of the successor states passing laws that to a greater or lesser extent marginalise Russians. New citizenship laws in countries such as Estonia and Latvia have made many of the approximately 25 million Russians residing in the newly independent states of the FSU feel insecure and unwanted in countries in which they might not only have been living and working for many years but might even have been born.[49]

One final, and sad, observation about the sense of insecurity among today's Russians is that some analysts have linked the declining life expectancy and increasing levels of ill-health in Russia to this factor.[50] While many of these health problems, especially in males, relate to even more alcohol abuse recently than is traditional in Russia,[51] the question arises of the extent to which such increases are related to the negative psychological effects of higher levels of insecurity.

13. Unfortunate Timing

In a sense, all the post-communist states were unfortunate in the timing of their anti-communist revolutions. One reason was that the West was just entering a recession, which worsened and spread from the English-speaking countries to continental Europe and Japan in the early 1990s. Hence, there were fewer funds for investment than there would be in an economically more buoyant phase. Second, the very fact that so many countries underwent revolutionary change more or less simultaneously exacerbated the general problem; Western investment funds were limited anyway, but might have been more effectively placed had only one or two communist states moved to post-communism at a time.

But Russia experienced two additional problems because of the timing of its anti-communist revolution. First, being later than most of the countries of Eastern Europe, it was further down the queue for Western funds. Second, since its revolution did not clearly start until 1991, it suffered indirectly from the post-euphoric mini-depression that was affecting many parts of Europe. On the one hand, many citizens in post-communist Eastern Europe were already becoming cynical about the short-term future of their countries, and some of this appears to have filtered through to Russia. On the other hand, one of the strongest countries in Europe, and the one so many East Europeans had seen as more sympathetic to their plight than other Western countries, was experiencing far greater economic difficulties than almost anyone had foreseen. That country was Germany, whose unification process was already proving to be considerably more complicated and expensive than the Bonn government had predicted (at least publicly).

14. Legitimation Problems

At least ten legitimation modes can be seen to be used by contemporary states. Of these, seven (old traditional; charismatic; goal-rational or teleological; eudaemonic; official nationalist; new traditional; legal-rational) are basically domestic, while the other three (formal recognition; informal support; existence of an external role-model) are primarily external.[52] Since I have considered legitimation problems in post-communist Russia at some length elsewhere,[53] only a truncated version of the argument is provided here.

All post-communist states face significant legitimation problems. The reasons are numerous, and many that apply to other states also relate to Russia. Thus, in terms of the domestic legitimation modes, the economic problems Russia has experienced in recent years render eudaemonism a quite unrealistic aspiration for the present Russian leaders. While the confusion and directionless leadership they have experienced in recent years might mean that an increasing number of Russians will soon be craving a common and dominant *telos*, it is not yet clear where that would emanate from or what it would be. Moreover, the one form of legitimation that is often held to be the only appropriate one for a modern state – legal–rationality – is currently out of Russia's reach; the continuing tensions between the President and parliament that have resulted in a so-called 'war of laws', and Yeltsin's closure of the Constitutional Court in October 1993 when he considered it disloyal to him,[54] are two clear indications that a law-based state is still a distant aspiration. Unfortunately, since both old and new traditionalism are for different reasons also inappropriate at present, this leaves only charismatic and official nationalist legitimation. Both of these are problematic. In the past, they have often been associated with a coercive phase in Soviet and Russian history, as during the Stalin era; while this is not to say that they will necessarily be connected with a highly coercive regime in the future, this precedent should not be overlooked. Moreover, both tend to be relatively short-term legitimators (to the extent that they are effective anyway), and of regimes rather than of systems. Hence, while they could act as legitimating modes in today's Russia, they are unlikely to be effective in the longer run, and could well have detrimental effects.[55]

What of the external modes of legitimation? Russia enjoys formal recognition by the world community, and looks set to continue to do so. But this is not a very powerful legitimating agent on its own. Turning to external support – although the West has fairly consistently sided with President Yeltsin when he has come into conflict with his parliament and other politicians, this support is ultimately tenuous. It is legitimising a regime rather than a system. Admittedly, the support is largely based on the assumption that the Yeltsin regime is the one most likely to succeed in transforming Russia into a modern, law-based state. But it is based on a hoped-for future, not an already-achieved present. The fact that the

West becomes nervous when Yeltsin's position appears shakier than usual is evidence enough of the fragility of this mode. Finally, it would be difficult to argue convincingly that Russia still has an external role-model that the elite uses to guide its policies and legitimise itself. While the West was in the earliest days of post-communism a model for many of the leading politicians, there was always a substantial and influential group who preferred to see Russia as *sui generis*. These divisions within the political elite have not narrowed in recent years. At the same time, there appears to be more doubt even among the 'Westernisers' than there was in the recent past; while Yeltsin's own shifts can be seen to be as much a function of political in-fighting as of ideological shifts, both he and other 'progressives' do appear to have become more sceptical about the West as a role-model, and more sensitive to traditional Russian concerns and ways of doing things.

In sum, all legitimation modes are at present problematic. Given this, plus the fact that all states rule on the basis of a mixture of coercion and legitimation, there is a risk that Russia's leader(s) will in the future decide that rather more coercion is required than is currently to be found in the country. A more optimistic scenario is that Russia continues to muddle through and the economy gradually picks up, so that eudaemon-ism and eventually even legal–rationality will become more salient. But a third possibility is not clearly any better for the average citizen than the first scenario: this is that the state becomes so weak and marginal that it seeks neither to legitimate itself to any meaningful extent nor to rule by coercion. This could ultimately result in the break-up – possibly violent – of Russia into many new states, *de facto* rule by organised criminal groups or both. Hence, Russia's legitimation problems are not merely of abstract theoretical interest; they reflect broader issues with potentially disturbing ramifications.

Conclusions

Some readers may believe they have found a contradiction in the above analysis, in the references to a rejection of teleologism and the possible future search for a *telos*. This is not necessarily a contradiction. One reason is that teleologism, as used here and in many analyses, refers more to the ideology that is employed to create the *telos* and justify a system geared to its achievement than to a popular desire for a new goal. Citizens may well want an objective and a leadership that appears to have one, yet be unwilling to pay the ultimate price of permitting a teleologically-oriented authoritarianism of the sort they once had. To acknowledge that many Russians currently want order more than freedom, as surveys consistently indicate, is far from accepting they are seeking a teleological regime. No doubt some Russians do want this; but clearly enough were concerned about the possibilities of it to vote against Zyuganov in the 1996 second-round elections. But a second reason it is not a necessary contradiction does highlight an aspect of the approach adopted here that is problematic and must be recognised as such. In attempting to highlight the salient features of post-communism, there is an almost inevitable tendency to deprive it of its own dynamism. Thus, it is difficult to encapsulate the changing nature of the beast; the overt inclusion of the dynamism factor is probably the most that can be done. This said, if the establishment and consolidation of a teleological regime and even system in Russia were to occur, then Russia would no longer be best described as a post-communist country. For now, the point can be made that Russia may be experiencing the stages that other post-communist states have gone through. The first, the euphoric stage, is short-lived. The second, the pessimistic and highly cynical stage, is now giving way to a third in countries such as Poland. This is a realistic stage, in which many citizens realise that progress can be made, but at a slower pace than they had once hoped for. Russia *may* be entering this stage; but the uncertainties surrounding Yeltsin's position in late 1996 make it unwise to be over-confident about this or to make predictions.

At various points in the above analysis, similarities between the Russian condition and that in other post-communist states have been mentioned. Even in some areas where the Russians might be thought to be in a unique position, care should be exercised before reaching conclusions. Hence, Russia is often seen to be in an almost unique position (along with former Yugoslavia) concerning the continuing uncertainties about its boundaries. But there are many latent territorial disputes elsewhere in the post-communist world, which could become major issues if elites perceive a possible advantage in making them so.

While this appears highly unlikely at present, Hungary could one day seek to incorporate Transylvania, or parts of Slovakia or Serbia, for instance. While the issue of ethnic difference and potential conflict is quantitatively more substantial in Russia than anywhere else, the difference is of scale rather than of kind. This leaves the identity issue in Russia, as the only country to have lost an empire, as the sole distinguishing feature. It can be questioned whether or not this constitutes a true crisis at present. But if Russians choose an extremist leader who not only promises greatness but is also prepared to create scapegoats of minorities and threaten neighbouring states as part of the package, then those who refer to an identity crisis will have been vindicated. Since it is such a large country, in all senses, that still has a nuclear arsenal (admittedly a deteriorating one), such a development would be of even greater international concern than such a development in a smaller, non-nuclear country.

Notes

1. Leslie Holmes, *Post-Communism: An Introduction* (Cambridge: Polity Press, 1997), pp.15–21.
2. For a controversial statement of this position, see Philippe C. Schmitter and Terry Lynn Karl, 'The Conceptual Travels of Transitologists and Consolidologists: How Far to the East Should They Attempt to Go?', *Slavic Review* **53**, no.1 (1994), pp.173–85.
3. See Valerie Bunce, 'Should Transitologists Be Grounded?', *Slavic Review* **54**, no.1 (1995), pp.111–27, who criticises the article by Schmitter and Karl. Schmitter and Karl responded to the criticisms, while Bunce then retorted in what proved to be a very lively debate: see Terry Lynn Karl and Philippe C. Schmitter, 'From an Iron Curtain to a Paper Curtain: Grounding Transitologists or Students of Postcommunism?', ibid., **54**, no.4 (1995), pp.965–78, and Valerie Bunce, 'Paper Curtain and Paper Tigers', ibid., pp.979–87.
4. Although there were some similarities with Serbia in this sense, these should not be exaggerated. The Serbs did not rule over a huge, centuries-old empire, and Yugoslavia had never been treated as a superpower. Nor did nearly as high a percentage of Serbs perceive themselves as Yugoslavs as Russians considered themselves to be 'Soviet'.
5. For a sophisticated analysis of some of the problems of consolidating a post-Soviet Russian identity, and of the way the whole issue is manipulated by political elites, see Michael Urban, 'The Politics of Identity in Russia's Postcommunist Transition: The Nation Against Itself', *Slavic Review* **53**, no.3 (1994), pp.733–65.
6. Details relating to the development of the CIS and the special relationship with Belarus are provided below.
7. This change of policy was almost certainly made in part to placate demands from sections of the military, including Yeltsin's own Defence Minister at the time, General Pavel Grachev. Whatever the primary motivation, however, the President was prepared to concede to nationalist demands to become more assertive towards the West, even though he risked alienating some of his Western supporters by doing so.
8. For survey evidence of a desire for strong leaders in Russia and two other FSU states, see W. Reisinger, A. Miller, V. Hesli and K. Maher, 'Political Values in Russia, Ukraine and Lithuania: Sources and Implications for Democracy', *British Journal of Political Science* **24**, no.2 (1994), especially pp.191–2.
9. For survey data on public attitudes towards Gorbachev, see Yuri Levada, 'Civic Culture', in D. Shalin (ed.), *Russian Culture at the Crossroads* (Boulder, CO: Westview, 1996), especially p.310.
10. For evidence of the decline of confidence in Yeltsin, see L. Sedov, 'Boris Yel'tsin pal

zhertvoi Borisa Yel'tsina', *Segodya*, 8 April 1995, and 'Rossiyane o prezidente Rossii', *Ekonomicheskie i sotsial'nye peremeny: monitoring obshchestvennogo mneniya* (hereafter *EiSP*), 1995, no.4, p.6. For details on the rapid rise in support for Yeltsin in 1996, even though many people had low levels of confidence in him, see Yu. Levada, 'Struktura rossiiskogo elektoral'nogo prostranstva', *EiSP*, 1996, no.3, pp.7–11, and N. Zorkaya, 'Prezidentskie vybory: elektoral'nye ustanovki rossiyan v aprele 1996g.', *EiSP*, 1996, no. 3, pp.11–16.

11. For survey evidence to suggest that a clear majority of Russians (approximately two-thirds of those polled) believed that only a strong leader could save Russia, see *Kommersant Daily* cited in *The Current Digest of the Post-Soviet Press* **XLVIII**, no.5, (1996), p.21. A November 1994 poll revealed that some 80 per cent of respondents wanted order in Russia at any price (*lyuboi tsenoi*), again suggestive of the faith in and desire for strong leadership: see Yu. Levada, 'V Rossii ustanovilas' "demokratiya besporyadka"', *Segodnya*, 15 April 1995.

12. Assuming General Anatolii Kulikov's allegations that Lebed was planning a military coup prove to be groundless, Yeltsin's dismissal of the latter was in many ways ill-advised, since it tended to make a martyr of Lebed. Given that Lebed is seen by many both as the least corrupted member of the political elite and as the one person likely to be able to solve the Chechnya crisis, his already high level of popularity in early October will probably increase still further as a result of his dismissal, unless there is a major scandal surrounding him. Conversely, Yeltsin's action suggested he was fearful about having as part of his team a 'clean' and decisive leader, which will not help the President's standing.

13. For survey evidence from January 1995, see Sedov, 'Boris Yel'tsin pal zhertvoi Borisa Yel'tsina'.

14. For a leading analyst arguing this, see Archie Brown, 'Political Leadership in Post-Communist Russia', in Amin Saikal and William Maley (eds), *Russia in Search of Its Future* (Cambridge: Cambridge University Press, 1995), pp.28–47.

15. For details of the charges, see O. Rubnikovich and I. Rodin, 'Nevidannye masshtaby korruptsii v Rossii', *Nezavisimayia gazeta*, 19 August 1993; for Rutskoi's instant refutation of the charges, see 'Rutskoi oproverg obvineniya', ibid., 20 August 1993.

16. For details of the charges against leading military officials, see P. Fel'gengauer, 'V voennom vedomstve gotovitsya bol'shaya chistka', *Segodnya*, 6 July 1996. It should be noted that Grachev very soon acknowledged that he had indeed been involved in corruption – primarily in improperly providing his chief accuser, Rokhlin, with a Moscow apartment and medical treatment for a heart complaint (this included an aircraft to fly Rokhlin from Volgograd to Moscow for medical assistance – see the interview with Natalya Konstantinova in 'Doklad L'va Rokhlina solidarno oprovergaetsya voennymi', *Nezavisimaya gazeta*, 9 July 1996)! It is also worth noting that the chief military prosecutor of Russia, Valentin Panichev, informed the Duma on 19 July that initial investigations had revealed some misdoings, but also no clear wrongdoing on the part of several generals who had been scrutinised; although many of these had received very large sums from banks for building dachas, Panichev pointed out that existing legislation provides no guidance on how such generals should be permitted to seek to borrow and on what terms. See A. Veslo, 'Generalov portit dachnyi vopros', *Nezavisimaya gazeta*, 20 July 1996.

17. 'Skhvatka dvukh klanov v rukovodstve Rossii mozhet privesti stranu k polnoi anarkhii', *Nezavisimaya gazeta*, 28 August 1993.

18. For analyses of corruption in late-communist Russia and the USSR, see William

Clark, *Crime and Punishment in Soviet Officialdom* (Armonk, NY: M.E. Sharpe, 1993), and Leslie Holmes, *The End of Communist Power* (Cambridge: Polity Press, 1993). Since corruption is often closely linked with organised crime, which is typically called 'mafia' activity in Russia, it is also worth reading Arkadii Vaksberg, *The Soviet Mafia* (New York: St Martin's Press, 1991), on the Soviet period. For a highly readable overview of corruption and 'mafia'-type activity in post-communist Russia, see Stephen Handelman, *Comrade Criminal* (London: Michael Joseph, 1994). An invaluable source written by one of Russia's leading experts in this field is A. Gurov, *Krasnaya mafiya* (Moscow: Samotsvet, 1995), while V. Razinkin's *'Vory v zakony' i prestupnye klany* (Moscow: Kriminologicheskaya Assotsiatsiya, 1995) is also useful. Those interested in a more sensationalist, indeed terrifying, study of economic crime in the former Soviet Union, and of its relationship to the globalisation of organised crime, should see C. Sterling, *Crime Without Frontiers* (London: Warner, 1995). Much shorter and specific analyses of corruption, organised crime, or both, include L. Shelley, 'Organised Crime in the Former Soviet Union', *Problems of Post-Communism* **42**, no.1 (1995), pp.56–60; V. Yasmann, 'Corruption in Russia: A Threat to Democracy?', *RFE/RL Research Report* **2**, no.10 (1993), pp.15–18; V. Yasmann, 'The Russian Civil Service: Corruption and Reform', ibid., no. 16, pp.18–21; and the special issue of *Demokratizatsiya*, 1994, no.2/3.

19. Ralf Dahrendorf, *Reflections on the Revolution in Europe* (London: Chatto & Windus, 1990), especially pp.24–37, contrasts various 'systems' with the concepts of 'open society' and 'normal politics'.

20. This point deserves much fuller consideration than is possible here. For some starting-points in the debate on the relationship of post-communism to post-modernity, see S. Eisenstadt, 'The Breakdown of Communist Regimes', *Daedalus* **21** (1992), pp.21–42; Z. Baumann, 'A Post-modern Revolution?', J. Frentzel-Zagorska (ed.), *From a One-Party State to Democracy* (Amsterdam, Rodopi, 1993), pp.3–19; Leslie Holmes, 'On Communism, Post-Communism, Modernity and Post-Modernity', in ibid., pp.21–43.

21. Levada, 'Civic Culture', pp.301–2.

22. Attitudes in post-communist Russia may already be much closer to Western attitudes, however, for the results of a survey of 2,200 Russians, conducted shortly after the June–July 1996 presidential elections by the Russian Independent Institute for Social and Nationality Problems, suggest that equality of opportunity is more important to most Russians than equality of income and living standards: see M. Gorshkov, 'Poslevybornaya Rossiya: obshchestvo trekh tretei', *Nezavisimaya gazeta*, 8 August 1996.

23. Cited in Jerry Pankhurst, 'Religious Culture', in Shalin, *Russian Culture at the Crossroads*, p.149. The figures are for all Russian Orthodox congregations throughout the USSR and beyond, not just Russia. The number was higher still by January 1995, at some 14,300, of which approximately 6,400 were in Russia itself. However, such figures are not definitive. Moreover, the increase in the number of congregations has in some areas been accompanied by a decline in the average size of congregation – all of which means that no authoritative picture of the overall state of Russian Orthodoxy can be painted. For the more recent data, and an analysis of the problems of measurement, see N. Davis, 'The Russian Orthodox Church: Opportunity and Trouble', *Communist and Post-Communist Studies* **29**, no.3 (1996), pp.275–86. A full-length study up to the end of 1994 is Jane Ellis, *The Russian Orthodox Church* (London: Macmillan, 1996).

24. Igor Kon, 'Moral Culture', in Shalin, *Russian Culture at the Crossroads*, p.185.

25. A May 1996 survey of 2,405 respondents in Russia revealed that 28.5 per cent believed that a 'crisis of morals, culture and morality' was one of the most pressing concerns in their country; the figure was much higher among those with a completed or incomplete higher education, at 46.7 per cent. Data are from 'Informatsiya', *EiSP*, 1996, no.4, p.59. The figures were higher – considerably so in the case of the better-educated – than those from a similar survey conducted in May 1995: see 'Informatsiya', *EiSP*, 1995, no.4, p.57.

26. Kon, 'Moral Culture', p.190.

27. Claus Offe, 'Capitalism by Democratic Design? Democratic Theory Facing the Triple Transition in East Central Europe', *Social Research* **58**, no.4 (1991), pp.865–92.

28. The approximately 4,000-kilometre-long Sino-Russian border was in essence finally agreed by Moscow and Beijing only in September 1994.

29. For survey evidence, see L. Gudkov, 'Etnicheskie stereotipy naseleniya: sravnenie dvukh zamerov', *EiSP*, 1995, no.3, pp.14–16.

30. See the 1991 quotation from anti-Yeltsin nationalist hardliners cited in John Dunlop, 'Russia: Confronting a Loss of Empire', in Ian Bremmer and Ray Taras (eds), *Nations and Politics in the Soviet Successor States* (Cambridge: Cambridge University Press, 1993), p.56.

31. At a CIS summit in February 1995, the Ukrainian President Leonid Kuchma described the CIS as a 'shapeless organisation' that had no future: cited in *Keesing's Record of World Events* **41**, no.2 (1995), pp.40419–20. In contrast, Belarus, Kazakhstan, Kyrgyzstan and Russia signed a treaty in March 1996 committing themselves to a deepening of integration in the economic and humanitarian fields. But as one indication of how fragile the CIS remained, the Uzbek and Azeri presidents publicly dismissed this treaty in June 1996.

32. The two states not present at that meeting, and which therefore did not agree to this, were Georgia and Moldova. It is worth noting in this context that Georgia and Russia signed a military–technical co-operation agreement in July 1996.

33. For a nuanced analysis of the differing levels of continuity between the old communist *nomenklatura* and the various 'new' Russian elites, see Olga Kryshtanovskaya and Stephen White, 'From Soviet *Nomenklatura* to Russian Elite', *Europe–Asia Studies* **48**, no.5 (1996), pp.711–33. It is relevant to mention here Archie Brown's point that even the quintessential 'radical free marketeer' of post-communist Russia, Yegor Gaidar, was not only a member of the CPSU, but also a journalist on its main newspaper (*Pravda*) and its theoretical journal (*Kommunist*): see Archie Brown, 'Foreword', in A. Grachev, *Final Days* (Boulder, CO: Westview, 1995), p.x.

34. One important symbol of the dramatic improvement in East–West relations by the end of 1991 was the establishment in November of the North Atlantic Co-operation Council. This brought together in one organisation all of the NATO countries and former members of the WTO, including all of the former Soviet republics except Georgia.

35. For examples, see D. Clarke, 'Uncomfortable Partners', *Transition* **1**, no.2 (1995), pp.27–31. For NATO's September 1995 'Study on Enlargement', see *Transition* **1**, no.23 (1995), pp.19–26.

36. John Mueller has claimed that most of the countries of Central and Eastern Europe have already in essence completed their transition to democracy and capitalism: see John Mueller, 'Democracy, Capitalism, and the End of Transition', in Michael Mandelbaum (ed.), *Postcommunism: Four Perspectives* (New York: Council on Foreign Relations, 1996), pp.102–67. Mueller is able to reach his conclusion by adopting a

minimalist approach to democracy that would be unacceptable to many. For our purposes, the mere existence of the structural (institutional) elements of democracy are insufficient for the application of the term 'democracy' to a given state and society; there must also be, *inter alia*, a dominant democratic political culture.

37. On Poland, see Louise Vinton, 'Walesa Applies Political Shock Therapy', *RFE/RL Research Report* **2**, no.24 (1993), pp.1–11. On Kazakh politics in the mid-1990s, including the closure of parliament, see B. Eschment, 'Das "Chanat Nazarbaevs"', *Osteuropa* **46**, no.9 (1996), pp.876–99, and I. Bremmer and C. Welt, 'The Trouble with Democracy in Kazakhstan', *Central Asian Survey* **15**, no.2 (1996), pp.179–99.

38. For listings and analyses of the political parties in the last days of the USSR and the earliest days of post-communist Russia, see Vera Tolz, *The USSR's Emerging Party System* (New York: Praeger, 1990), and V. Pribylovskii, *Dictionary of Political Parties and Organizations in Russia* (Washington, DC: Center for Strategic and International Studies, 1992). For a broader listing, see Bogdan Szajkowski (ed.), *New Political Parties of Eastern Europe, Russia and the Successor States* (Harlow: Longman, 1994).

39. On regionalism and federalism, see for example G. Lapidus and E. Walker, 'Nationalism, Regionalism, and Federalism: Center–Periphery Relations in Post-Communist Russia', in Gail Lapidus (ed.), *The New Russia* (Boulder, CO: Westview, 1995), pp.79–113.

40. See, for example, the results of a survey on perceptions of the political scene in March 1993–May 1996 in 'Informatsiya', *EiSP*, 1996, no.4, p.51. Also useful is the series of New Russia Barometer findings published jointly by the Centre for the Study of Public Policy at the University of Strathclyde and the Paul Lazarsfeld Society in Vienna.

41. On welfare policies during the communist era, see V. George and N. Manning, *Socialism, Social Welfare and the Soviet Union* (London: Routledge & Kegan Paul, 1980). For an analysis of the housing situation, see J. Sillence (ed.), *Housing Policies in Eastern Europe and the Soviet Union* (London: Routledge & Kegan Paul, 1990); B. Turner, J. Hegedus and I. Tosics (eds), *The Reform of Housing in Eastern Europe and the Soviet Union* (London: Routledge & Kegan Paul, 1992). And on health care, see C. Davis, 'Priority and the Shortage Model: The Medical System in the Socialist Economy', C. Davis and W. Charemza (eds), *Models of Disequilibrium and Shortage in Centrally Planned Economies* (London: Chapman & Hall, 1989), pp.427–59.

42. By late 1994 the official rate in Russia stood at 2.1 per cent and in the Czech Republic at 3.1 per cent; this compared with 14.3 per cent in Slovakia, 14.4 per cent in Slovenia and 16.5 per cent in Poland (all figures from *Business Central Europe*, December 1994–January 1995, p.73). Even though the *actual* rate in Russia at that time was almost certainly much higher than the official figure suggests (perhaps as high as 7.1 per cent according to Head of Federal Employment Service F. Prokopov cited in P. Morvant, 'Unemployment: A Growing Problem', *Transition* **1**, no.6 (1995), p.46), this was still low in comparison with most other post-communist states.

43. The Federal Employment Service estimated in late 1995 that the real unemployment rate in Russia would reach 10.8 per cent of the potential work-force by 1997, as enterprises were forced to become more efficient: see Ye. Murtazev, 'K kontsu 1995 goda v Rossii nabralos' primerno 6 mln bezrabotnykh', *Segodnya*, 9 December 1995.

44. According to a March 1995 survey, 17.4 per cent of employed respondents had received no wages recently for their work, compared with 7 per cent in March 1993. The survey further revealed that in March 1995 only 43.3 per cent of those employed

had been paid in full and on time recently, compared with 61.5 per cent in March 1993. Although the March 1995 data were slightly better than those for March 1994, it is quite clear why increasing numbers of ordinary Russians feel financially insecure and bitter. Data are from N. Pichkhadze, 'Monitoring obshchestvennogo mneniya', *Sotsiologicheskie issledovaniya*, 1996, no.1, pp.157–8.

45. It is worth noting in this context that Yeltsin signed a decree in July 1996 intended to ensure that old-age pensioners actually received the money due to them from the state: see A. Zil'bert, 'Prezident Yel'tsin otpravlyaet k pensioneram "neotlozhku"', *Izvestiya*, 13 July 1996. This was clearly in response to problems of non-payment, and constitutes clear evidence of why even those dependent on state financial support should feel insecure about their incomes. For survey evidence to suggest that a majority of Russians were seriously concerned about unemployment, see O. Savel'ev, 'Rossiya "kusayut" tseny, Moskvichei "dostali" ugolovniki', *Segodnya*, 23 February 1996.

46. V. Mikhalev, 'Social Security in Russia under Economic Transformation', *Europe–Asia Studies* **48**, no.1 (1966), p.8.

47. These figures have been compiled by the author on the basis of statistics provided in various issues of the *EIU Country Report: Russia* and *Business Central Europe*.

48. For a survey of the Moscow homeless, including an analysis of new reasons for homelessness, see S. Sidorenko, 'Moskovskie bezdomnye – pervye shagi v izuchenii problemy', *EiSP* 1995, no.4, pp.46–9. According to this analysis, some experts have estimated there are approximately four million homeless people in contemporary Russia. It also points out that homelessness was officially forbidden between 1960 and 1991; this is not to say it did not exist, but the scale was much smaller.

49. An analysis of the position of Russians living beyond Russia itself, in what are now often described as the successor states, is provided in J. Chinn and R. Kaiser, *Russians as the New Minority* (Boulder, CO: Westview, 1996).

50. See, for example, N. Eberstadt, 'Demographic Disaster: The Soviet Legacy', *The National Interest*, 36 (1994), pp.53–7, and *The Economist*, 7 January 1995. For detailed analyses of health problems since the 1980s, see C. Davis, 'The Former Soviet Union', *RFE/RL Research Report* 2, no.40 (1993), pp.35–43, and M. Ellman, 'The Increase in Death and Disease Under "Katastroika"', *Cambridge Journal of Economics* **18** (1994), pp.329–55.

51. On the long history of alcohol abuse in Russia, see David Christian, *Living Water* (Oxford: Oxford University Press, 1990), and Stephen White, *Russia Goes Dry* (Cambridge: Cambridge University Press, 1996).

52. Since I have considered these at length elsewhere, I shall not repeat this exercise here. For detailed elaboration, see Holmes, *The End of Communist Power*, pp.13–18 and 58, and Holmes, *Post-Communism*, pp.42–5.

53. Leslie Holmes, 'Normalisation and Legitimation in Postcommunist Russia', in Stephen White, Alex Pravda and Zvi Gitelman (eds), *Developments in Russian and Post-Soviet Politics* (Basingstoke: Macmillan, 1994), pp.323–30.

54. The court became operational again in February 1995, following July 1994 legislation. But it will take a long time before the court's judges feel confident that they can seriously challenge the President's actions without running the risk of again being shut down.

55. The potential dangers of official nationalism do not require elaboration; one need only consider the effects of Serbian official nationalism, or indeed of the confused version of official nationalism pursued by Yeltsin and its ramifications for both Chechnya and

the rest of Russia. The possible drawbacks of charismatic legitimation are perhaps less obvious. But there are several potentially negative effects of a highly personalised and officially-eulogised form of power, including the delaying of a law-based, modern state, the hindrance of the development of civil society, and the greater possibility of dictatorship.

Index